Pim

The G

authorHOUSE®

by James Robinson

Pimpin' wasn't easy, but someone had to do it!
Jimi Starr

Pimp Tales: Book One

Book Proposal Overview

Gentle People,

    These revealing, and dramatically shocking inner-city tales contain the painstaking memoirs of my life story. I am Jimi Starr, Master Pimp, retired. From the vantage point of a pimp, this uniquely raw and intriguing manuscript gives a descriptive and rare bird's eye view of the street life across America that pimps call "The Game." In the innocence of my own ignorance, and over a period of twenty years, I led a crew of whores and faithful followers across America on a rampage seeking fame in the Game, while pillaging and plundering wealth and devouring the morality of all that I have met. The morbidly gripping and chilling contents of these writings detail my driving ambitions and, at times, sadistic quest to be the best. The contents of this dossier capture elements of my early childhood and focus on the life and death struggles of my ascension to fame, wealth, and power in the Black Underworld, to claim the coveted title of The Master Pimp. This manuscript's taboo genre takes the reader there. It is a vividly colorful inner-city novel, which describes in great detail, the thoughts, sights, sounds, and scents of the underworld. This work is reflective of my relationship with my mentor, Filmore Slim, the Black Underworld Icon, who was and is a legend and institution in the Game. These writings introduce my encounters with the most foul and degenerate characters of Mimi, the dirtiest bitch in the world, and Anna, her sexually depraved mother; two of the most despicable, and unscrupulous whores who ever squatted and pissed between two feet.

    This gut-wrenching manuscript graphically details my interactions with larcenous and murderous peers and my on going mental manipulations over all that I have met. Witness the step-by-step building of my crew of notorious cross-country whores, who were known throughout the Black Underworld as The Gabors.

    In conclusion, this exposé discloses my eventual spiritual resurrection, and retirement from the life-style known as the Game and the illuminated realization that the simplicity of my humble beginnings would become my ending.

    Reader, this is the book! There has never been a book quite like this. After this, there will never be another! These chilling and descriptive contents are meant by in no means to glorify, but on the contrary, to vilify.

    This small and unworthy novel contains the content and substance of a real pimp's story.

AuthorHouse™
1663 Liberty Drive
Bloomington, IN 47403
www.authorhouse.com
Phone: 1-800-839-8640

© *2012 by James Robinson. All rights reserved.*

No part of this book may be reproduced, stored in a retrieval system, or transmitted by any means without the written permission of the author.

First published by AuthorHouse   09/21/2011

ISBN: 978-1-4634-5293-3 (sc)
ISBN: 978-1-4634-5292-6 (hc)
ISBN: 978-1-4634-5291-9 (ebk)

Library of Congress Control Number: 2011917218

Printed in the United States of America

Any people depicted in stock imagery provided by Thinkstock are models, and such images are being used for illustrative purposes only.
Certain stock imagery © Thinkstock.

This book is printed on acid-free paper.

Because of the dynamic nature of the Internet, any web addresses or links contained in this book may have changed since publication and may no longer be valid. The views expressed in this work are solely those of the author and do not necessarily reflect the views of the publisher, and the publisher hereby disclaims any responsibility for them.

Table of Contents

Dedications 1
In the Morning of the Dawning 3
Pimp Tales: Book One 5
    The Gospel of the Game 5
Preface 7
Chapter 1 9
    The Majestic Green 9
    Sweet, Sweet Mama 13
Chapter 2 17
    New York, New York 17
    Bianca 27
Chapter 3 30
    Shake Dancer 30
Chapter 4 41
    Squirrel, the Dirtiest Bitch in the World 41
Chapter 5 49
    Don Vito's Revenge/The Naked City 49
Chapter 6 57
    Pimp or Die 57
Chapter 7 63
    Rosebudd 63
Chapter 8 72
    Dog Dick Sucker 72
Chapter 9 80
    Mother Squirrel's Curious Boodie 80
    Quality 84
Chapter 10 95
    High Stakes Game 95
Chapter 11 107
    New York Mugging, California Style 107
    Young Dummy 122
Chapter 12 130
    Portrait of a Prostitute 130
    Spokane 134
    International Shiloh Chicago 138
    Incestuous Twins 139
Chapter 13 150
    It Takes a Thief 150
    Easy Money 153
    Farewell to Manhattan Mike 162

Chapter 14	168
Pretty Boy Floyd	168
The House of Newbill	170
Frisco Slim	175
China	180
Red	185
Chapter 15	190
The Oops Game	190
Chapter 16	204
California Dreaming	204
Chapter 17	218
Revelations	218
Chapter 18	226
The Last Hurrah	226
Reno	230
Las Vegas	236
The Rat	239
Chapter 19	244
The Judas Package	244
Chapter 20	250
Rescued in the Name of the Game	250
Reflections	252
Epilog	254

Dedications

This small informative novel is dedicated to the life forces and powers that have guided me throughout this growing and learning process that man call's life. I would first give thanks to the Creator by whom all positive things and changes are possible.

I present a special acknowledgement to my mother and father, Carrie and James Edgar. From the beginning, you physically nurtured and psychologically supported me. I will always love you for your spiritual comfort and for believing in me when I failed to believe in myself.

Thanks to the incomparable Dr. Nathan Hare who's concerned, dedication, and guidance assisted in the assimilation of these meager scribings. Your kindness, sir, and earnest mentoring will never be forgotten.

To the flamboyant pimps and players across America whose colorful paths I've crossed, which enriched my existence.

To my longtime pimp pal for being a beacon of light in the darkness and allowing a fellow writer to tap into the creative brilliance that is unmistakably Rosebudd.

Finally, to those whores whom I have known, both living and dead, who believed and supported the ideology that made me the man that I was, which ultimately led to a spiritual metamorphosis creating the changed man that I am today. I salute you one and all as I embrace times past and, bittersweet memories, and present my humble heart-felt thanks.

Jimi Starr

In the Morning of the Dawning

To all of you whores, I give you fair warning. In the morning just before the dawning when the suckers of the world are still asleep and before the proverbial squares start yawning, you had better have my money, bitch.

Now, listen up, you dizzy-ass bitch, and don't you ever try to switch. Don't you ever try to give my money to another man, or perhaps you'll become a bitch with just one hand.

Now Daddy sends you forth out the door, whore, I don't care who you have to suck or fuck for a buck. But you better hope that you break luck, and you had better come when Daddy calls, and you had better have my money, bitch.

Ho, please remember, don't you ever try to bring me half, I've got to have it all. And darling, you better come when Daddy calls, and remember you had better have my money, bitch.

Ho, you must understand I don't give a rat's ass about the freezing snow or your beloved family member that passed or your menstrual flow, Ho. You still got to go; I really and most emphatically got to have my dough.

Now Ho, you have had fair warning; in the morning just before the dawning you better have my money, bitch.

Darling, yes, before the squares start yawning, in the morning, you had better have my money, bitch.

Just one last mental flash about Daddy's cash, bitch, you had better be peddling your ass and you had better be selling it fast, fast, fast, or Daddy will become upset and have to beat that ass. Just before the dawning in the morning, you better have my money, bitch.

With daybreak's first golden rays of morning light comes the new day's dawning, shinning bright. When Daddy awakes from sweet sleep's embrace, you had better have my money, bitch.

Jimi Starr

Pimp Tales: Book One

The Gospel of the Game

Preface

This book is for the intellectual understanding of my esteemed and earnestly anticipated readers, and to those with a vast knowledge of the Game, or perhaps only with a curious mind and eye. I extend full salutations to one and all. Be you of the masses of women's libbers or the professionally educated, be you the President of these United States, or a common everyday laborer, or perhaps even a buffoon, for your station in life does not matter here, nor will it matter on the journey we are about to embark upon. To the gentlemen pimp and to the novice. I bid you greetings and salutations from Jimi Starr, Master Pimp, retired.

In this novel, I will attempt to take you into the underworld of the pimp, so that I might impart to you some form of intelligent understanding of the otherwise grossly misunderstood. My dear reader, venture with me into this unknown void of darkness and danger in and of the streets across America. Venture with me deep into this abscess within the asshole of the world, which oozes forth its putrid puss that pimps call the Game. Come with me, if you dare. Come with me, curious one, and dine on vanity and arrogance. Realize the thrill of a fool's victory and feel the devastating agony of a wise man's defeat. I will solve for you the age-old riddle of why women sell their bodies and give men the monies. I will share with you my rise to power, wealth, and fame. I will share with you my fall, and my spiritual resurrection. Curious one, you will learn that pimping wasn't easy, but someone had to do it.

This small insignificant novel represents and reflects but a portion of my prior unsavory existence. The contents of this unworthy yet priceless manuscript are not by any means an attempt to glorify the life-style known as the game but, to the contrary, it is to vilify.

My thoroughly anticipated, misinformed, and perhaps naïve or curious readers, understand this now and remember it in the spiritually enlightened, socially educated, and morally informed times to come, that the contents of these vividly descriptive and emotionally stirring writings are factual and drawn from a predatorial and narcissist period past, in my colorful and eventful existence. I refer to this life's journal as the Gospel of the Game because I lived it. These writings are the undisputed, uncorrupted, and uncorroborated truth of my prior existence and the life style known as "the Game."

There is an age-old pimp cliché that reads: "From the time of conception, man spends his first nine months trying to escape the physical confines, odious stench, and umbilical restraints of a pussy. Alas, upon man's predetermined escape, man spends the entirety of his existence, trying to re-enter the confines of the womb."

The physical and psychological drive, and thirst for pussy is monumentally apparent. Sex is precedent in the species of man from the womb to the tomb.

Reader, these are the life and times of Jimi Starr. The story about to be unfolded and revealed to you is painstakingly true. The names have been changed to protect the innocent and the dead.

Forward…

Chapter 1

The Majestic Green

Distant stars twinkled in the midnight skies over New Jersey. The powerful engine whistled as my customized Biarritz Eldorado missiled east on Interstate 80. I looked into the rearview mirror at the three fabulous young West Coast whores who sat at the edge of their seats in anticipation of their New York whore debut. Bianca, my most reliable and bottom whore, sat at my side. Looking into the vanity mirror, she adjusted her makeup, preparing herself for the evening's events.

We were on The Garden State Park Highway, racing through the outskirts of Jersey City when I witnessed the fullness of her majestic beauty for the very first time. It was as if she and her island had risen up from the depth of the dark and icy ocean floor. She stood completely frozen on the horizon, draped in her gown of undeniable royalty. In the hand of her outstretched arm, the golden flame of her torch blew in the wind. Upon her regal head, she wore a crown of unquestioned majesty. She reigned over all America as a symbol of freedom for all men to see. She was unmistakably and undeniably Lady Liberty. I was momentarily awestruck and astonished at the realization of the totality and of what she represented to me. Somewhere, there on Ellis Island, is a plaque that reads: "Send me your cold, your tired, and your hungry." Well, I was cold, most probably as cold as they came. I was tired, tired of being on the West Coast, and I was hungry, hungry for a suitcase full of fast cash produced by fast-stepping New York whores!!! According to the pea-green bitch's majestic mandate and prerequisite, I met her full criteria and, in that instant, I knew for a certainty that I understood her and she me, and I also knew the lucrative streets of New York City would soon become mine. There was no doubt in my mind that regal and majestic green bitch had given me the nod of acceptance and a key to the city. I knew for a certainty that shortly there after, the elements of New York, New York would test my psychological prowess, my manhood, and my pimp hand. I also knew for a surety that my pimping and me would test true.

The shinning chrome Dayton star wires and the expensive Vogue tires spun as my two-toned customized Cadillac Biarritz Eldorado hurtled down the highway towards a date with destiny or perhaps fate.

My mind reflected back through lessons learned and hundreds of thousands of pages of mental dialogue and retrospect, and focused on my mentor, the legendary Filmore Slim--Pimp, Philosopher, and Grand Master of the Game.

"Jimi," Filmore would begin, "always remember, pussy will sell when cotton and corn won't. When a trick won't buy food to feed his family or buy food even for his own belly, he'll beg, borrow, or steal some cash to take care of his dick. Jimi Starr, pussy is powerful stuff; most men got to have it," he would say. "However, pimping is even more powerful. Prostitution is the oldest profession in the world. The sale of pussy in America is just as lucrative as shares of stock in any Fortune-500 Company. Jimi, prostitution is just as big and just as lucrative as U. S. Steel," he would conclude. After all these years, I can still remember Fillmore's stirring words burning my ears and ringing in my mind.

America is comprised of suckers and tricks. It's like P.T. Barnum once said, "there is a sucker [trick] born every minute." Socially in this country, young women are unwittingly brought up to be common whores, however, never knowing or realizing it. Why? It is an American mindset, and is therefore the norm. Children grow through watching, and they emulate their mothers and fathers every day of their adolescent lives, especially on payday. The weary and dutiful father brings his paycheck home and the grateful mother prepares him a big meal. For his services rendered, after dinner Mom and Dad retire to the bedroom retreat where Mom rewards Dad for his labor, and not to mention his cash, with a shot of her hot pussy that she's most probably given to the mailman, milkman, a co-worker, or a passing handsome stranger for absolutely free. You can call it a wife's duty or you can call it whatever you want; however, the facts are what they are, and I like to call the transaction of sex for cash prostitution. Let us call a spade a spade. Had that poor working sap failed to get a paycheck, he would have had to sleep on the couch, or even worse.

Young girls in this society are traditionally taught to give themselves to the highest bidder. The social mindset and rule of thumb is, don't give yourself to the poor man; save yourself for the generous guy who takes you to dinner and buy's you gifts and gives you cash. Again, you can call it what you want, but the recipient of those gifts and cash is a cock-sucking whore if there ever was one.

On the flipside of that same coin, a young man is systematically and methodically taught to pamper women and lavish and give gifts and cash, with the hopes that he will be rewarded with a shot of some parasitic bitch's stinking pussy. You can call it what you want, but this young man is a trick, and being groomed for a lifetime of doting trickery. After careful scrutiny and analyses, I find the truth is that this society is knowingly raising and cultivating tricks and whores; it is a way of life. It is an institution and therefore it is acceptable.

Unfortunately for society, this scenario creates a climate that is tailor-made for a person of predatory cunning like myself, a pimp. Pimps have reversed the Game on society. For the most part, we don't give a shit about lavishing a bitch, nor does a real pimp give a shit about her stinking pussy, for that matter. The pimp, himself, is looking to be pampered and lavished. He wants the verbal blandishments, jewels, the gifts, the cash, etc. Why should some bitch have these valued assets that are so highly esteemed and prized in this capitalistic society? Anything of any real financial value that any woman affiliated with a pimp has in her possession, becomes the property of that pimp. From the onslaught, it must be realized just what a pimp is. A pimp is a capitalist in the truest sense of the word. He realizes society's preoccupation and obsession with sex, and therefore, the pimp sees pussy as a product or a commodity that will sell in the open market place of the world. He obtains that pussy through mental cunning and finesse and realizes a monetary exchange value of seven hundred to a thousand dollars a day profit per whore or perhaps more. Reader, you must understand, that no matter how articulate I seemingly may be, for a thousand dollars a day, I will make your white-haired grand mother suck dick and sell some pussy in a doorway, to some school kids! Hell, for a thousand dollars a day, I'd have your old grand mammy sale some of that old asshole, too!

For all of you cynical women feminists and brainwashed, terrified, emasculated male feminist sympathizers, I will have you to know that it is better for man to survive on the labor of the woman, than for the woman to survive off of the fruits of a wise man's labor. This process is called the survival of the fittest, and it is the first law of the jungle beast. Via the Constitution of these United States, all women have been granted the freedom of choice. However, all women do not choose to be liberated. During the course of my extensive and prosperous career, I never held a gun to any woman's head, nor physically forced any woman to do anything, yet all of my women were gracious, and not to mention they, that were all exceedingly generous.

Reader, if you would attempt to understand; your mind would become truly enlightened to this revolutionary school of thought, and you too, my dear mentally liberated reader, can be free. Again, it all boils down to that age-old cliché, "the survival of the fittest." The strong man shall survive. The weak man shall perish. No matter how you slice it or try to dice it, whether you agree or disagree, it really doesn't matter. The pimp is the only American male, free from the bondage and servitude to a female's vagina. He is the last man standing and the only true man, black or white, in the American society today.

It is this one singular and confrontational mindset that sets pimps apart from most males and the reason why pimping is most readily identified with Black males. The lawmakers who are representative of the White masses find pimping intimidating because it indirectly exposes the White masses as the mental and sexual weaklings that they really are. American males are enslaved to their dicks. Therefore, their minds are bound to a relentless quest for sex. Pimps have elevated past and moved beyond that sexual enslavement. This in my opinion is the reason the lawmakers have deemed pimping and prostitution illegal. In most other countries of the free world, pimping and prostitution are legal. I do not find it strange, nor by any means confusing, that White men constitute the largest segment of tricks in the United States. Sex plays a major roll in the American society. Prostitution has existed from the dawning of recorded time until today.

We live in a society in which every thing is for sale. If you were to turn on your television set at three o'clock on any given morning, you undoubtedly will find a semi-nude and highly suggestive infomercial, a 1-800-sex line or a tele-evangelist sinfully selling the blessings of God, from one dollar to a thousand dollars, to an audience of millions. It is all capitalistic exploitation; that's what the American economy and society are all about. How then, can pimping and prostitution be economically or morally wrong in a nation that has, over the course of time and throughout history, economically enslaved and oppressed the entire world? America, in its blood-thirsty pursuit of world domination and profits, has tied the world to its purse strings, with a hangman's noose, while furthering its own capitalistic pursuits and endeavors around the world, pursuing and murdering millions of innocent people via bombs and drug addiction, racism, and aggression around the world. Now that's what I consider pimping, true exploitation and oppression. How could America point its filthy racist finger at pimps and whores and utter the word "morality"? How dare America even think the word morality?

The nation's economy is based on capitalistic exploitations; everything is for sale. The basic lust for sex is primal, it is psychological, and it is realized through the physical need to dominate, compromise, or utilize one's sexual partner. Do we remember Helen of Troy, the face that launched a thousand ships? Down through the ages, man has warred over pussy, and killed over pussy. Hell, man even eats pussy. It is of little or no consequence to find that man will pay for pussy.

It is no whispered secret that sexual immorality in the Oval Office almost destroyed the former President of these United States. Yes, my dear reader, pussy is a commodity, not to mention some extremely powerful and devastating stuff. He, who can control the pussy, is he who holds the key to controlling the entire civilized free world.

In 1998, the then President of these United States endured impeachment proceedings, stemming from immoral acts while in the Oval Office. Had the woman in question been a whore of mine or someone like myself, I can honestly say that, without doubt, and for an absolute surety, there would be a pimp in the White House, standing behind the President, controlling the activities of America today. I challenge the readers of this novel to ask yourselves, is this scenario possible or probable? Then ask yourselves, are you controlling that pussy in your home or is that pussy controlling you? This, my dear and enlightened Reader, is my reason why.

As a child, while other kids played baseball and football or the cherished innocent youth dreams of becoming police or firemen, I would hang out in the barber shops and pool halls of the ghetto shining the shoes of the flamboyant pimps and players in the hopes of hearing their vividly colorful cross-country tales. In my childhood, pimping was a preoccupation, my fantasy. As I matured pimping became my life's ambition and, ultimately, my reality. I had but one desire--to pimp, pimp, and pimp expanding my pimpdom. I was now living the dream. As far as I was concerned for me, it had to be whore money or no money at all. I was a man driven and I was a man possessed. I was going to pimp or die. My entire life's scenario was just that cut and just that motherfucking dry.

Sweet, Sweet Mama

From out of the heavens and from a point somewhere beyond my limited understanding, the icy winds began to howl, rolling over the awakening face of Manhattan. Like a huge golden ball, the sun began its ascent on to the horizon to sit at its high point in the sky, only to descend at the end of the day. Cars made their way up and down the Harlem River Drive. People scurried, rushing frantically throughout Manhattan. They seemed to be going everywhere and ending up nowhere. I began to think to myself, what does it all mean and where would it all end?

In my mind I find myself reflecting back to my childhood and the voice that carries my sweet mother's words, "Jimi, it's a long road that doesn't have an ending." Mama did everything within her power to turn me away from the Game. I vividly remember Mama once knocking me down on the kitchen floor and physically washing my mouth out with Ajax and a dishrag. I had used the word "pimp" in her presence and in her household. Yes, my sweet mama tried all she could to turn me from the path leading to a life of parasitic pimping and pandering. Mama had strong spiritual convictions, as do I. Would you believe that Jim Starr, the legendary pimp, had attended and graduated from a school of theology? Perhaps that best explains why I was able to maintain throughout my career some minute degree of mortality.

I was sired by Ollie James Robinson, and born into this world on the second of April. I'm a product of the 1960's. My mother and my stepfather, Edgar Allen, whom I love dearly, raised me and, if the truth were told, Edgar Allen is the only father that I have ever really known. For the greater part of his life, Edgar Allen, has held two jobs as a longshoreman and a civil servant. My mother is and was the director of an emergency human services organization for abused youths. My parents were both extremely strict and yet, very loving.

Unlike Robert Beck, the author and patriarch of novels such as this, I was not sexually abused, nor abandoned, nor a victim of a broken home. In fact, my life was quite the contrary. I grew up and attended school in the upper Haight-Ashbury district of San Francisco. I was reared in a solid middle-class home and community with one brother, a dog, and a loving mother and father. For the most part, I was denied nothing that my loving mother and father could provide. For a Black kid in the late 60's, this was as close to the average American family as it would get. We were living the American dream.

I can recall one singular event from my childhood, which stands out, in my mind. It was the absolute first day of school. The excited mothers dragged, carried, or pulled their young crying and whining children to attend their first day of formal education. I can still remember the dimly lit echoing building and the highly waxed hallways and stairwells. The curious children shyly held their mothers' hands or clutched unto the hems of their mother's dresses.

Mrs. Jacobs, my kindergarten teacher, stood in front of the class, addressing the students and parents. From behind her thick, bi-focal glasses, she viewed the huge nametag that my mother had pinned to my plaid, flannel shirt. In an attempt to make me feel more comfortable, the teacher asked me, "Jimmy," she said, " What are you going to be when you grow up?"

It is unknown to me why or where these words came from, I only know they were expressed. As I stood holding the hem of my mother's dress, the words came from somewhere deep within the fiber of my being, "I'm going to be a poisonous butterfly and fly all over the world, spreading my poison everywhere," I said.

Looking at my life in retrospect, I wasn't far off. Mrs. Jacobs's eyes widened in curiosity and heightened suspicion. Her face turned beet red and her mouth fell wide open. I remember this incident vividly, as if it were yesterday. I can still see Mama standing there, embarrassed and with that look in her eyes that said, "Your ass is a mine, little smart-mouth nigger! Wait until I get you alone."

I can truthfully say I wasn't like most kids. I didn't give a rat's ass about baseball, football, being a cop or a fireman. I didn't want to fly a rocket ship to the moon. I simply wanted to pimp whores and that was my childhood preoccupation.

Mom and Dad were and are good people. It seems they live their lives helping others in need. Perhaps that was it. Perhaps somewhere deep inside of me I didn't want to be wrapped up, warm and pampered. Through the trial and errors of living life, I have come to know I was resisting structure and authority.

Jimi Starr

Chapter 2

New York, New York

We were leaving Jersey City, New Jersey; the two-toned maroon and white customized Biarritz Eldorado slowed to a stop at a signal light. The overhead sign read Lincoln Tunnel. A family of curious motorists, seeing the out of state license plates, pulled along side of the custom hog and began gawking through the tinted windows in the hopes of getting a closer look at perhaps what they thought was a Hollywood movie star. No such luck.

"No, Dad that's some kind of a goddamned pimp and his whores," I distinctly heard a disenchanted male voice say.

I decided to let the tinted window down so that this "All-American" family of squares could get a good look at what a real live pimp looked like, live and in living color. Father Square hurriedly turned his head away in the hopes that he would not be recognized by some whore he had previously dated. Placing my fingers on the automatic window control, I let the window descend. My diamond-encrusted hands gripped the steering wheel as my shoulder length hair blew in the New Jersey breeze. I profiled in Hollywood fashion and flashed the family of squares a diamond-toothed smile. Father Square turned beet red. The Mother Square gasped and stared in wide-eyed elation. In an attempt to save face with Father Square, she turned her face away as if she didn't see me as she waved her hand in front of her face, attempting to catch her breathe. Perspiration broke out on the goofy, freckled-face, and buck-toothed son's forehead as he secretly fondled his genitals. It was as if he was in a daze or perhaps wanted to pray; silently he starred at my whores mesmerized, as if he were staring into the face of God. He was most probably thinking about asking Father Square for an advance on his weekly allowance. Mother Square was sneaking another peek; I managed to make eye contact. Mother Square shivered and goose bumps broke out all over here body; she was sizzling hot and I knew it. Nasty little blonde-haired, blue-eye Daughter Square sat in the rear seat of the family utility vehicle, fondling her firm, and round breasts as she licked her lips, sticking her tongue out at me and wiggled it at me in suggestive fashion. Nasty little daughter square began to fan her legs open and shut, a sure-fire sign of sexual arousal. The whole goddamn, sexually perverted, All-American square family was sizzling and burning up hot. The angered and intimidated Father Square sped away, his wheels screeching into the congested traffic.

Cautiously, I made my way through the merging traffic into the two-lane tunnel, inching towards a hot date with fate. The dim overhead lighting seemed to flash off and on. At the end of the tunnel was a light showing me the way as I slowly forged my way through the stagnant traffic and towards destiny. A destination sign read, "You are now entering the City of New York, New York", as we exited the Lincoln Tunnel and entered the city.

It was 1:30 in the morning and the vaporous heat of the city and its tall buildings seemed to rise from the sidewalk straight up into the darkness, ascending into the star-lit the heavens. Anxious hoards of vibrant people, discovering the city, tourists and locals alike; roamed the streets as if it were 12:00 noon; taxi cabs and limousines were everywhere, and a sea of angry horns blew as the traffic bottle-necked and came to a stop at 24th Street. Wide-eyed, my curious and anxious whores surveyed their initial view of Manhattan as we made our way through the hustling and bustling midtown area.

Cautiously, I made my way through the reckless and sporadic traffic of Tenth Avenue, towards the Times Square area. The voices and sounds of the horns and the traffic were almost deafening. I eased my customized Eldorado to the curb at the intersection of 29th and Park Avenue, which would later become a point of rendezvous for my crew of notorious West Coast whores.

Under the cover of darkness, I cut off my engine and turned off my headlights. In complete silence, I solemnly and studiously stared out my tinted windows. I was bedazzled at the sight. The parade of tricks was endless. They bee-lined and zigzagged back, forth and back across the intersection, pursuing whores of all nationalities, shapes, and sizes. The streets were lined with cars and there was a whore sucking or fucking a trick in what seemed like every one of them. Half-naked whores in mink coats, wearing silk lingerie, sucked dicks in doorways, while other aggressive whores pulled cunt-hungry tricks into illicit hotels.

The atmosphere was thick with ambitions and excitement. There was an odious stench of sex and fast cash hovering in the midnight air. Hum, I thought, had I found myself a honey hole or perhaps the proverbial bird's nest on the ground?

The overhead streetlights shone down on my customized Cadillac and through my tinted windows, causing flecks of blues, reds, and yellows to sparkle from my diamond encrusted dukes. Bianca placed her hand on my thigh and nudged me gently. She was ready. I looked in the mirror at the three young whores in the rear seat who anxiously awaited my any and every command.

Wickedly, I smiled then spoke. " A woman is the product and the reflection of her man's teachings. So hear me and hear me well. You are the best flat backers and thieves in the country. You have held your own against top flight whores all across America. We have come to New York because it is the Mecca of pimps and whores. I have faith in your abilities; I'm sure you will all fare well. While you whores are out there getting my money this evening, I want you to remember this; the Game never changes, just the faces and the places. Always remember, a familiar face is not always the best face," I said. "Now I want you whores out there selling pussy out of both draw legs, sucking them, fucking them, and jacking them off," I continued. "Now go, whores, and get me the cash I mothafuckin' need."

With my manicured, diamond-encrusted hand I motioned them out of the door and into the cruel lucrative streets of Manhattan. New York was a city with a population of eight million people who had eight million stories; I didn't know nor realize it then but my story would soon become one of them.

Bianca and I exchanged knowing glances as the three got out of the car. These four whores were known across America to be notorious thieves and flat backers. The players of the game had nick-named my infamous crew of whores The Gabors.

The air conditioner blasted. It was an unusually warm, humid, mid-summer Saturday night as my whores left the car and I pulled from the curb and began my survey of the fast life in Manhattan. Through out the city, in the shadows of the tall buildings and in the darkness of the night, whores, hustlers, and an assortment of thieves plied their craft, searching for a mark with a plump pocket full of cash.

It was a strangest thing about the Game; it didn't give a fuck who it took advantage of or robbed. I was determined it wasn't going to be me. I cruised along 45th Street. At the intersection of 8th Avenue, while I was sitting at a red light, a dark figure approached my hog. There was a tap on my window. New York was well known for it's gank artists and stick-up kids.

Startled, I reached under my seat in contemplation of the worst-case scenario, and I wrapped my hand around the grip of my blue steel pistol. At that point, I heard a loud and familiar cheerful voice. "Jimi Starr, you dirty California pimp you!!!" It was K.J., a homeboy from Sacramento, California. He was a high-powered, Rolls Royce driving pimp, renowned for his crew of cutthroat, murderous and thieving black whores.

"K.J. my dirty California pimp pal," I said smiling. I stepped from my customized Biarritz Eldorado. We embraced and exchanged pleasantries.

"How long have you been in the town, baby?" K.J. asked.

"I just pulled up," I replied. K.J. pointed across the street.

"There's an after-hours across the street; park your car and let's have a drink and some powder and I'll run this town by you. Jimi, I guarantee you haven't ever experienced nothing like it. This is the city so nice they've named it twice. New York, New York," he said enthusiastically, as he smiled and grabbed his right and left front pants pockets, exposing the imprint of two huge bankrolls. It was at that point that I noticed that he wore no jewelry.

In a concerned tone K.J. began to speak, "Jimi, you are known for wearing that flamboyant jewelry, but as long as you are here, always remember where you are. Nigga, this is the Big Apple; these mothherfuckers don't give a fuck about you being Jimi Starr, the high-powered pimp, nigga. A cop or the man on the street will attempt to rob your ass in this city," he continued. "In the City of New York, you never want to be searched by the police. Any cash or jewelry they find, they may be prone to keep. As a matter of fact, there is a crew of dirty cops in this area that have been robbing pimps and whores left and right for their cash and jewelry as if it were the thing to do," he concluded.

"If I were you, I'd take my jewelry off until I knew the city and how to move around in it." I heard K. J.'s words of concerned wisdom and surveyed my immediate surroundings. I also realized that the quickest way for a man to make a mark out of himself and stage himself for a robbery was to attempt to take his jewelry off in the middle of the street, in front of scrutinizing eyes.

On 45th Street at the intersection of 10th Avenue, under an overhead streetlight and a royal blue canopy, had a sign that read The Big Dipper in white lettering. Colorful pimps, dope dealers, con men, and thieves and their women drifted into and out of this popular illegal establishment of underworld congregation.

It was Saturday night in New York City and, as if it were high noon, people curiously strolled the avenue in search of fun and excitement in the Big City. Taxicabs, passenger cars, and busloads of people passed and nobody noticed. It was almost as if nobody cared. It had to be buzzard's luck. We had walked no less than fifty feet when we saw, parked at the curb, an unmarked police vehicle containing three police officers that sat with their engine idling. In the front seat, two muscular blonde detectives anxiously rifled through and greedily counted a young renegade whore's trap. At their side was a clipboard with a picture of a fifteen-year old girl listed as missing.

In the rear seat of the unmarked police vehicle and in dog fashion, their sweaty, red head partner was nude from the waist down as he feverishly and brutally jack-hammered his swollen dick into the tender pink, puckered butthole of a hysterical, wide-eye teen-age runaway who, oddly enough, looked a great deal like the girl in the photo. It was the young girl's eerie wailing and tortured screams that captured my attention. Without thinking and not knowing it was a police car, I foolishly glanced into the rear seat of the car. What I saw and heard caused me to hesitate momentarily, not really sure of what I had quite unintentionally witnessed.

I heard a voice with a heavy Irish accent roar, "Freeze, niggers!" The front doors of the unmarked vehicle slammed shut as the two blonde rouge detectives in the front seat exited and stepped away from the car towards us, with pistols drawn.

"Get your hands up!" The sight of their cocked blue steel pistols, the tone of the undercover officer's chilling words, and his pale blue and angry racist eyes brought us to an abrupt and immediate halt.

"Nigger, did I see you looking into the window of my car?" " Nigger, did I." The blonde mustache detective angrily quizzed.

"Just what in the fuck were you looking at, you goddamned Peeping Tom Jigger boo?" the rouge detective threateningly snapped, flashing angrily pale blue eyes.

"Do you niggers see anything see anything out of the ordinary?" The blonde mustache detective questioned.

The red headed detective in the rear seat never looked up and never missed a beat, as he manically continued to viciously stroke and punish the tender schoolgirl rectum of the horrified juvenile runaway, and as she continued to wail like a Banshee.

"No, we don't see anything," K. J. nervously replied. "Not a thing, sir," K.J. responded again in an intimidated tone. From the sound of K.J.'s jittery voice and the shaken look in his eyes, I sensed that these police were real live fools and that we were in immediate danger.

"Listen, officer," I began, "I truly meant no one any harm. We were simply walking down the street and I happened to see and hear your buddy making love to his girl in the back seat of the car. I'm not from around here, sir, the event caught me by surprise, and momentarily I hesitated and curiously glanced into the window. Again, Sir, I meant you and your associates no harm," I concluded.

With pistols drawn the two detectives stood, listening and watching my every move. The blue-eye cop spoke and concluded. "I like you, nigger, because you were honest and didn't lie to me." He and his partner began to put away their pistols.

"When niggers lie to us, it really makes my partners angry. When they think that niggers are trying to put some shit over on us, then we have to hurt them to keep them honest," the cop continued.

His mustached partner anxiously remarked, "That's some real nice jewelry that you have there, nigger; do you have any money?"

Blue Eyes spoke, running interference on his partner and most probably stopping a robbery at the hands of New York's Finest.

"Boy, I know every pimp in the borough of Manhattan and I've never seen you before, so I assume you're new around here. How long have you been in the city?"

Answering only what I had been asked and volunteering no information, I said, " I just arrived tonight officer," I answered.

"I like this Moolie, he's intelligent and he's honest," the officer said to his partner, then looked at me and continued, "You can go a long way around here, boy." " My partner is eager to shake you down for your cash and jewelry, but for some strange reason, I'm feeling exceptionally generous. So I'm going to welcome you to the city and warn you, we rob pimps. The next time you see us, have something for us. If you don't have our money the next time we see you, we'll take you niggers for a ride in the patrol car, kick your ass, and take it all. Perhaps no one will ever see your black assess again," he said. "Because you just got to the city tonight, this one time only I'm going too give you jigga boos a pass and let you go." He continued, "You boys remember me and how good I've been to you, because you're going to be seeing me again."

K.J. excitedly nudged me towards the street. The blue-eye detective concluded, "Remember, if I ever catch you degenerate peeping-Tom niggers looking into another window inside the City of New York again, I'll blow your black goddamn brains out. Now get the fuck out of here before I kick you in your ass."

Throughout the entire conversation, the red headed detective never looked up and never missed a stroke. He continued to punish the tender, young butt hole of his horrified, screaming adolescent captive.

"Jimi, keep walking. Don't look back or they might give you a ride in the rear seat of that cop car. This is New York," K.J. began. "You might see or hear anything at any time. Always remember, whatever you see or hear, don't stop; it's none of your business. See no evil and speak no evil."

He continued, "Those two blonde detectives are infamous. They go by the names Baloney and Cheese. They don't just rape and rob whores; they rape, and rob pimps and dope dealers too. Jimi, whatever you do while you're in the City of New York, stay out of their way. If they ever find out who you really are, you're in real trouble, pal. Pimps have been seen getting into the back seat of their patrol car that were never seen again."

I stopped at the curb to smoke a cigarette. K.J. continued into the after-hours. I watched an endless flow of traffic on 45th Street.

The sweaty cop in the rear of the police car was still feverishly socking his cock into the whore. What kind of cop would fuck a screaming baby in the ass? Only in New York, I thought to myself.

I put out my cigarette and stepped through the door into a small informal nightclub setting. There was a white guy on the stage doing a

Frank Sinatra impersonation as a room full of Italian-looking people applauded. There was an elevator directly to the right as I entered the building. A huge well-dressed Italian bouncer began to pat me down, searching for weapons. I glanced around the room as I realized the players I had seen enter the building were not here. Turning around, I shrugged my shoulders and spoke.

"Excuse me, partner, I must be in the wrong place," I implied to the bouncer.

"You must be the new guy in town," the bouncer responded with a heavy New York accent. "K.J. told me you were coming in right behind him, so I'm going to excuse you and I'm going to forget about it," he said with the confidence and poise of a polished pimp.

The bouncer pressed the button for the elevator and the doors slid open, exposing a hidden entrance to the building next door.

Cautiously, I stepped through and the elevator door slid shut behind me. Before my eyes could focus, I heard the sound of dice rattling and heard them rolling across a table crashing into chips.

On the other side of the door, before my vision could adjust, a grinning Puerto Rican, holding an Uzi, greeted me. He was security.

"Turn around and put your hands on the wall, I'm going to pat you down," he said. The hair rose on the back of my neck, it was if time itself had stopped. There was something about his voice and demeanor that led me to believe this guy had used these words before, under other conditions.

"Sure," I said as I nervously and obliged.

I looked around the room as he patted me down. There were four other Uzi-toting Puerto Ricans floating around the crowded room. I began to hear the joyous chatter of the street people. A live jazz band played on stage.

"That's some real nice jewelry that you have there, buddy; you look like King Tutt," the Uzi-toting Rican snidely continued. "Be careful that one of these New Yorkers doesn't take that jewelry away from you, King Tutt,".

There was something very cold and very sinister about this grinning gangster. I made a mental note to remember him.

In one corner on the far side of the room, gamblers surrounded a crap table. There was the sound of rattling and rolling dice and the Italian stickman's voice that yelled, "Seven, unlucky seven. Sorry, nigga, you lose."

In a darkened corner on the far side of room, a Hispanic man sat at a wooden table, under a bright light that hung from a cord that was dangling from the ceiling. On the table was a triple beam scale. On either side of the man sitting at the table were two huge trashcans; one that was full of cash and the other was full of powdered cocaine. Inside of the After Hours, directly behind the man that sat at the table was an open cabinet that was filled with neatly stacked with bricks of cocaine. In his hand, the man held a large scoop.

"You must be new here," he said eyeing me. "This is why they call this establishment the Big Dipper, he added. Smiling, he asked, "Can I help you?"

"No thanks, buddy," I replied. I had never seen that much cocaine or that much cash at one time in my life. I stood momentarily looking at this underworld wonderment.

"Excuse me, my man." I turned toward the sound of the friendly voice. "Aren't you the Jimi Starr nigga?"
He questioned.
"I might be," I cautiously replied.

" I'm Gorgeous Gary and this is my partner Top Cat. We call him T.C. "We're from Boston, Massachusetts. Perhaps you've heard of us, as we've heard of you." He questioned. When I didn't answer, he went on. "The word is that you've been doing some marvelous pimping all across the country, Jimi Starr. Your name and your reputation proceeds you," G.G. concluded.

"Sure, I've heard of you guys," I smoothly replied as we shook hands and they escorted me to their table in the VIP section of the After Hours.

It is a strange thing about the life pimp's call the Game, if you are a successful pimp and you are pimping to any degree in a major city or on any major track in the country, your name will precede you. Because of the nomadic nature of pimps and whores and their comings and goings to different cities and destinations, someone in every major city knew you. Likewise, if you were a perpetrator, that label would precede you also.

In the candle-lit booth, Paul Price, Lil' Kim, T.C., Kenny Diamond, K.J., Gorgeous Gary, International Blue and I, cross-country pimps all, sat and exchanged thoughts until well after sunrise. I didn't know it then but looking at life in retrospect; that night, among the pimps who sat at that table, a powerful alliance in the Game was forged that would last for years to come.

K.J. and I pulled up out of the speak easy at about 7:00 a.m. He went his way and I went mine. We had partied, tossed thoughts, and kicked the civilized world in the ass 'til the early morning hours. There were many cross-country players, pimps, con men, dope dealers, and thieves there that whom I knew. I had been well received by New York's underworld elite. This would be the first of many such sessions. This was New York, New York, the Big Apple, and Jimi Starr had arrived.

Over the years, it has been said that the West Coast is the best coast. However, I am a man who has traveled the length and breath of the continental United States on a numerous amount of occasions. It has been my personal experience that, be it east or west, the Game never changes, simply the places and the faces. East Coast or West Coast, Madison Avenue, Hollywood Boulevard, or perhaps Pennsylvania Avenue in front of the White House, the Game is where you find it.

Night's darkness fled as the gleaming golden sun brought a new day to the City of Manhattan. My crew of enthusiastic whores anxiously stood in the early morning shadows of the Empire State Building as curious workers entered and left their places of employ. At the corner of 32nd Street, a blonde, stringy-hair police detective in plain clothes wearing a plaid shirt, tied off, inserted a needle into his arm, and drifted into a drug-induced euphoria. Meanwhile, whores and tricks alike passed him by, paying no attention to the disgusting scene; they entered and exited the illicit hotels. Slowly and methodically, horny johns, each searching for the whore of his choice or perhaps the girl of his dreams, circled the block on Madison Avenue. Early morning customers entered grocery stores. On the streets, early morning customers patronized hot dog and pretzel vendors who were opening shop, preparing for the day, unconcerned, as if nothing was happening. Horny tricks and money-hungry whores continued to do what they were doing. It was just another day in the city. Inside parked cars, on either side of Madison Avenue and in doorways in broad daylight, aggressive whores in broad day light openly and without shame practiced their craft as if they had a license in the light of the rising sun and in the shadow of the Empire State Building. New York was truly a city that never slept. Only in New York, I thought to myself. The tricks were still riding as I pulled to the curb. Excitedly, my enthusiastic, bright-eye, giggling whores rushed the car.

At the corner of 32nd Street and Madison Avenue, parked directly in front of my customized Cadillac, a famous professional basketball player was getting his groove on in the rear seat of a limousine with a three foot six-inch midget with flowing blonde hair. She stood nude and wide-legged, bracing herself with her arms while her head hung out the window. The illicit midget became the recipient of a slam-dunk fucking from the famous NBA star.

"Daddy!! " Daddy, Manhattan is just like you said!" Boom Boom, my youngest whore, proudly announced. "We've been getting money hand over fist."

Yes, it had been just like I said. I checked $3,200.00 that morning, not to mention a watch that turned out to be an 18 carat gold Rolex Presidential. It had been a long day. It had also been an informative and now a prosperous one. I was tired and I was hungry. I pulled my car from the curb, and headed towards my sub-leased penthouse apartment in West New York, New Jersey for a good hot meal and some much needed sleep.

Bianca

In the bedroom of our dimly lit penthouse apartment, not far from the banks of the Hudson in West New York, New Jersey, with curtains open, we watched the light from the first of many beautiful red sunsets reflected in the windows of the skyline of Manhattan. Tugboats pulled barges up and down the Hudson River. Methodically, stagnant traffic made it's way past the U.N. Building on Franklin Delano Roosevelt Drive. Bianca and I lay nude and uncovered in the sweltering warmth of the New Jersey evening. I ran my eyes over her beautifully toned and textured chocolate body. It had been seven years, but it seemed like only yesterday. She had been a premiere runway fashion model with a nationally known black fashion organization. I would never forget that sensationally entertaining evening in San Francisco, after an elegant all-stars occasion in one of San Francisco's finest concert halls. I could still recall the moment that I presented her with one dozen long-stemmed red roses.

Holding her hand, I whispered these tender words of endearment into her ear, "If your mind and your heart are half as beautiful as you are, then you are someone that I would love to know." She gasped for air and waved her hand in front of her face as if to catch her breath. I put my hand around her waist and pulled her closer to me.

Breathless, she stood before me, dazzled and amazed. Attempting to resist the inevitable, she whispered, "I already have a man." I placed my finger to her luscious ruby-red lips.

Looking deep into her beautiful chestnut-brown eyes, I enfolded her in a romantic lover's embrace and whispered, "Yes, you do have a man; that man is me. To resist me and to resist your own destiny is futile." With that statement, I passionately kissed her sweet, sweet quivering lips, and we've been together from that day to this.

I have never been one who was known to kiss and tell; however, just this once I'll make a rare and informative exception. Out of the infinite scores of whores that I have bedded, during the course of my career and throughout the course of prescribed time, Bianca Starr has the sweetest pussy that I've ever had the pleasure or opportunity to encounter, or that my legendary penis has ever entered. The taboo ride on Bianca's cherry poom poom was so magnificently exquisite that I can find no words to express my mental or sexual elation through verbal or written articulation.

Jimi Starr

Chapter 3

Shake Dancer

It was 7:30pm Sunday and, like every Sunday, my crew of notorious whores and I sat at the kitchen table having family dinner. I had only been in New York two weeks and, up until last night things had gone relatively smooth. Last night I had a whore come up missing. The three whores at the table chatted gaily. I wiped my mouth with a napkin and began to speak. Their mouths fell silent as they sternly listened attentively; all eyes were on me. Whores don't just disappear from the face of the planet; one of these devious whores knew something and I was about to find out who.

Standing up from the kitchen table, I walked to the sliding glass door and slid it open. I stepped out and stood on the balcony. The golden sun had begun its breath, taking descent into the red skies over Manhattan. I watched a lone night hawk soar into view. The hawk appeared to freeze on the evening breeze. Just as swiftly as the hawk appeared, it soared away. In the distance I could see the cars making their way up and down Harlem River Drive and the seemingly never ending traffic congestion of Midtown and the Times Square area. At the intersection in front of my penthouse, stagnant traffic came to a stand still.

My crew of seasoned whores watched in mixed anticipation as the hawk soared away on the breeze. For the proper mental effect, I grabbed the railing on the balcony with both hands, squeezing it until my knuckles protruded. Slowly and deliberately I turned and growled, "If it's one thing I can't stand, it's for a whore of mine to lie to me or attempt to deceive me. It makes me angry. For lying to me, one of you whores is going to learn how to fly this evening."

With my manicured hand, I pointed to Suzie Q. She was a gorgeous Cajun whom I had acquired while I was in New Orleans last year. She and Tina were the best of working buddies. They were a team. If any one knew anything about Tina's whereabouts, Suzie Q did. I motioned her to me. Slowly, Suzie Q wobbled out of the penthouse onto the balcony towards me. She and I stood taking in the view of the cityscape as I wrapped my arm around her. The hawk returned to view and soared motionless over the city. I pointed at the hovering hawk as it glided on the breeze, motionlessly over the city.

"Can you do that Suzie?" I asked.

Her eyes almost leaped from her head; she swooned from puzzlement and fear.

In response, Suzie Q whispered and questioned, "Can I do what, Jimi?"

In mischievous fashion, I glared into her horrified eyes and spat, "Can you fly, bitch?"

She had tears in her eyes and her entire body was shaking as if she had the palsy when she flatly stated, "Jimi, no one can fly."

Suzie Q tried to make direct eye contact with me, hoping I was joking. However, I maintained that distant look, keeping her off balance.

"Sure you can fly, Suzie Q," I said continued. "Now climb up on the rail and hop off the side of the building and fly for Daddy," I demanded.

Suzie Q climbed up onto the only chair that sat on the balcony; cringing, she peeked through one eye; she peeked over the edge down at the congested traffic below. She was trembling; her body jerked as if she was having convulsions as the tears streamed down her terrified face.

"Suzie Q cried, "If you tell me to fly, Jimi, I'm going to die. It will kill me; kill me dead. I don't want to die," she whimpered.

I asked, "Am I your man, Suzie?"

"Yes, Daddy, you know you are my man," she sobbed.

"Is there something you'd like to tell me, Suzie, before you test your wings and leap off the side of the building?" I questioned.

Suzie watched as the hawk gracefully soared away on the breeze.

"Yes, Jimi, yes," Suzie Q pleaded, "I want to tell you something, Daddy. I want to tell you something right now," she cried. "I can't fly, Jimi, and I do not want to die for that crazy gangster robbing bitch."

The truth is, I wanted to laugh so badly it was hurting me. I would never have let her jump nor pushed her for that matter. Case in point, she didn't know that.

"Jimi, Tina's been robbing mobster tricks," she said.

My mind reeled as Suzie's informative words slapped me like a hammer, instantly making everything crystal clear. This explained the ridiculous amounts of cash and the fine jewelry Tina had given me, over the course of the last year. My mind flashed through the recent past. It was a good thing that I was on the highway or the celebrated mobster, Don Vito, most probably would have maimed or murdered me by now.

Don Vito was an aging and renowned drug-trafficking gangster who owned a chain of topless bars throughout America. He was legendary known for his horrifically sadistic exploits. He had the respect of every criminal in the country.

I reflected on the stacks of cash, Rolex watches, and almost countless number of diamond rings that this whore had given me. I realized there had to be hoards of enraged and murderous drug dealer gangsters, searching high and low, across the length and the breadth of the continental United States for this unwise and foolish bitch. I was hell bent on finding that bitch fast, putting her on a jet, and sending her as far away from me as possible.

Over the years, if the Game has taught me anything, it was not to fuck with anybody's shit that's mob connected. I headed straight to the safe in my bed room and removed every piece of jewelry this confused, wanna be slick whore had ever given me, putting the jewelry into a large red velvet jewelry pouch, placing it into the inside pocket of my leather jacket that lay on the bed.

Tina had been a shake dancer in a San Francisco tittie joint when I initially knocked her. She was selling pussy to the flashy big spending syndicate types of the exclusive establishment on the under. Her claim to fame was the fact that she had once been with young Bowdy, the same youngster who ran the David and Goliath act on the Bear, in Ace's Barber Shop, turning the ferocious Honey Bear into a toothless and whining bear cub.

I distinctly remember my first encounter with Tina. She proudly boasted that Bowdy was the man who turned her out.

"No, baby," I corrected her. "Bowdy is simply the nigger that turned you lose. Jimi Starr is the man who's going to turn you out." I replied.

Tina's skin was softer and smoother than a newborn baby's ass. She was tall, dark and slender and had huge silicone-implanted breasts that would have made Dolly Parton blush. Some in-love syndicate trick known as Don Vito had purchased her a set of jiggling, humongous titties while she was dancing in that ritzy shake joint in San Francisco. From the beginning, Tina went straight koo-koo for my pimping and me. If the truth were known, I kind of liked that big-tittied black bitch, too.

However, try as she may and pimp as I did, her whoring abilities never really matured, nor was she what I would call a true thief. However, she was consistent with her cash flow. What I didn't know was that she was robbing the underworld figures that she had met in the bar in San Francisco. She was simply stealing from people she knew who had trusted her.

It was the strangest thing. Over the course of the year that I had possession of and pimped on Tina, at least twice a month, like clockwork, no matter where I was in the country, that bitch would surface with ridiculous amounts of cash and fine jewelry. Over the course of the year I had simply written off her seemingly good fortune as a counter balance for her obvious lack of skills, attributing it to the luck of the draw. I was all the way across country and in New York before I had a hint or realized what Tina was doing.

The music from the stereo blared as I made my way from Jersey City, through the Lincoln Tunnel, and into Midtown. It was Sunday evening and the traffic was unusually light. In Manhattan, there was a track on Eleventh Avenue that was open 24 hours a day. It was still daylight so I decided to put some work in on Eleventh until the sun went down; then I would move my crew of skillful whores to Madison Avenue.

Seasoned whores always carried a change of clothes just in case they got lucky; i.e., robbed a trick and had to change identities, getting away in a hurry.

I turned off 42nd Street on to Eleventh Avenue, pulling to the curb at 39th Street. The track was on full. A U.S. Postal Service truck sat parked at the curb; the stark naked Asian mail carrier was fucking the shit out of a fat, pale, bleached blonde, perhaps he was on his lunch break.

Directly across the street from, the U.S. Postal Service truck was parked a blue police cruiser was parked, containing one of New York's Finest. In the rear seat of the car, the blonde hair officer frantically socked it into a set of black thighs. I can only imagine some naive whore was trading her sex for her freedom.

Always and without fail, there was Rubber Man. Rubber Man, at first glance, appeared to be a derelict. He wore a long, black overcoat, uncombed hair, and scraggly beard. Rubber Man walked the track day and night selling dick rubbers to whores in need, at a marked up price. In a city like Manhattan and a track like Eleventh Avenue, I can only surmise that though he looked like a derelict, in reality he was most probably a millionaire.

It was business as usual. Sassy and virtually naked, voluptuous whores walked the streets in sheer sexy underwear and wearing spiked high-heel shoes, aggressively waving at and pursuing sweating and horny stiff-dick tricks. Eleventh Avenue, during that time, was a nationally known meat rack whore's stroll. Whores from all over the nation converged there to practice their lewd craft. In the cars parked along the illicit avenue or in doorways and even against buildings, no less than one hundred whores sucked and fucked tricks right out in the open and in broad daylight, as if they had a license and as if there were no tomorrow. Discarded and soiled rubbers lay three to four inches deep in some places on the sidewalk and the streets. The stench of sex and seamen was in the air. Some might equate this perverse scene unto that of Sodom and Gomorrah. New York was a city with eight million people and on any given day there were two million tourists from around the world. In a city of ten million people, I think it was safe to assume that five million of them wanted to fuck daily. If a pimp couldn't get a minimum of $500.00 a day per bitch and $1,000 per bitch per day on the weekend, then that nigga simply wasn't pimping or that bitch wasn't whoring. There is an old pimp cliché that reads, "If there is a slacking in your macking, there will be no showing in your whoring."

I dropped my whores off on 39th Street and made my way through the traffic of Midtown toward 45th and Broadway. It had always been a mindset with me that a runaway or missing whore always returns to where you found her, trying once again to become the person that she was before she met you. When I met Tina in San Francisco, she was a dancer of some renowned local notoriety. If the bitch had her rathers, she would rather still be dancing. I assumed if she were missing, I would find her in a shake joint somewhere in the city, shaking those huge titties that the notorious mobster trick had bought her and that she was so arrogantly proud of. I pulled to the curb at Broadway and 45th and parked. At the very first bar I came to, the marquees on the overhead read Venny Valachi's Poom Poom Room.

Lively, melodic and soulful music drifted out of the Poom Poom Room and onto the bristling streets of Times Square; sweaty-faced voyeuristic customers rapidly stepped from the sidewalk into the mob-run establishment, escaping the heat of the sweltering city into air-conditioned darkness of the exotic dancing establishment.

The two three hundred pound bodyguards were twins. They were well dressed, black suited twins, with hands the size of small hams. They stood at either side of the black draped entrance of the doorway.

A gray-haired, hump backed, yellow-toothed, cigar-smoking barker, in a plaid sports coat was standing at the curb calling out to curious passers-bys, "Step right up, sir; and come on in and witness this indescribable, once in a life time sexual odyssey with your own eyes. Come in and feast your starving eyes on the ninth wonder of the world, the black Dolly P. For a two-drink minimum, you too, sir, can experience the once in a lifetime thrill of witnessing her sensually, incomparable, jiggling gyrations. Experience the thrill known as Chocolate Love, the velvet black beauty with the Dolly Parton titties. She walks, she talks, and for enough money, she will crawl on her belly like a reptile," he humorously concluded.

I stepped through the door. A gold-framed picture featuring Tina and her humongous renowned tits hung from the wall. There was no doubt about it. It was Tina all right. I sat down at a table at the rear of the room until my eyes adjusted to the darkness. A silver mirrored disco ball hung, spinning from the ceiling over the stage. A brass pole ran from the floor of the stage to the ceiling. After a minute or two, my eyes adapted to the darkness and there she was, live at center stage in a red thong and matching spiked high-heel shoes. Tina bumped and grinded and gyrated, but most of all she proudly shook her renowned titties. A long-legged cocktail waitress, wearing a blue bra and thong, with pale blue eyes brought a drink to the table.

"This is from your friend," she said, pointing.

I looked up and caught a glimpse of my old pal, Butch Stone, private eye, leaving the gangster owned establishment.

Like an acrobat or perhaps a contortionist, Tina wiggled her ass while jiggling her famous tits in opposite directions and sliding her pussy up and down the length of the brass pole. Out of the darkness into view, I moved to a stage front table as Tina did her act. Damn, this bitch is fantastic, I thought to myself. It's a damn shame I've never appreciated big tities or pole dancing either, for that matter. Tina and I made eye contact. At the end of her act, she sat down next to me.

"Jimi, how did you find me?" She asked.

"Never mind how I found you," I said, "The fact is that I found you." Coldly I staed at her and continued, "You left without saying goodbye." Leaning over the table, questioningly I whispered, "Out of all the places in the world for a runaway whore to go, why would you come to a place where the motherfuckers want to kill you?"

"Before you say anything Jimi, may I please say something?" she asked.

"Sure, go ahead, Tina," I responded.

"Nigga, I risked my life, stealing those gangsters jewelry for you! It is because of you that Vito was looking for me in the first place. I stole jewelry from him, and his friends to make you happy. You have street whores, and too many of them as far as I'm concerned. I have ruined my career and all but lost my life, and I have never gotten any attention from you. Jimi I am a dancer. I cannot compete with those street whores of yours and now Vito tells me he forgives me. Even though Vito did question me, asking me the whereabouts of the jewelry, I never divulged that information. If these Diego motherfucker's were looking for me to kill me, I think you should at least get a good ass-whipping out of it."

Coldly I stared across the table and calmly said, "Are you finished, Tina?"

"Yes, motherfucker, I'm finished," she said, shaking her head in ghetto fashion.

"Tina, coming here is not the wisest move that you ever made. These people are known killers; they've been looking for you to kill you," I concluded.

In an elevated and arrogant tone Tina responded, "When I talked to Vito, my Italian sugar daddy, he reassured me that everything was okay. He even told me to look up his cousin Venny, who gave me a job here at the Poom Poom Room, dancing and all was forgotten. He's flying in from San

Francisco to night. Tomorrow Vito is going to take me shopping and rent me an apartment. Vito's rich and he will give me anything I want."

I looked across the table into her eyes and thought to myself; surely this bitch doesn't believe this shit?

"When Don Vito gets here, bitch, he's going to give you something, all right, and you are not going to like it," I said. "Now get your shit, Tina, we're getting out of here, now, " I continued.

"Why?" she asked.
"So you can take me some where and kick my ass?" she spat.

"No Tina, I don't want to kick your ass. I'm your man. I'm your family. I'm trying to save your ass, dumb bitch. Understand, I'm in danger and my own life is in jeopardy just being here," I said. Tina gazed at me in a confused kind of way, as if I were speaking to her in some foreign tongue.

"Jimi, these people look out for me. They are my family. Vito has already forgiven me for my temporary loss of loyalty and assured me that no harm was done," Tina said.

"Wake up, ignorant nigga bitch! You've robbed the mob!" I said. "You've been watching too many of those goddamned godfather movies. You're no fucking Italian, whore, and even if you were, these murderous sons of bitches will not only kill, but have been known to mutilate the corpses of ignorant mother -fuckers who have robbed them. If you believe that because you gave Vito some of your stinking pussy, it's okay to rob the mob and you'll be forgiven for it, then you're already a dead bitch. Now, Tina, get your shit and lets go," I concluded.

The two giant Italian bouncers waddled across the room and stood over the table and one of them questioned, "Are you all right, Chocolate?"

"Sure, Joe, no problems," she confidently responded. "This is simply an old friend who was just leaving." She intentionally let me see her wink at one of the giant; no-neck bouncers and he nodded, which I perceived as a signal to the twins that if I got out of line, they should give me a real good ass whipping.

This foolish whore really thought that she was plugged into and had clout with the infamous Don Vito and the racist Italian mob? Go figure.

"I'm going to walk him outside to his car. I'll be right back," Tina concluded.

"Sure Tina, I understand." One of the three hundred pound Italian bouncers mean-mugged me, slamming his ham-like fist into the palm of his open hand. I stood and walked to the door. Tina followed me and the two giant, sadistic bouncers followed close behind her.

Neon light's, fresh air and the sounds of the flowing Midtown traffic met me as I left the shake joint. My car was parked at the curb directly in front of the bar.

"Tina, I may never see you again," I said. "I have something in the car that belongs to you. Who knows, it might even save your life."

"I am not going to allow you to trick me. I'm not going to get in any car with you, you dirty black nigga pimp!" She said loud and arrogantly, in doing so summoning the two giant Italians. Tina was hell bent on causing me some confusion.

Hurriedly, I got into my car and rolled down the window. Reaching into the pocket of my leather coat, I produced the red velvet bag.

"Say whore," I said, "this is every piece of jewelry you've ever given me." Leaning into the window, she attempted to use her body as a shield to prevent the two giant Italians from seeing the bag. Clumsily, Tina dropped the red velvet bag, spilling the golden glimmering contents onto the front seat of my luxury car. It was unknown to me, at the time, that even though Tina had attempted to use her body as a shield to conceal the bag, the oversized bouncers had eyed the contents of the red velvet bag. Nervous perspiration broke out on Tina's face as she hurriedly raked the jewelry off the seat and stuffed the glimmering contents back into the red velvet bag.

Tina never realized her attempt to conceal the bag and her Italian buddies had observed its contents; she stood arrogantly at the curb between the two-three hundred pound Italian bouncers.

She placed her hands on her hips and said, "Now get the fuck out of here before I have a couple of my close friends do something real bad to you!" The giant, no-neck bouncers glared from the curb as she added, "You dirty fucking pimp!"

"Tina, good old fashioned common sense and a healthy respect for the Italian Mafia tells me I will never see you again," I said solemnly. Then I whispered, "Goodbye Tina," as I pulled away from the curb and into the Manhattan traffic.

Filmore Slim

Chapter 4

Squirrel, the Dirtiest Bitch in the World

Insane Wayne and I sat poised and positioned at the end of the bar, looking through the window as the summer storm blew the people up and down the street.

A full yellow moon sat low in the jet-black skies over the City of Manhattan, New York. There was not a star in the heavens. It was an exceptionally warm night and, from nowhere, strong winds began to stir, blowing the people of the night to and from their illicit and illegal destinations as a heavy and rare summer rain began to fall on the city.

"Jimi, this looks like hurricane weather," Wayne said.

I glanced around the room at the red velvet and mirrored fixtures and at the many booths that housed the drenched and colorful cross-country pimps and their giggling whores, dope dealers, thieves, and other vivid characters of the night.

I had been in New York thirty days and those four whores of mine were working hard on that suitcase full of fast cash. I truly had them selling pussy out of both draw legs and taking everything that wasn't nailed down. The statuesque pea-green bitch had not only given me the nod of acceptance, the bitch had unconditionally surrendered. Body, soul, she was mine. The only reason I didn't have her heart is that the bitch doesn't have one. I was doing some of the most magnificent pimping of my career. Truly I had risen to the occasion.

I raised my wrist and looked down at my diamond-embezzled watch. I rose from my seat and straightened my royal blue Stetson hat and matching blue ensemble. My long time friend and pimp pal, Insane Wayne, and me put on our over coats and began to walk towards the door and the ongoing storm. The winds began to whistle, rattling the windows, and at just that point in walked Satan in a red satin dress. Through the double doors, she swayed wide-legged from side to side with her rear protruding as if she had just been fucked in the ass and the dick was still in it. The wet dress clung to her body like cellophane, exposing and exemplify her shapely frame. She was medium height, slender, half-Latin and half-Black. She was heading my way. I had never seen this bitch before in my life, but at first glance, I knew for a certainty that she was going to be mine. She swayed and stopped directly in front of me.

She looked into my eyes and with the face of an angel and in a schoolgirl's voice asked, "Jimi Starr, may I buy you a drink?"

"Excuse me Darling," I curiously asked, "but do I know you?"

"No," she replied, "but I know you. You're the notorious, hope-to-die pimp from San Francisco, California. You're Jimi Starr. You have a crew of thieving whores known as the Gabors that have been stealing everything in New York City that isn't nailed down, all the whores in the city are talking about you." It was blatantly obvious to me that this unknown strumpet had done her research. We sat down at the bar and with a smiling face I said, to the bartender "Remy."

If I had only known and if I could turn back the hands of time, I would have said "arsenic." I would have been better off. We engaged in conversation, and the Latin vixen sat mesmerized, after a few minutes I informed her she was "out-of-pocket." I demanded full financial compensation for my time. I believe that it was at that point, that I placed her under "pimp's arrest" and demanded to know who her man was. She responded with some off-brand sucker I had never heard of.

After further conversation, I informed her that a sucker couldn't have a real whore's money.

Wittedly, I spoke these words. "Ham and eggs go together, doctors and nurses go together, pimps and whores go together, and bitch, your nigga ain't no pimp, so you're going to have to choose the truth this morning. Bitch, give me my money," I concluded.

Reaching under her red satin dress, from between her smooth golden thighs she produced a large wad of moist bills.

"If my man ain't no pimp, well whose whore money is this then?" she sneered sarcastically.

With confidence, I extended my diamond-encrusted hand and relieved her of her cash. Smugly, I stared her down as I slowly folded her money, placing it in my pocket while I responded to her question, "Oh, this? This is mines, baby." Confused and unable to believe what had just happened, she looked on in disbelief.

"When you get some real money, you could be mine too. Now, are you going to be a smart whore and follow your money or a damn fool who gives her money to strangers in bars? Now get to stepping', little broke, undiscovered bitch. You're fucking with a star this morning," I snapped. "Get the fuck out of my face, so that some real whore could reach out and touch my pimping this morning."

In placing the scrilla (whore money) in my mitt, this fresh young Latin whore had chosen me. This particular event almost rendered me to sexual climax. I was mentally elated with this strange twist of events. This was how true pimps received their thrills. It was the thrill of the hunt and the capture of the Game. I stared at her and profiled as I exuded calm, confidence, and poise.

"TRAMP!" the word snapped from my mouth demanding attention.

In life you will find three types of men. There are males, who are born by the dozen, and being a male doesn't necessarily make one a man. Then there are pimps, who are born by the few. And then there's me, you bitch.

"Undiscovered insignificant whore, you can't be with me for no chicken shit two or three hundred dollars," I said. I saw astonishment rise in her eyes. The bitch had bit, swallowing the bait, hook, line, and sinker.

"I am not that unknown comic mothafucka' you call your man," I said. "If you want to choose me, then get at me when you got some real money," I continued. "Now, little bitty bitch, until you get my cash, you're dismissed." I concluded."

She was dumb founded. She stood up, her knees wobbled, her mouth moved, but nothing came out. There was an undercurrent of sarcastic laughter from the ear flapping patrons who had obviously been eavesdropping on our conversation.

There was an old snaggle-tooth, has-been Mack drinking from a bottle. He raised his head from the table, wiped his mouth on his soiled and tattered sleeve and, in a loud and excited voice said, "pimp son!" then dropped his head back to the table with a thud.

I motioned to the whore, pointing my manicured finger toward the door. She stared at me for a moment, and then dropped her head in submission, embarrassment, and disbelief. Slowly she stood up, her rear protruding, and swayed toward the door. She still had that dick in her ass.

"Get at a real pimp when you got some proper choosing money," I exclaimed.

Again, the old drunk has-been Mac rose his head from the table, stomping his foot on the floor and laughing. "Hee hee, that nigga's really pimping," he said. "You've got to keep on pimping, son," the drunk continued. "Bitch, you don't come around here playing like that with no pimp!" With that the drunken has- been Mac concluded as he slid from the table, striking his head on the floor, slipping into unconsciousness.

The way a whore comes is the way a whore goes. The way that you catch them, that's the way you hold them. This bitch, out of her own vanity, had prodded and tested me with her curvaceous body and that moist wad of bills. However, I had rejected her, humbled her, broke her, and humiliated her, rejected her. This whore had been thoroughly checked. I had tested true to the Game, that I was pimping for real!

Wayne and I stepped out of the double swinging doors into the falling rain and the cruel streets of Manhattan, leaving the loud hysterical chatter of the people of the night behind us. The plummeting rain continued to fall, as dutiful whores lined both sides of the streets, practicing their illicit craft. Some stood in the doorways robbing tricks and others turned dates in cars. I had knocked my fifth whore.

Wayne, my long time pimp pal and road dog said to me in a questioning and articulate voice, as we left the bar "Jimi Starr, I think you should have taken that money and rushed that fine, young Latin bitch straight to the sheets."

I responded jokingly, "You see, Wayne, that's the difference between you and me. You're a cum freak and me, well, I'm really pimping. Hear me, Wayne, and hear me well, never let a bitch have you and you don't got the bitch!"

During the course of my lengthy and colorful career, Wayne and I were constants. I never traveled any where for long without him or he without me. Insane Wayne motherfucker that he might be, he was and is undoubtedly one of the best and most trusted friends that I've ever had the pleasure to be acquainted with in the Game and in my life.

Wayne and I climbed into my customized Biarritz El Dorado, which was parked, at the curb. We rode the track and snorted cocaine and exchanged ideologies all night long. Wayne was medium height; brown-skinned, from Phoenix, Arizona, and was a turnout artist. He had the uncanny ability to meet any woman, be it a nun, schoolgirl, teacher, or the wife of a corporation president, but by the end of the night, she'd be a whore. With articulate style, elegance, and grace, he psychologically out maneuvered them and captivated them. He led them to believe that he was a "Don Juan," a gentleman with style, education, and grace, only to at some point expose Wayne's horrible reality. Wayne's darkest, deepest secret was that he was a psychotic and sadistic gorilla pimp.

My mind flipped the pages of retrospect, summoning up my first remembrance of Wayne's sadistic streak. It was Oakland, California, and his tender young victim was Tina Marie Fontaine. Oh yes, how well I do remember, hum.

Wayne and I shared a penthouse in the hills of Oakland. I remember this event in the totality of its fullness. At the time, Wayne had three whores and I had Bianca, my career woman, who just happened to be a turnout at the time. It was Friday night. Wayne and I had just sent our game off to work. As we sat and discussed life, popped game. My pal Wayne began to do a strange thing. He began to rub his hands together and rock back and forth in his seat.

I will never forget the look of sadistic depravity in his eyes when he morbidly said, "Jimi, I know I'm going to have to murder those whores this morning, I just know it." *Murder!* I thought to myself, my pal's kind of way out. He was still rocking back and forth in his seat, rubbing his hands together when I leaned over and looked in his eyes. He was crying real tears. I looked deeper. Oh shit!!! The lights were on, but there was nobody home.

The first rays of daylight had just begun to shine through my bedroom window when I heard Bianca's soft, raspy laughter in the outer room. Her gaiety provided a mental security that the evening had been smooth and she had fared well. In elevated excitement she entered the room smiling and set $1,500 and a gold Patek Phillipe watch on the bed. Bianca was a born thief. I was honing her to become a professional cannon.

Wayne rushed into the room, with a wire hanger in one hand and dragging two nude whores in by the hair; he manically glared at my night's receipts lying on the bed. That's when I heard it for the first time, the sound of the wire hanger as it cut through the air and the popping sound it made upon contact with bare flesh.

In a calm, clear voice Wayne said, "You skanks let that black bitch Bianca out whore the both of you. Now you've made daddy have to punish you."

The terrified whores cringed, trembling in fear. I'm sure you lousy mother fuckers will never allow this to happen again. The hanger went up and came down repeatedly. I witnessed the horror in their eyes, and heard their shrieks and screams of pain and anguish, their sympathetic tearful pleads for mercy. Like two limp, broken and welted dolls, Tina and Marsha lay sprawled out on the floor in the bedroom. Marsha, with her back propped to the wall, had a horrible gash on her left breast. I looked again, as the blood trickled down her welted body. The nipple of her left breast had been whipped off.

I realized one thing for assuredly and as certainty, that in the realm of Wayne's pimpdom, he had complete dominium over his whores. The unique punishing device opened windows in my mind. I would find out later that together the two whores had produced in excess of $1,200, but in retrospect, readers, the man had asked for $1,200 a piece. The lesson here is that a true pimp must ask for the impossible and expect it. Was Insane Wayne a mad man or a genius? In my opinion, he was the latter. I can only convey to you the truths of which I have personal knowledge of the subject matter; let the reader be the judge.

958521952

Jimi Starr and International Blue

Chapter 5

Don Vito's Revenge/The Naked City

Midtown traffic froze, coming to a complete stand still. In the distance I could here the sound of police and ambulance sirens. The entire Times Square area had become a huge congested parking lot. Motorists, whose cars were frozen in traffic, seeing and hearing the police and ambulance sirens, got out of their cars peering into the distance, toward Eleventh Avenue, to see what was causing this untimely congestion.

My cell phone rang, "Yes?" I dryly spoke into the receiver.

"Hello, Daddy? It's me, Bianca," she said excitedly. "Are you sitting down?" she questioned?

"Yes, I'm sitting down and it looks as if I'm going to be sitting down for a while. I am stuck in a major traffic jam at 42nd Street and 8th Avenue in front of the Port of Authority. Something strange is going on," I continued. "Traffic is backed up everywhere."

The phone was silent. "Bianca, are you there?" I questioned.

"Yes, I'm here." she said. "Jimi, they found Tina in an abandoned building, that is a known trick spot for whores. Her tongue was cut out and stitched into the crack of her ass; her thumbs and index fingers were cut off both hands and were missing from the scene. Her implants were cut out, and pinned to the skin of her empty and sagging left breast was a piece of notepad paper that simply said 'thief'.

From my head to my toes, an icy shivering chill crept over me. Damn, that's retribution! I thought to myself. The angry trick had taken his Dolly P tities back from Tina. Ain't that a bitch!

"Jimi," Bianca went on, "the truly cold and ironic part of the story is that even though they had manically butchered Tina, they left her alive."
"I tried to tell that ignorant bitch that Don Vito was a sadist. Like a hog, they led her to slaughter, ooh wee. "Nobody robs the mob, baby," I respectfully whispered into the cell phone.

Bianca's voice cracked, "Daddy, do you think it's time we blew this town?"

"No, not right now," I responded. "Tina might still die, and that constitutes murder. Any major player who leaves the City of New York right now is an automatic suspect. That's enough on the phone. I will see you when I get there."

Slowly, I made my way through the congested traffic. Looking on to the floor, I saw a diamond ring with a three-caret solitaire stone that had obviously fallen from the red velvet bag. Leaning over, I retrieved the shimmering solitaire three caret treasure and looked at it. Damn, this ring or a ring like this one had cost Tina her prized Dolly P tities, her tongue, fingers, and most probably her sanity.

On Harlem River Drive, I screeched to a stop, and pulled to the side of the road and walked to the water's edge. Reaching into the pocket of my leather coat, I retrieved the diamond ring. With a phenomenal burst of energy, I threw the ring into the Hudson River. I never saw it splash. Perhaps in my attempt to get the diamond solitre as far away from myself as possible, I had thrown it all the way across the Hudson to Jersey City, New Jersey.

Amidst the humidity of the sweltering summer heat, the stagnant traffic dredged its way through the Lower East Side of Manhattan. In the distance, spooked pigeons flew in formation through the archway of Washington Square as my stable of whores and I made our way through the crowd. I glanced down at a man who was sleeping soundly on the street. Briefly, I turned to look again, he wasn't sleeping, he was dead. There were buzzing flies walking on his fading pale blue eyeballs. An unknowing and uncaring crowd pushed on and so did I.

A young rookie policeman, in full winter uniform, sweated as he directed traffic in the center of the intersection. All around me I heard the deafening sounds of the heavy, and ongoing New York street traffic and the chatter of the people of the street, as they beckoned and motioned to the passers-bys, offering promises of diamond rings, furs, washing machines, and everything else from a submachine gun to a newborn baby. In the city of New York, New York any and everything had a price.

Through the roaring sounds of traffic and the chattering of the street people, I could hear the faint ringing of the bell of a hot dog vendor at the corner.

We were on the Avenue of the Americas Out of the bank, and from the corner of my eye, a masked bandit swiftly emerged carrying two bank bags full of cash in one hand. In his other hand he brandished a pistol. Just as swiftly as he had appeared, he spun and fired into the bank. I can only imagine that someone in that bank fell to the floor dead, undoubtedly.

From behind a newspaper, an elderly priest sat on a bench at the bus stop salivating and masturbating as he eyed the behind of a young fat-butt boy. The masked bandit rushed past the preoccupied priest and entered and escaped into the subway. The rookie policeman, paying the shots no heed, nonchalantly continued to direct traffic in the hot summer sun. This was New York. I candidly touched my crouch, feeling for my pistol. Yes, it was still there. It was just another day in New York.

Slowly, we strolled through the store-lined area of Eighth Street, off Sixth Avenue. I stopped and observed my reflection in a storefront window. I wore a white Panama hat on my curly shoulder-length hair, a red silk shirt, white linen slacks, and white lizard shoes. As always, I had my jewelry intact. Looking at my reflection, I smiled at the five whores who stood behind me. This was "Family Day." I had promised my stable of whores a shopping spree. Intoxicated with excitement, my whores, in the spirit of the shopping spree, began to run in and out of different stores, asking prices, trying on clothes and buying things. In a rare moment of sarcasm and anger, Bianca approached me.

"Jimi," she demanded harshly, "I want you to let that Mimi bitch go. I want you to fire that whore, right now! Today!"

"Bitch," I said roughly, "I think you're beginning to believe that you have more say, so than you really do in my business," I harshly continued. "If you ever ask me to fire one of my whores again, Bianca, I'm going to fire you."

Gathering her composure, Bianca calmly replied, "Daddy, if you don't let that bitch go, she's going to destroy you."

Bianca looked up at me with concerned, piercing chestnut-brown eyes, and continued, "Mimi is the dirtiest bitch that I've ever known or that you've ever had. Jimi, last night I saw that vile, disgusting bitch eat a pile of human shit," Bianca concluded.

I laughed so hard at Bianca's statement, I almost cried.

"That whore is giving me six or seven hundred dollars a day, each and everyday of my motherfucking life," I said. "Why would I dismiss a good-paying bitch behind a jealous whore's larceny-hearted lies?" I snapped viciously.

With a cracked voice and a tear in her eye, Bianca said, "Jimi, I've never lied to you. There is no reason for me to start now. That skank, half-Latin and half-nigger bitch eats shit."

If I had only sensed the tip of knowledge or the true sincerity and reality of what Bianca tried to convey to me, or perhaps with all my foresight and perception, had began to perceive the depths of Squirrel's sexual depravity, I would have grabbed Bianca by the hand and run screaming out of the lower eastside, out of Manhattan, out of New York, and out of the Game.

Bianca began to reveal the bizarre tale of the past evening's events and of Mimi's sexual depravity. This was a tale so morbid, so morally disgusting; it was almost impossible to believe. Bianca's rendition of the previous night's events entailed a horrific and shocking story that ran something like this.

The colorful ladies of the night had lined both sides of the street of Whore's Row as they waved at passers-by, hopeful of a chance to practice their craft. The tricks smiled and made catcalls as they drove through the red-light area, some of them openly masturbating as they rode through. The heat of the sweltering summer evening released the pungent stench of stale piss from the sidewalk into the midnight air.

Bianca and Mimi stood wide-legged, as their short skirts revealed their pantied pelvises. In a red pickup truck parked at the curb, a sweaty, red-headed, freckled-face trick masturbated frantically, moaning and cooing as he rhythmically socked it into the palm of his hand while watching the toned legs and jiggling bottoms of Bianca and Mimi.

"That trick in the red truck is a big spending regular of mine," Mimi said, as Bianca attentively listened. "He likes to sit, jack-off, and watch before he spends any money. He's one of my biggest spenders," Mimi continued as she held her head high in the air, attempting to look important.

Mimi and Bianca approached the truck, and through the open window, Mimi wittingly engaged the trick in conversation. "Hey, Red, where have you been, you two-timing fucker? I haven't seen you in a week. You haven't been giving my money to one of those chippy-ass bitches, have you? Am I going to have to cut off that freckled pecker?" Out of the humor that had been conveyed, the two whores laughed.

Confused by Mimi's statement, Red scratched his head in true hillbilly fashion and responded, "Heck, no." The freckled faced trick replied in a tone of country and down-home honesty, "Mimi, you know you're my only girl. Besides, I swear I can't find nobody else who will suck a fart out of my ass but you Mimi," the said smiling, and in his slow hillbilly drawl.

Surprised at the statement, Bianca thought to herself, Wow! Suck a fart out of his ass? What's really happening with this disgusting whore, Bianca thought to herself? What kind of freak bitch is this whore really she questioned?

Mimi climbed into the truck. An apprehensive Bianca followed. A giant, green, shit-eating fly buzzed past Bianca's face. Mimi closed the door behind them.

Bianca began to speak in her sultry and raspy voice. "Hello, handsome. Would you like some company tonight?" she asked softly.

"Why, sure I would," the freckled-face trick replied as he sat there holding his weeping penis in his hand, expressing no shame or humility.

"You know I'm so hot tonight. If the price is right, I'll lick that dick for you just like it was a vanilla ice cream cone and then my girl friend here is going to fuck you," Bianca said. The red-headed trick's green eyes lit up like a pinball machine. In animated fashion, he moved his eyes back and forth between the two women. He began to pound his pud again.

"Oh my, oh my," he said, while drooling. "I've always wanted two girls."

"I'm hot, and this pussy's tight, and you know how I love white dick," Mimi said.

"Let's get the money out of the way," Bianca responded. With that, the trick reached under the seat and produced a brown paper bag. Bianca, seeing the bag, had the mental flash that any true whore would. This might be the big one, Bianca thought to herself. As the trick brought the bag into full sight, Bianca fanned her hand, waving the pesky buzzing green fly away from her face. The fly landed flush on the bag as the grinning trick calmly spoke.

"Hey, Mimi, does your girlfriend do the scats, too?"

"Sure I do," Bianca, replied, eager for a look at the cash in the bag, not knowing the true meaning of the word scats.

"Great," he responded. Withdrawing his hand from the brown paper bag, he produced a small, green, odious piece of shit. He threw back his head and tossed the shit into his mouth. He began to chew, and smack as if the shit was some kind of rare delicacy.

"Umm, and it's so tasty, too." He held out the open bag towards Bianca. "Here, have one. I have plenty."

Bianca's mental flash of fast cash and pie in the sky were instantly gone. Her eyes opened wide, and the hair rose on the back of her neck as she slipped into the survival mode. Gagging from the trick's disgusting act, she leaped over Mimi's lap; Mimi calmly sat unmoved by the trick's repulsive actions. Bianca opened the door and leaped to the sidewalk; tears filled her eyes, as she wretched in disgust. Her hot puke splattered on the ground, splashing on the toes of her open- front spike-high-heeled shoes.

Between her wretches, these words managed to escape Bianca's mouth, "You sick, Peckerwood shit-eating, motherfuckin' trick, you!" She turned and wretched again, wiping puke from her mouth; she prepared to read the redheaded, freckle-faced trick the riot act. Returning her vision, peering into the open cab of the truck, she saw the most disgusting and obscene sight of her life. The trick squatted over Mimi's face, grunting and shitting profusely into Mimi's waiting, wide-opened mouth. Mimi lay sprawled out on the seat of the truck with a fifty-dollar bill in her hand. With her free hand, she frantically masturbated as she made gurgling sounds. The odious feces filled her mouth and slowly rolled down her face and neck.

The sour stench of human feces hung heavy in the air. "You nothing, shit-eating bitch," Bianca said feebly. In a state of mental confusion and complete and utter disgust, Bianca turned and wretched her way down 11th Avenue.

Filmore Slim and Jimi Starr

Gangster Brown, Pimpin' Ken, and Kenny Redd

Chapter 6

Pimp or Die

It was the strangest thing about this Mimi bitch. In all the months that I had her, I could seldom find her on the track. However, she always had acceptable money whenever she surfaced. Mimi is the type of whore that is always crazy hot; she loved it up the ass. That degenerate bitch could and would sit down on a horse's dick with her asshole, if she chose to. In fact, Mimi used to say that her asshole was better than a lot of whores' pussy that she knew. But the real kicker was that in the initial months that I had this perverse bitch, I never knew her to go to sleep. When I get the time, I'm going to have to further investigate this foul whore's entire story, I made a mental note.

Like the stars in the heavens, bright shimmering lights twinkled like diamonds, silhouetting the magnificent skyline of Manhattan. Automobiles raced north on the FDR Drive towards Harlem. Tug boats and well-lit barges busily made their way up and down the Hudson River. Buster Price and Gorgeous Gary had just seated themselves in my living room as I walked Mimi to the front door. She placed her head on my shoulder and placed her arm around my waist in dreamy-eye, school-girl fashion. It always makes a pimp feel good to know he had a good looking whore who is paying him well; not to mention that descent sex is always a plus.

Softly and confidently I whispered to her, "Now you go get my money."

I opened the door for Mimi to leave and Wayne, Kenny Diamond, and some vagabond want to be pimp, who called himself Manhattan Mike stepped through. Wayne and Mimi made eye contact, and nervously Mimi dropped her head, hurriedly racing out the door. The hair rose on the back of my neck; something was wrong.

At least twice a week, our crew would get together to play cards, have a drink, talk or just kick the pimping in general. We called these events "Round Table sessions." We used these sessions to keep each other pimping. These sessions were also a good way to keep up on current events, who was in town, who had gone to jail, who had a lose bitch, who wasn't pimping, and even who was going to be the next President of the United

States, etc. A round table session, to some degree was similar to confession in a Catholic Church. Over the years, I had verbally roasted many mispimping perpetrators, dragging them across the red- hot coals of the legendary Round Table. Not until now had I ever had a turn in the hot seat. After all, to be in the hot seat, you had to mispimp, and I was pimping, right? Wrong! Prior to this point in my career, my pimping had never been in question. I was revered and my word was respected throughout the Game. But that was about to change.

Without fail, these social gatherings would always turn into a cocaine session.

It was 12:00 midnight as we sat snorting cocaine and admiring the skyline of New York, New York. I am of the opinion that, Manhattan after dark, has the most breathtaking and picturesque skyline in the world. I fell in love with the incomparable view the first time I saw it. I was admiring that sight when Wayne's verbal assault came from out of nowhere.

"Jimi," Wayne began as the room fell silent; you could have heard a pin drop. "I have a good friend with a tremendous ego, who has a whore that's been chipping on him. The dirty bitch has been fucking his friends and associates, not to mention giving them his money. Hell, the bitch has even given his flunkey driver some money. This friend of mine is a well-known and well-respected pimp who's known for taking care of his business. However, lately, he's been spending too much of his time with this out-of-pocket whore, and we believe perhaps that whores pussy has clouded his judgment " Wayne concluded. "Jimi, if I want to maintain the friendship, what advice do you suggest that I give my old friend?" Wayne questioned.

I nonchalantly looked around the table at the cold scrutinizing eyes that were locked on me. The hair rose on the back of my neck. My gut feeling told me something was wrong. Carefully I analyzed the question. Filled with years of wisdom, I began to speak.

"Wayne, your friend is a sucker for that bitch. If he's your friend, tell him that he's got a problem. If he doesn't accept it, then knock him off," I said. "There are no exceptions to the rule. My bitch, your bitch, or anybody else's bitch, Wayne, the rules and regulations of the Game still reads the same." I continued, "A lose bitch is like a lose tooth that must be pulled." As I spoke those words, every eye in the room fell on me. Wayne's next words shattered my reality.

"Jimi, my friend, you are that sucker," Wayne snarled coldly and continued, "and we all think you're starting to like that Mimi bitch a little too much. You're ranking your style, and if you continue slipping like this, you will blow your real whores behind that perpetrating skank. It's not easy for me to come to you like this, but if I don't, Jimi, who will?" He questioned. I had no answer for him. He went on, "Jimi Starr, that bitch has been out-of-pocket and paid not only myself, but also every pimp at the table."

I looked around the room; all of my pimp pals stared arrogantly at me in return. Yep, there was no doubt about it that dirty bitch Mimi had disrespected me proper, I thought to myself. Bianca's words haunted me. Jimi that bitch will destroy you, she is the dirtiest bitch you've ever known. Any bitch who would clown herself through eating a stack of human shit, didn't give a fuck about clowning me. That bitch I liked so goddamn much and, that I was so mother fucking proud of was a hater. It was at this point that I realized Mimi hated my fucking guts, and she wanted to defame and destroy me.

"Every pimp at the table has seen the dimple in Mimi's left butt cheek," Wayne continued. " That tender, Latin asshole you believed that only you were getting, we've all had some of it, not to mention we've shared your cash. I'm telling you this because I love you and you've been out of character lately," he concluded.

I was totally shocked and caught off-balance. However, I retained my composure and rapidly ran this distasteful scenario through my mind before speaking. I realized in that instant, that a punk bitch could make a good pimp's pimping look real bad, real fast. With the calm and confidence of a brain surgeon, humbly I began to speak.

"My pimp friends," I began, looking around the room, "I appreciate your concern in this matter. I truly wasn't aware that I had this type of flaw in my business, and you can all be assured that I will immediately address this situation." I said as I looked around the room.

This was double-talk for I was going to put the wire clothes hanger to Mimi's stinking and perverse ass. I could only come up with two conclusions; either Wayne had gone bad and wanted the bitch for himself, or the bitch was everything he said she was.

In retrospect, everyone in the room couldn't possibly be lying. I studied the tone of their razor-sharp words and my associate's physical demeanor before I spoke. It is never easy to let a money-getting bitch go. Before I made any decisions or drew any conclusions, I had to investigate.

"Jimi," Wayne suggested, "save yourself and dismiss that bitch and continue to pimp." The raw cocaine made his stinging words echo in my mind. All but the vagabond pimp stood up, got their coats, and began to leave. Gorgeous Gary tried to soften the blow as he left.

"Pimps keep pimps pimping," he whispered softly and confidently as he winked his eye, shrugged his shoulders, and shut the door behind him. Momentarily I sat in silence. It was the first time I had been mentally spanked and verbally disgraced by my peers; I didn't like it. The distasteful situation presented me with two clear alternatives. I could fire the bitch and save what was left of my recently besmirched reputation, knowing that by the end of the night, one of these very niggers in this same room would have her on his line. Or I could really pimp, absorbing and accepting the personal defamation and upping her quota and keep getting money. I was seriously considering the latter.

Let there be no doubt that I am now and have always been an egotist, but as I matured in the Game, I realized my purpose. I was pimping for real and money was my true motivation and my reason why. Based on that, I knew what I had to do.

Gangster Brown and Filmore Slim

Filmore Slim

Chapter 7

Rosebudd

In the darkness of night, a lone star and a quarter moon sat high in the skies over the city of Manhattan. The sweltering heat and humidity were almost unbearable. It was the fifthteenth straight day of Manhattan's current heat wave. The electrical power was out in various sections of Midtown. Frustrated and tense, police directed traffic at all major intersections as the people of the city opened their windows or sat on stoops, praying for a hint of a cool summer breeze. At the intersection of 30th Street and Madison Avenue, in front of the Blarney Stone Bar, water sprouted from an open fire hydrant. Cross-country pimps, driving Cadillac's and Mercedes Benzes screeched to a halt and pointed their fingers, backing up traffic all the way to 12th Avenue.

Directly across the street from the Blarney Stone Bar, screaming and ecstatic whores began to rush down the sidewalk. Parked at the curb were a Rolls Royce and a vintage Auburn. You would have sworn that the swarming pimps and whores thought it was the second coming of Christ. It was Rosebudd and his road dog and partner in crime, Shonté, two of my homeboys from Hollywood, California. They were grossly overdressed for the current weather. They were wearing wool sports coats complete with plaid vests, silk mohair slacks, straw Panama hats, and sported alligator shoes. These two niggers were totaled out. They were completely Hollywood and as colorful as they get, profiling like movie stars and from behind large dark glasses, in true Hollywood fashion. Rosebudd and Shonté smiled and nodded at the on lookers as they took a leisurely pimp stroll along the sidewalk, surveying the Manhattan street scene. Curious whores looked them up and down and licked their lips hungrily as if the two men were something to eat. From the other side of the busy street, I could hear whores murmuring the name, "Rosebudd."

Budd earned his stars and bars in the cruel lucrative streets of Los Angeles, California, rising to fame in the Game in the city of Hollywood. It was there that he laid his anchor and called it home. In his home in the high-hills over Hollywood, Budd lived a posh life, surrounding himself with exquisite luxuries and glamour. In the Game, he had mastered the art of pimping white women and risen to the pinnacle of street success. In the process, he had become a legend, a pimp icon, and some say a Ghetto god.

Rosebudd and I had vivid history. My mind reflected back to the fledgling days of our pimping and our zealous rivalry, which culminated in a lifetime of mutual respect and friendship. It is with this friendship in mind that I vividly reflect on the early days of our longtime careers and of the colorful times of our arrogant youth, long since past.

Music blared from the jukebox as the immaculate pimps, in tailor-made attire, and their dutiful whores strolled into and out of the popular restaurant and hang out. Rose's Soul Food Kitchen, during this particular time, most probably served the best soul food in Oakland, not to mention all of Northern California.

Budd's pea-green Brougham had screeched to a halt directly in front of the busy restaurant that night. Budd was dark-skinned and of medium physical stature. He was new in town and his name was ringing like a bell. He had really been getting his pimping in and his rollout on his prize white girl, Sandy. It was widely rumored that this fine peckerwood bitch was giving that nigger money hand over fist. Budd and Wayne were cool from the beginning. I had met Budd through Wayne a couple of months earlier when he had initially arrived in town. Wayne and I sat at a table in the window of Rose's Soul Food Kitchen. We were waiting for our whores to meet us for dinner. As we sat, we watched Budd's every move.

Sandy sat tall and proud in the front seat of Budd's new pea-green hog. Her flowing blonde hair blew in the gentle breeze; there was something about Sandy's hair that reminded me of a giant blonde Afghan hound. From my advantage point in the window, I could see Budd smile as his mouth moved a mile a minute. In the rear seat of Budd's hog sat his new Black turnout whore, pouting with her arms crossed. At that point Budd did the unthinkable; he leaned over and romantically kissed Sandy on the cheek. I could see the steam rise from the top of the turnout Black bitch's head. I didn't know it then, but in latter times, this turnout whore would profess to me that she was Rosebudd's wife. Whether or not her passionate confession was true, perhaps I'll never know the answer.

"That Nigga's getting his pimping in," Wayne said.

"That Nigga is going to blow that Black whore, quick," I replied. "He's in love with the white whore and the turnout is feeling it. All that bitch needs is a reason to choose." I concluded.

From the beginning, I have always been a master of illusion. I had the rare an uncanny ability to make a whore see things that didn't even exist. I wouldn't have to wait long to test my theory.

"This Nigga, Rosebudd, is a white whore's pimp and a man after my own heart," Wayne loudly exclaimed.

The Black turnout, Marietta, gritted her teeth as Budd entered the restaurant with the six-foot white girl with flowing blonde hair and blue eyes, who could have easily been a centerfold for any adult magazine. It wasn't personal, but I was skilled in the art of observation and mental manipulation, not to mention conversation. I was the Grand Master of tricknology. I bided my time. I was going to have that turnout.

Budd strolled to the counter and seated his whores. "What's on the menu Rose?" he asked. Rose, the owner of the café, smiled at him, and he and she began a conversation as he seated himself. Budd didn't know it then, but he was next on the menu. At that moment in time, Budd was so caught up in his pimping, he didn't realize he was fattening up the frog for the snake. Budd was cruising for a bruising.

A yellow cab pulled to a stop in front of the café. Bianca and Tina Marie Fontaine, Wayne's main woman, got out of the cab and hurriedly entered the establishment. Our hungry whores enjoyed the food here. It was the best soul food in the city. We ate and made conversation. In the center of the floor sat a pool table on which Budd was exposing his skills. He was actually very good. If he ever became whoreless, he could still make a descent living shooting pool.

Wayne and I were preparing to leave the restaurant when Budd approached us and said, "Hey, it's my birthday and that fine peckerwood bitch just bought me that brand new hog; she's been paying me like she has a printing press. Or perhaps she has a key to the mint. Today is my birthday and I want to celebrate," Rosebud playfully exclaimed. "Let's hook up at 12:00 o'clock at Janelle's Lounge for a drink and some powder."

"That sounds like a plan," Wayne replied as they shook hands and we left the establishment, stepping into the night.

Budd was a good pimp; however, he was caught up in the moment. Sandy had just ridden him in a brand new Fleetwood Brougham Cadillac. He was young, Black, nigger-rich, and feeling the intoxication of his burgeoning pimping. He was in a state of euphoric bliss, which rendered his game slightly off- center. If Budd could be knocked, now was the time, while he was adjusting, to his successes in the pimping and his game was off-balance. His fastest move would be way too slow.

Parked on a side street and under the discreet cover of darkness, I sat watching the intersection of MacArthur and Grove streets, waiting for Rosebudd to drop his whores off. I knew for a fact that once Sandy, Budd's prize white girl hit the track, some horny trick would scoop her up, leaving Budd's Black turnout whore vulnerable and defenseless. Sandy was dropping her drawers for those tricks on MacArthur Boulevard so fast; I knew she couldn't possibly be on the track long. This was going to be real easy pickings; trimming Budd for that tun-out was going to be a walk in the park.

I looked at my watch, checking the time; it was 9:39 p.m. I lit a cigarette. It was 9:50 p.m. when Budd pulled to a stop in the intersection; Sandy was at his side. A rumpled, sobbing, confused, and slightly battered Marietta got out of the car. Budd was intoxicated on the Game and truly felling his pimping as he popped his collar and screamed from the open window, "Don't you ever try to make demands on my dick or me, Black bitch, or I'll whip your ass again. Now get my money, whore!" Budd screamed.

His chrome wheel covers flashed and his wheels screeched as his Cadillac Brougham fishtailed away from the curb into the flowing traffic, towards Janelle's Cocktail Lounge. Like flies on shit, my whores surrounded Marietta. I can honestly tell you, neither she nor Budd ever stood a chance. Without a doubt, the turn-out would be mine tonight.

"Girl, you need to leave that Nigga. Leave that Nigga tonight," Red, my second whore said. "You don't have to put up with this kind of shit and pay a Black-ass Nigga your money, a Nigga who's obviously white-girl struck," Red concluded.

"Dumb bitch, you're on the whore stroll while Rosebudd and the white girl, he's in love with, are going to the birthday party. Bitch, who do you think is going to get the birthday dick tonight?" Bianca spat, "Girlfriend, every whore in the city is laughing at you. You got your ass-whipped and have to work tonight; meanwhile the White girl's being wined and dinned with your money and then she's going to get fucked tonight," Bianca sarcastically spat.

China, my third whore interjected, "You're a laughing-stock, bitch. That nigga has made a clown out of you. Where's your pride, where's your dignity? You've got to be the dumbest whore in the entire world." China concluded.

Budd was a great guy, but he was a terrible egomaniac and a narcissist, as are most gentlemen of our profession. My whores knew it, and it wasn't difficult to capitalize on this fact.

My main woman, Bianca, and the rest of my crew of whores had been putting work in on Budd's fledgling strumpet for the last week. Marietta was light, bright, and damn near white. She had the potential to be a sure enough moneymaker under the proper guidance; however, in her developing stages, Budd was not giving her that extra bit of attention she needed to grow. She was new to the Game, which presented the reality of the fact that she was weak anyway, automatically putting her at a unique disadvantage, like a lamb amongst wolves. Budd's egotistical actions, over the last 24 hours, had all but cinched the certainty of his blowing of the fine young turnout.

There is an old pimp cliché that reads, "A lose bitch is like a lose tooth; it has got to be pulled." If I didn't get the bitch from Rosebudd, some other pimp would. She was already blown. If a whore picks today to leave a pimp, it doesn't necessarily mean that he lost her today. He blew her yesterday; she simply chose today to leave. Budd had to be dope-sick and hallucinating to kick that turn out in the ass and then drop her off in a nest of seasoned, larceny-hearted, white-girl hating, Black whores. There was no way on God's earth that the tender turnout would still be there at Budd's return.

I started my engine and turned on my headlights, pulling through the busy intersection. With her back turned to the curb, Marietta bitterly wept as I stepped from my white Coupe Deville and opened the door on the passenger side.

With my hand I touched her shoulder, she leaped into the air and screamed, "Please don't hit me again, Daddy; I'll get your money!" she continued.

Her tears rolled freely from swollen eyes. She had thought I was Budd coming back for her, with another ass whipping. I reached into my coat pocket and retrieved a handkerchief and handed it to her. I could hear my whores in the back- ground urging Marietta to choose.

"Now, bitch, you got the opportunity to pick a real pimp," Bianca said. Once she accepted the handkerchief, I knew I had her.

With a soft voice and through teary eyes Marietta said, "Jimi Starr, I don't have any money, but I want to be with you."

I led her to the car. She slid into the front seat and I shut the door behind her. My crew of seasoned whores piled into the rear, shutting the door behind them as I pulled from the curb.

"You may not have any money right now, but you will shortly," I said smiling confidently as I made my way through the traffic.

This fledgling bitch knew she had to pay me before her choosing could be officially recognized in the Game and before I could properly serve Rosebudd. I got on the freeway and cruised across the Bay Bridge to San Francisco, to another track and another opportunity at financial freedom.

It was a week later, as I sat on the end of the bed; as Marietta got out of the shower draped in nothing but a red satin robe and, stepped into the bedroom. Although she was attractive, there was something about her character that made me think of a schoolgirl.

"Jimi, I'm the mother of Budd's baby. I've been his woman for a while. He brought me here from Pittsburgh, California and made a whore out of me. He told me when we got to Oakland he was going to marry me." She wept bitterly.
Sobbing, she went on, "I never thought Rosebudd would do anything like this to me."

Attempting to put a lock down move on the Marietta, I fed her naive and displeasure with deceit and gained her confidence.

"Marietta, I didn't want to tell you that Budd and I have talked about you in great depth. He's told me that he never loved you and that he never had any intentions of marrying you; he only brought you to town to make a whore out of you. He and that white girl laughed at you the night Budd turned you out. Budd let that white girl spend your money. I know it's hard to believe, but baby, I saw them, I heard them. Marietta, the things that nigger said and the way they clowned you made me so angry, if I wasn't pimping, I would have given that fella Rosebudd, the ass-whipping of his life," I concluded in my best sympathetic bullshit fashion.

Budd's novice whore, believing she had been abandoned and betrayed, tears streaked her unknowing and confused face, as she invitingly dropped the red satin robe onto the plush shag carpet, revealing her small- framed and yet well-defined nude body.

"All of the things I swore to Rosebudd I would never do with anyone else, I want to do those things with you right now, tonight," Marietta concluded. With those words, she climbed into the bed, turning out the lights.

Because of the nature of their relationship, Rosebudd and Marietta were ultimately reunited. When he got her back he put her in his car and raced out of town. I never saw her again from that day to this. Over the years, it never crossed my mind weather Budd had taken this situation personally. My preplanned intrusion into the domain of Rosebudd's pimping wasn't personal. It was just pimping. Soon afterwards, in the pursuit of destiny, Rosebudd pointed his pea-green Brougham towards the city of Hollywood and hit the highway. Over a period of time and in the name of the Game, he became a master pimp and, some say, a legend. He never looked back. I'm sure the lessons he learned in Oakland, California assisted him in his various mental conquests and triumphs over the years. Pimps don't get angry; they learn from their mistakes and, through their pimping, they get even.

In my initial encounter I had rattled Budd's confidence, teaching him a life's lesson. On any given night under the proper circumstances, any bitch could be had.

Gangster Brown

Jimi Starr

Chapter 8

Dog Dick Sucker

The days of summer flew and my reputation grew as I rapidly tired of the fast lane in Manhattan. It had been a nonstop party and 24-hour cocaine binge from the moment I set foot in the town. Having had received my suitcase full of cash, my mission was accomplished here. I had done everything I had come to do. I longed for the cool Pacific Ocean breeze and the warm and golden California sun.

I pulled to the curb and entered the bar at 23rd and Madison Avenue. Seating myself at the bar, I was approached by Sultan Mac Mohammed, an Arab pimp and pal of mine, approached me and sat down. I ordered drinks for the two of us. With his Middle Eastern Arabic heavy accent he said, "Jimi, I stumbled into some knowledge you might be able to use." Focusing my attention on other activities in the room, yet with a diligent ear, I listened.

"Starr, it seems that you have a bitch that is a crack monster. She's been in the dope house for the last two weeks freaking for crack cocaine. Mimi is her name," he said.

"Mohammed," I began, "you must have me mixed up with someone else. I'm Jimi Starr, man. I do not know nor do I possess any drug- using whores. I don't need a prop to keep a bitch."

"Jimi, I figured you didn't know about it. That's why I'm pulling your coat," Mohammed continued.

Reaching into his inside pocket, he removed a photo and placed it on the bar. "If you don't believe me, believe this," he said.

I picked up the picture and glanced at it nonchalantly. It was Mimi, all right. She had her head buried deep inside some blonde white girl's ass. This nasty bitch is a bigger freak than I imagined. I thought to myself. I realized and knew within myself that any bitch who gets $700 a day, each and every day of her life, would be difficult to let go of and even more difficult to replace. What was I going to do?

    Mohammed began to relate and exhorted, expressing to me a tale of sexual depravity so profound and of acts so vile and so revolting that since the dawning of time, they had neither been matched, witnessed, nor performed by neither man nor beast. Lost in deep thought, I reached the conclusion that this vile, disgusting and scandalous bitch might possibly be the Anti-Christ. Mimi had truly earned her moniker, "Squirrel, the absolute dirtiest bitch in the world!" Mohammed ran his spiel in a kind of horrific elation. I clung to his every word, believing, but not wanting to believe, hearing things that were too despicable to hear, but they were the manifested revelation of the truth. Before leaving the bar, Mohammed gave me the word on when and where I could catch this degenerate whore's next freak show.

    It seems Mohammed's family owned a chain of transient hotels throughout Manhattan, and that he and his brother ran one. The two brothers were as different as night and day. One brother was a trick and a dope dealer. The other brother was an aspiring pimp. We agreed to meet at 4:00 in the morning and Mohammed would grant me entrance into the hotel. In exchange, I agreed not to harm his brother.

    Alone in the Manhattan darkness, I rode through the city endlessly, reflecting on Bianca's words, "Jimi, this is the dirtiest bitch you have ever had or that I have ever known. She will destroy you." If I had realized Bianca's truth and sincerity and the depths of Mimi's depravity, I would have grabbed Bianca's hand and ran screaming out of the lower eastside, out of Manhattan, and out of the Game.
    I circled the track and picked up Bianca and explained my current situation. She and I had and have an open and honest relationship. I had no problem admitting that I had been slipping and that it was time to make the best of a bad situation. We headed for Sultan's hotel.

    Manhattan was a city that truly never went to sleep. It was 4:00 am and the tricks were still rolling when I pulled to a stop in front of the Seaton Hotel on 20th Street. I told Bianca to slide under the wheel and keep the engine running just in case I came out in a hurry.

    As previously agreed, Sultan opened the hotel security door and with honest concern he excitedly said, "Jimi," George is my brother. You promised me, you wouldn't hurt him. You're just going to check the bitch and go, right?"

    "Yeah, right Sultan, I just want to check the bitchs."

We made our way through the rat-infested dimly lit corridors of the trick hotel and up two flights of a dilapidated staircase to the third floor. We stopped in front of Room 312. Sultan turned the knob and we stepped through the door. What I saw next was completely mind-boggling. It was the first time in my career that I was ever confronted or bore witness to, something that was stronger than the truth, so incredible. In the dimly lit filthy room, George sat nude in the center of a round table with his back to the door. The window had been painted black. In his right hand, he held a small butane torch. On his left, a curious glass pipe sat at his side. There was a plate covered with small white pebbles. Mimi made kissing and sucking sounds. Her head was buried deep in Rosebudd's blonde white girl's ass.

The Arab blew smoke from his mouth and said, with an Arabic accent, "Mimi, stick your tongue up a real white girl's ass, you half-nigger bitch, and perhaps I will let you have another hit of crack cocaine."

It was one of the damndest things I had ever seen in my life. With the promise of another hit, Mimi became like a giant anaconda, waving her tongue in the air. It leaped from her skull 7 or 8 inches and buried itself deep inside the white girl's waiting, opened, pink, puckered asshole. I had seen all I had cared to see. Anger began to rise from the tips of my toes, flowing throughout my entire body. Was it because this bitch represented $700 a day to me or perhaps because I liked her? I truly don't know the answer. What I do know is that I snapped and pulled my razor from under my coat.

Sultan screamed in anticipation and fear, "No, Jimi, he's my brother!" Foolishly, Sultan grabbed at the blade of the razor, splitting the palm of his hand wide open. With the rage of a savage jungle beast, I swung, knocking Sultan Mac Mohammed to the floor unconscious. In rhythmatic pulses, his blood squirted to the floor, on to the walls, and on the filthy furniture. Mimi began to scream at the top of her lungs. Looking at his brother lying on the floor unconscious and bleeding, George rolled his eyes toward the ceiling and leaped from the table, throwing his hands in the air and began to call on the name of Allah, Allah...

"Get your clothes on, you nasty, disgusting bull-dagging bitch!" I said sharply.

Mimi began to plead and lie, with tears in her eyes and with the voice of a schoolgirl, "No, Daddy, you don't understand. This Arab, baby, he made me come up here and made me smoke some dope; then he raped me, and fucked me in the ass. Don't kill me, Daddy!" she pleaded.

In the midst of my rage and confusion, I spoke in a soft, somber voice. "I'm not going to kill you, but I'm going to fix it so you don't come here again."

George was on his knees rocking back and forth, still calling on the name of Allah when I handed Mimi the pearl handled razor, telling her, "It's him or you, bitch; now who's it going to be?"

Mimi sliced, hacked, and hewed poor George from the top of his head to the tips of his toes. The pearl-handled razor was dripping with blood as I removed it from her trembling hand. I grabbed her by the arm and we stepped through the door, knocking Rosebudd's bug-eyed white girl to the floor.

For a gambling man, the odds would be one thousand to one. At any given time, there are no less than one thousand cross-country whores in the city of Manhattan. I found it exceedingly strange, if not impossible to believe, that out of all the whores in New York, Mimi, the dirty bitch that she was and is, would wind up out-of-pocket with Rosebudd's bleached blonde, bug-eyed, crack head, white girl. From a gambling man's perspective, the odds of a bizarre encounter of this nature would be one million to one. In my mind, this obscene and distasteful event had definitely taken some scrutinizing, not to mention preplanned, and devious orchestrating.

My mind flashed through the past to Oakland, California and Marietta, Budd's sensual, hot and horny, young, dumb, and full of cum little wife. In retrospect, Bud had never forgotten this scenario. Over the course of time, Budd had obviously learned some scurrilous new tricks, becoming a master of orchestration and manipulation. I respected how the man had grown. This incident was definitely preplanned retribution. After all, pimps don't get angry, they learn through their mistakes and get even, through their pimping. This conclusion was not only possible, but also probable.

Mimi was still nude as I led her down the dilapidated staircase and through the dimly-lit corridors to the street. Directly in front of the hotel, parked under the streetlight, Bianca sat with the engine running. I opened the door and threw Mimi's stinking degenerate ass in the back seat. Sliding under the wheel, I screeched away from the curb and into the traffic. This had to be the absolute most disgusting night of my life.

"Jimi let me explain," the drugged out Mimi begged.

"Shut up, you disgusting, degenerate bitch!" I barked. Bianca studied Mimi's shit- smeared face and blood- stained hands. It was at that point that Bianca gave me a puzzled and questioning glance.

"No," I said coldly. "I didn't kill anyone."

Bianca peered at me through narrow concerned eyes and excitedly spoke in her raspy voice, "I told you, Jimi. This bitch is the dirtiest bitch in the world!!"

I pulled to the curb at 32nd and Park Avenue and Bianca got out of the car. "Be careful, Daddy," she said caringly. " I'll see you later on this morning."

In the silence of the early morning darkness, we rolled along FDR Drive, taking the George Washington Bridge to Fort Lee, New Jersey and to Mimi's apartment. I gave her my coat to cover her bareness. Her $600 poodle sat poised in the second floor window. He began to bark excitedly as he watched her exit the car. I opened the door to the apartment and went straight to the bathroom. Mimi's little apricot-colored poodle scurried by me barking. I looked at my watch as I relieved myself. Over the sound of the roaring piss, I could hear the dog racing around the room, yapping, excited at Mimi's return. Little did I know how happy the frisky little dog truly was.

In the complete and total innocence of ignorance, I sarcastically called out to Mimi from the bathroom, "You dirty bitch! If you could suck a white girl's pussy and ass hole for an Arab dope dealer, certainly you could suck that $600 dog's dick for your man."

Reader, when I made this verbal humiliation, that's all that it was, in thought and deed.

I stepped from the bathroom and into the bedroom and into a more complete realization of Mimi's sexual depravity. She was stark naked, on her knees at the end of the bed. Her head bobbed frantically up and down. The poodle was on it's back and the slick, pink dog's dick slid in and out of Mimi's open and wanton mouth.

Yikes!!! I thought to myself, what kind of degenerate bitch is this? I looked on in shock, horror, and disbelief. I wretched, sending puke splattering across the hardwood floor. In between wretches, I tried to speak, but I could find no words. Mimi sucked the dog's balls. I puked again. I flashed through endless pages of dialogue and retrospect. I found her reminiscent of a character from the pages of *The Exorcist*. She looked at me as if for some kind of approval and began cooing and moaning and jacking the dog off.

"Umm," she said, as her eyes rolled back in her head. "I like doing things like this." The dog lay on his back with his tongue hanging from the side of his mouth. He appeared to be smiling. With her hand, she pushed her hair out of her face and leaned over and stuck her tongue deep into the dog's asshole. Disgustingly, the cum from the dog's dick shot six feet high. The dog whined, his eyes rolled into the back of his head, he whined again, and then he fainted. The sight of this morally sick and twisted event caused me to wretch until I was almost unconscious. Puke splattered on my shoes and splattered across the floor. It was no joke. Squirrel truly was the dirtiest bitch in the world. In my quest for fast cash, could I have possibly chanced into the Anti-Christ?

Bianca's words haunted me, "Jimi, you've never known a bitch like this. Don't let this bitch destroy you."

Mimi was the kind of whore you had to pimp hard and fast, getting all the money you can as fast as you can and getting rid of her, letting her become some other pimp's problem. Just when I thought it was all over, Mimi climbed up into the bed getting on all fours. Her canine lover had revived himself to consciousness and in a streak, jetted around behind her. Hooking her with his left paw and placing his right paw behind his right ear, he frantically socked his dog dick into her filthy, disgusting, degenerate pussy. My mind reflected back through the past on lessons learned. I found nothing comparable. I have traveled extensively across America and Canada, back forth and back. I have even spent a couple of years in Asia. I have exchanged tales with pimps and players all around the world. I have never heard about a more horrifically obscene tale of degenerate, depravity, and disgust.

Now that I realized what I had possession of and what I was confronted with, I knew for a certainty, from this day forth, Mimi and the poodle were to be a team inseparable.

Noble Dee, Gangster Brown, and Filmore Slim

Jimi Starr

Chapter 9

Mother Squirrel's Curious Boodie

The sleek, triple-black Brougham had just crossed the Canadian boarder and slowly made it's way down the slick and icy highway. Snowflakes flew and the wind blew as Manhattan Mike and I made our return trip from New York City to Montreal, Canada, to check a week's receipts from our whores. Mike, a tall, slim, brown-skinned brother, originally out of Cincinnati, Ohio, was a part of my "globe-trotting clique" and, unbeknownst to him, was about to become my full-time driver and a part of my personal entourage. I eased the black Cadillac to the side of the road.

"Mike," I said. "You have traveled with me all across America, from coast to coast and back again." Coldly I continued, "Brother, that bitch you got ain't no whore." I opened the door and got out of the car, walking to the rear of my automobile. I took a long piss on the side of the road. How could I tell my friend, who was so passionate about his pimping, that he was no pimp and probably never would be? I opened the door, reentered the warmth of my plush hog, making myself comfortable in the rear seat, staring at the back of Mike's head. The straightforward approach is always the best approach.

"Like I said, Mike, that bitch of yours ain't no whore and you, Mike, well, you just ain't no pimp, not today, anyway."

Mike sat there with his mouth opened. He was in shock, unable to believe the words that were coming out of my mouth.

"Keep plugging away at the Game, baby," I smoothly continued, "until you perfect it. But as long as I have to carry you and that nothing, sorry-ass bitch, you're just a pimp's helper. Mike, if you can't be a good pimp, there's no harm done in being the driver of a great pimp. Now slide under that wheel and drive the car, baby."

With a tear-streaked face, he slid under the wheel, started the car, and pulled from the side of the road onto the highway. I found it utterly distasteful to address my friend in such a manner; however, it had to be done. He had a no-money getting bitch, which who had starved him all across country. She wasn't a bad-looking woman, but she lacked "trick appeal." That, combining with the fact that she was a straight coward, prevented Mike from getting any note worthy amounts of cash. If she saw the police six blocks away, Shirley would break and run. Manhattan Mike's bitch, Shirley, was truly a punk, in the first degree and for a fact; the sorriest bitch in history to ever claim the Game and own a pair of whore shoes.

We slowly motored through picturesque, snow-covered downtown area of Montreal. I sat comfortably in the rear seat of my black Cadillac as Mike maneuvered his way through the slick streets of the city. Miles Davis softly blew his horn over the CD player. After his initial sobbing came silence between Mike and me, with his realization of his newfound occupation.

"Turn here on St. Catherine," I said, "and pull into the driveway."

The penthouse suite that Bianca chose was exquisite. As always, she had chosen a place with an overview of the city. Manhattan Mike and I had observed the snow covering of downtown Montreal from our newfound advantage point.

My four primary whores and Mike's worthless skank bitch listened to music and giggled and made whore small talk. They were happy. I was happy at that point. My life was like a bed of roses and it seemed as if everything I touched turned to gold. Pimps and whores clung to my every word as if it were the gospel. I had become a legend in the Game. Mike stared across the room at his worthless whore, Shirley, as he fanned his legs open and shut and subconsciously squeezed his swipe with his hand.

I sat down next to Mike and spoke softly and honestly, "Mike, that's why you're homeless and broke. You're a slave to your dick and a goddamned cum freak. You just can't keep your dick out of that bitch. Don't you think your whore Shirley knows it?" He dropped his head in shame and acknowledgement.

"Pimping ain't for everybody and everybody cannot do it," I went on. "Mike, you know I love you like a brother, but you've ruined that bitch. And know for a certainty, I would not fuck with that nothing bitch for money. Mike, you're standing in some pimp's way. Let her go, Mike, let her go in the name of the Game!" I said as the phone began to ring. It was a boohooing young Casanova. He had been incarcerated in a jail in Montreal. Back in New York, the season was changing; there was a stiff chill in the air. The brisk wind blew over the face of Manhattan. At the corner of 125th and Lexington, I motioned Mike to the curb. Getting out of the car, I wrapped my scarf around my neck as my shoulder-length hair blew in the wind.

The melodic jazz sounds of Miles Davis's hit tune, "Human Nature," flowed from behind the closed doors of The Baby Grand Bar and Lounge. It was like a peacock parade as the colorful players strutted back and forth in tailored, hand-made suits. The Baby Grand was a known haven for street players. Manhattan Mike and I walked towards the bar. A raggedy young woman, of slight build with flowing black hair, stood at the entrance holding a basket of flowers.

She cried out, "Flowers, Mister? Flowers for the woman in your life?"

I stopped. "How much?" I asked.

"Three dollars," she replied. I reached into my pocket and removed a $10 bill.
Placing the $10 bill into her hand, looking deep into her eyes I said, "Keep the flowers. You're going to be the woman in my life." Elated the flower girl was still smiling as Mike and I stepped into the bar.

Mike curiously began, "Jimi, why did you give that raggedy flower girl $10 for $3 worth of flowers and then let her keep the flowers, not to mention the change? You might just as well have turned a trick with her raggedy ass," Mike bitterly spat, "At least you would have gotten some pussy."

With sarcasm and confidence, I responded while seating myself at the bar, "Mike, that's why I'm pimping and you're just a pimp's helper! You exhibited a lack of vision when you saw the raggedy flower seller and the cum freak in you made you see a possible piece of ass. What I saw was a beautiful young woman, five feet five inches, about one hundred and ten pounds, with fair complexion and flowing raven hair who obviously has had some bad breaks and yet who has the ability and desire to have her own business. Mike, that raggedy bitch outside is going to be my next whore, so be careful what the fuck you say to me and about her," I snapped. Mike stared open-mouthed in disbelief.

Time flew and the music blared as the street chatter and gaiety of the flamboyant players continued into the early morning hours. From the darkened corners of the room or perhaps even from the vile pits of hell, slithered an unholy and hope-to-die nightmare. She swayed across the room. There was something familiar about her. She walked as if she had a dick buried deep in her ass. She stopped, and swayed in front of me. I looked on, with disbelieving wide eyes. My mind screamed, "Yikes!" It couldn't possibly be true, but there she was, a carbon copy but older version of Mimi.

With a strong Latin accent she began to speak, "Mr. Jimi Starr, I am so glad to finally meet you. I am Anna, Mimi's mother. Can I buy you a drink?"

"No," I said, wanting to get up and run from the bar.

"No?" Her eyes widened in questioned puzzlement at my response.

"Let me buy you one," I pleasantly replied. After much small talk and her second drink, Anna began to show the signs of what I perceived to be an apparent sexual depravity.

"Jimi, you know Mama been in the Game for more than twenty years. In all Mama's' life, I've been looking for a man just like you. You know my daughter Mimi is a dirty, dirty bitch. Some say perhaps the dirtiest bitch that ever lived. She doesn't know how to take care of a gentleman like Mama do." She placed her hand on my thigh while eyeing my crouch and hungrily licked her lips.

"If Mama were twenty years younger, I would make you rich, Mr. Jimi Starr. You make me feel young again," she said.

With those words, she began groping my crotch. Her eyes lit up and she smiled as her hot wandering fingers found the object of her perverse and freakish desires. I pushed her hand away.

"Listen up, Lady, I'm not that kind of guy. You are my whore's mother. Respect me and let me respect you," I said harshly.

Anna continued aggressively, "Mr. Jimi Starr, Mama ain't no broke bitch. I could pay for anything I want. I simply want a taste of that fine, Black pimp's dick. That black dick of yours is legendary," she drooled and hungrily licked her lips again.

Yep, she was Mimi's mama all right, I thought to myself. Standing up, I began to make my way to the door. Mike laughed and followed close behind. This bizarre freak scene was a little too distasteful for me.

I stepped from the club into the darkness of the Harlem night. I could still hear the roaring laughter of the street players and Anna's accented Latin voice, "I going to fuck you, nigger. I going to make you love it. Mama got the best pussy that you gonna ever get." She was clowning my integrity as a pimp, and for this, someday, she would have to pay.

Many pimps would have broken their necks, racing Latin Anna to the sheets just for the rare opportunity of having a mother-daughter team. But as for me, in this life of depravity, greed, and perversion, I had somehow managed to hold on to some degree of morality. After all, there were some things you just didn't do. I pondered the probability of pimping the Squirrel and her degenerate mammy. A mother-daughter team would definitely have to calculate into big dollars. No, I concluded to myself. I would probably loose money financing the upkeep of a kennel.

Quality

I sat in the warmth of the barbershop as the razor-sharp icy winds blew briskly, rattling the foundations of the borough of Harlem. As I watched from the window, the whistling winds seemed to push the multitudes of bundled people to and from their destinations. The pot-bellied stove roared, sending heat throughout the confines of the barbershop.

From my vantage point, I watched through the window as the children went to school. There were mothers and senior citizens carrying shopping bags, darting in and out of stores. The hustlers of Harlem practiced their craft on 125th Street. The street hustlers sold everything from babies to machineguns. The numbers runners entered the barbershop and made their drops in the rear room and left again. The flamboyant pimps loudly talked, telling their stories of conquest, profiling as they vainly glared into the barbers' mirrors in narcissist fashion, in love with their own image. I listened and looked at the people of my world. I reflected on the words of my mother and my childhood long since past.

"Jimmy," she would say, "it is a long road that doesn't have an ending."

At my profession, I was one of the all time greats. Some say a legend. I wanted for nothing and possessed more than most. I had turned my childhood fantasy into a reality. I was living the dream, yet something deep down inside of me cried out for a normal way of life.

A crack head stepped into the barbershop, pushing a shopping cart full of groceries. Reaching into the cart, he produced a huge bag full of skinny chickens.

From the window, I saw the attractive, raggedy flower girl making her way up the crowded street and entering the dilapidated building directly across the street from the barbershop. Zeb the barber, a middle-aged, slender, dark-skinned brother, took the last roller from my hair and combed it into place, styling my hair to perfection. Zeb knew everyone in Harlem.

"Zeb," I said, "give me the drawings on the flower girl."

"Jimi, she's not a bad looking woman, but she's a waste of your time. She is a teetotal square. She lives in a three-room tenement with her mother and eight sisters. She hustles flowers to help her mother make ends meet." he concluded.

I stopped the crackhead as he attempted to leave the shop and, for twenty dollars, I bought the shopping cart full of groceries. I had him follow me across the street. Once inside the building, the girl's apartment was not hard to find; I simply asked an old man in the hallway. I hadn't figured on her living on the top floor and the elevator not working, so I gave the crackhead a little extra and we wearily took the stairs. Out of breath, I straightened my apparel and produced a wide smile and knocked on the door.

A slender, middle-aged Black woman with long wavy graying hair opened the door. A hoard of kids stood behind her.

"Mother Amsted, my name is Jimi. I am a friend of your daughter, Quality." I'd learned the girl's name from Zeb. With a fifty-dollar bill in the palm of my hand, I extended my hand towards her, shaking her hand in friendship. Mother Amsted looked into the palm of her hand and smiled and then focused looking past me to the cart of groceries.

"Excuse me Mother Amsted," I said still smiling, "this cart is for you."

Her mouth opened in disbelief. Tears welled in her eyes. The kids shrieked in excitement and rushed the cart. A little girl ran past me, hugging the huge bag of skinny chickens.

"Son, you are a blessing from God. I truly had nothing to feed my children today," Mother Amsted said. I stepped into the apartment. Quality stood there smiling and shaking her head in puzzlement. She stood beside me as her mother and sisters excitedly unpacked the much-needed and appreciated groceries.

"Thank you for what you've done for my family. I'll truly never forget this moment," Quality said and then whispered into my ear, "What is your name?" I turned to her, pulling her close to me and looked deep into her eyes.

Smiling I whispered, "Oh, I thought you knew my name. For the records, it's Daddy," I confidently concluded. This was the beginning of a beautiful and lasting relationship.

The water roared as a steamy mist fogged the bathroom mirrors. Meanwhile, in the living room, red and yellow flames licked the inner walls of the stone fireplace. The lanolin-rich bubbly suds floated high in the tub of warm bath water. I relaxed, soaking and pampering myself as the melodic sounds of soft jazz from the stereo filled the silence.

I had seven whores. Squirrel was in jail doing 90 days; she was temporarily the problem of the City of New York, thank God. When she was released, I planned on giving her her walking papers. It was a bad policy to fire a whore while she was in jail, but I had grown tired of her disrespectful and disgusting antics. I was nigger-rich and had more money than I knew what to do with. I no longer needed Mimi, nor any problem bitch. I was at peace with myself; I was at peace with the world. The phone rang, ending my moment of luxury and solitude.

I picked up the receiver. "Speak," I said.

"Hello, Jimi Starr. Do you know who this is?" The Hispanic voice asked.

I knew from the onset exactly who it was. The voice on the phone purred with a strong Latin accent. Oh shit, it was Mother Squirrel. What could this antique, degenerate, Latin bitch possibly want with me? Her daughter Mimi was doing 90 days on Ricker's Island. The alarm sounded in my mind and flashed a red flag. She knew she wasn't here. What could she possibly want from me?

"Jimi, it's me, Anna, Mimi's mother. I have some important insurance papers that need to be signed in order for her to receive a settlement. I would like to drop this documentation off today, if it is at all possible."

In an earlier time, before the vile serpent, better known as Mimi, had slithered into my life, she had been involved in a slip-and-fall accident in a major hotel, falling down a flight of stairs and breaking her ankle. She filed a lawsuit against the hotel owners. My mind reflected on the truth and on what had really happened. She had robbed a trick for his cash and jewels, and the situation had gotten ugly. She was involved in a fistfight with a crazed knife-welding trick, which ended in a flight for her life. With the trick in hot pursuit, her foot caught a snag in the carpets, sending her tumbling headfirst down a flight of stairs, breaking her ankle. The crazed knife welding trick wanted to kill her. The commotion from the fall probably saved her stinking, worthless, life.

I returned my focus to the situation at hand. This is going to be easy money. "Sure, Anna, you could drop that paperwork off this afternoon," I said.

The melodic jazz tones of Miles Davis drifted throughout the confines of my sanctuary as I lavished myself in the luxury of the life style to which I had become so well accustomed. Stepping from the tub and drying myself, I sprayed my entire body with Trussardi L'uomo, my favorite Italian cologne. Then I slipped into a set of white linen pajamas and a red silk smoking jacket. I enjoyed this intimate moment of leisure. In a pimp's life, this was what it was all about, to pamper one self and rest and dress. I sipped the fine cognac from a snifter while taking in the picturesque vantage point of my penthouse apartment view of this great metropolis. It was 3:00 when the grandfather clock began to chime. It was at that point that the doorbell rang. Her voice came over the intercom.

"Who is it," I asked.

"Jimi, it's me, Anna," she purred. "Are you going to invite an old lady in out of the cold and offer her a drink, or should I leave these papers with the doorman? Are you going to buzz me up, Jimi Starr?" she questioned.

I pressed the buzzer, granting her entrance into the building. Moments later, Anna stepped through the front door of my penthouse apartment. She was wearing a full- length, white sealskin coat. As she crossed the room, her feet sank deep into the luxurious shag carpet. She handed me a large envelope as I handed her a snifter of fine cognac.

"I can't believe the panoramic and breath taking views of the city that you have from here!" she marveled, "and the French provincial furniture in your home. Jimi, your home is exquisitely furnished," she said. " I must say that you do have impeccable taste," she continued as she sat down in a French provincial chair. Gulping down her drink, she reached for the bottle, pouring another, then set her snifter on the table.

"Mr. Starr, you have fine taste in clothes, cars, and fine household furnishings, but I'm here to challenge your taste in women. I'm here to fuck you this afternoon and suck that big, black dick, nigger," she concluded.

Standing up from the chair, she dropped her sealskin coat to the floor, revealing her completely nude, slightly aged but voluptuous body.

Reader, let me tell you, any time you think you're getting a deal you generally get fucked. It's like that old cliché that reads, "Beware of Greeks bearing gifts." In my greed for fast cash, I had opened my door to the Trojan horse.

"Miss Anna," I began, as gentlemanly and politely as I possibly could. Calmly I said, "you're my whore's mother and you're intoxicated. I respect you. Cover yourself up and leave this place, immediately."

Veins bulged in her angry forehead as she spoke in a heavy Hispanic accent and through gritted teeth, "What's wrong with you, you conceited nigger? You think Mama and her money is not good enough for you, Mr. Starr?"

Picking her coat up from the floor, reaching into her coat pocket, she retrieved five one- hundred dollar bills and placed them on the table.

"Look at this firm body, nigger. Is you crazy?" She demanded, while slapping herself on the ass.
"Now give it to me like you have been giving it to my baby." She repeated herself. "Give it to me like you have been giving it to my baby!"

"Anna, you're drunk," I firmly stated. "Get the fuck out of my house before I loose my temper and kick you in your hot Latin ass!"

With her heavy Latin accent she screamed, "Choo no do the pimpie, choo fucking punk!"

With Anna's last statement, any dignified end to this distasteful situation was gone. Anna had disrespected my pimping and my manhood. In my mind, it was time for Anna's aggressive, Latin ass to pay the piper.

With lightning speed and ill intentions, I rushed across the room and knocked her to the floor. She opened her mouth and attempted to speak; I slapped the next words right out of her mouth. Her eyes grew wide with fear and excitement. In keeping with my word, I jerked her up from the floor, threw her down on the couch, face first, then I kicked her dead in her hot Latin ass. She wailed as her tears flowed freely. The flowing tears that she shed were not tears of pain they were tears of joy.

Whimpering, she chanted, repeating herself, "I'm going to be a good bitch, Daddy. I'm going to be a good bitch," as her eyes rolled back in her head and she masturbated frantically.

I thought to myself, yep, Anna was definitely Mimi's mother all right. It had become blatantly obvious to me that Anna was some kind of masochistic freak. Being armed with the fact that Anna was a masochist, I exposed my repressed sadistic streak and continued to kick her in her hot freak ass.

Chill bumps covered her entire body as she shuddered. In her heavy Latin accent Anna cried out, "You're giving Mama an ass-whipping royale! That's it! That's it!" she panted and continued. "Now quick, give me what you been giving my baby," she cried, weeping real tears.

Throwing her on her belly and standing behind her, I asked, "You don't really want what your baby's been getting do you, you funky bitch?" I sadistically questioned.

"Yes, give me what you've been giving my baby! Wahoo, Wahoo!" She screamed out in pain as I penetrated her, burying my bone deep in her firm, round butt.
"Oh no, oh no, that's Mama's ass hole," Anna shrieked. "That's my asshole," she cried.

"I know what it is, I know, I know, I know," I recanted as I mechanically and methodically pile dived and jackhammered myself deep into Anna's hot Latin bowels.

The hot Latin jazz blared from the stereo. I stepped from the shower into the living room. In the kitchen, Anna prepared a meal of steak and eggs. She wore nothing but my red satin smoking jacket. She sang and danced, doing a samba around the table like a teenage girl in love. We sat down at the dinning room table. She stared into my eyes in a girlish romantic kind of way. When I fucked them, they stayed fucked, I thought to myself.

Romantically, Anna began to speak, "Although you tore my bottom, I've got to let you know, that was the best sex I ever had in my life. You caused me to have multiple orgasms. Not only did you make love to me in every hole in my body, you made me love it."

She continued, "Jimi, you are the most intense lover that I've ever had or have ever known of. I think I fell in love with you before I ever knew you," she said dreamingly. She was coming off like a dreamy-eyed schoolgirl. Anna walked around the table. What is this crazy motherfucker talking about, I thought to myself? Love! From behind me, she placed her arms around my neck.

Tenderly, she kissed the side of my face and questioningly whispered into my ear, "what are we going to tell Mimi about us?"

Calmly I began to speak, "Anna, you must try to understand. What we had was a drink, you gave me some money, and then we had sex. That's all it was, sex. We aren't going to tell Mimi anything."

Anna's rejected eyes searched my face for compassion and found none. The veins again began to swell in her forehead; her eyes began to widen and she gritted her teeth, "Jimi, how can you say it was just sex? How can you say that you don't want me after all the vile, disgusting, and degenerate things I allowed you to do to me?" Anna asked.

She continued, "Jimi, if you reject me, I'll tell Mimi that you tricked me up to your penthouse apartment and drugged me. Then you savagely beat me, then forced me to suck your dick, then raped and sodomized me. Jimi," Anna confidently continued, "that nut house tramp will send you to the joint for the rest of your life," she smugly concluded.

With Anna's last statement, I realized I had allowed repressed sadistic tendencies, and not to mention my dick, to lead me directly into a plotting whore's trap.

Instantly, the morally unthinkable became a harsh reality. My immediate future had been cinched and etched in stone. I had been led through the maze and trapped like a rat. I was now locked into this morally unethical and psychologically unsavory situation. I had pimped myself into this distasteful dilemma. In time, I could only hope to pimp myself out of it. For the moment, the mother and daughter squirrels had just become stable sisters.

Jimi Starr and Robbie Crosley; aka RC

Jimi Starr at home

Filmore Slim and band member

Chapter 10

High Stakes Game

The blue and yellow flames continued to flicker, dancing and crackling across the face of the warm fireplace.

Mimi's tormented voice broke the serene silence as she shrieked, "You lying bitch! I know he wants me, and you know he wants me! I want to see him now," Mimi demanded.

"You've been dismissed, you insane, degenerate low life!" Quality snapped. "Jimi no longer wants you, nor has any need of your services, bitch."

Quality firmly stated, "Jimi informed you on the phone that he didn't want you, and now, you vile tramp, I'm telling you. You've been fired!"

The disturbing sounds of the elevated voices of these verbally embattled whores drifted up the stairs and down the carpeted hall into my dimly lit and warm boudoir.

"You opportunist tramp!" Mimi barked. "While I was in jail on Ricker's Island, you stole my man. You've poisoned his mind against me. You're the reason why he doesn't want to see me. You're the reason why he won't even talk to me on the phone. You've turned Jimi against me," Mimi ranted.

"Jimi doesn't want you," Quality began, "and he never did. Do you really think a man of his caliber wants to be seen or associated with a known shit-eating, bull-dagging, dog dick-sucking bitch that has chippied with every wannabe pimp and would-be dope dealer on this side of the American continent?"

Quality confidently put her hand on her hip and threw her head up high, then smiled. "No bitch, Jimi don't want you. Bitch, your mammy don't even want you," Quality shouted, "Now get out of here, before you wake my man up, and I have to cut you, bitch!"

The front door was wide open. The two angry whores stood in the walkway. Mimi's long, black hair blew in the wind as she pushed her hand deep into her coat pocket.

Quality raced to the fireplace and grabbed the poker and yelled out, "I told you you're not welcomed here, bitch."

With wide eyes, the two angry whores glared at each other and prepared to do battle until death. Stepping out of the door, Quality raised the poker from the fireplace high above her head and was about to send it hurtling towards Mimi's enraged and confused face. Stepping into the door behind Quality, I grabbed the poker, in mid-swing, most probably preventing a homicide.

"Jimi!" Mimi gasped. "This crazy bitch tried to kill me. She's been telling me hurtful horrible lies about things you said. She said that you don't want me anymore and I'm no longer welcomed here; you only wanted me for my money. Jimi, this bitch is trying to come between us, trying to destroy our relationship." Mimi excitedly cried.

With suave and diplomacy, I stood in the doorway intervening in a battle that may have rivaled the Holy field, Tyson fight.

"Didn't I make myself perfectly clear?" I said bluntly. "Bitch, you are the foulest, most vile, and most despicable whore that I have ever known, and quite possibly the dirtiest bitch that has ever squatted and pissed between two feet!"

Mimi stood shocked, wide-eyed, and open mouthed. "Personally, Mimi," I added, "I don't like you and, if the truth were known, I never did."

A lone tear rolled down her face as she whimpered, "Poppy, you know you want me."

"No, bitch, I don't want you. I don't even want your money," I concluded.

With my manicured hand, I pointed her out of the door and down the walkway. The tears welled up in her eyes as the reality of this final rejection began to set in. Quality and I reentered the house. I shut the door behind me. I could still hear Mimi talking to herself and crying outside.

"I just got out of jail and I'm down on my luck, but I'm going to get some money!" she cried. "You'll see, you're going to want me again, nigga. That Quality bitch is an opportunist and she has poisoned you against me."

Quality fast became a favorite of mine. Her flat-backing abilities were typical at best; she was a standard three hundred dollar a day whore. She lacked technique and concentration and most probably would never become a top-flight thief, but what she lacked in thieving ability; she made up for it in dedication and determination. She possessed both, character and loyalty; most of all what she brought to the table was peace of mind.

There is an old pimp cliché' that reads something like this, "What sense does it make to gain the entire world and lose your immortal soul?"

While Mimi's persona continued to diminish, just when I thought no one could sink to that level, that motherfucker would find a completely different and lower level of moral and sexual depravity. As Mimi fell deeper into her hellish world of obsessed, degenerate behavior, I realized one true thing about her character. For a surety and a certainty, it was flawed to the quick.

In the last year, I had made a whole shit load of money on her and her furry lover's antics. Some may have considered it a small fortune. I have often wondered if her pet believed that he was a man trapped inside a little dog's body. Hell, the dog didn't even like dog pussy. Mimi had turned her furry lover completely out on a strict diet and canine delicacy of human cunt.

One day while the door was open, the little dog left and never came back. I can only surmise that Mimi's level of sexual depravity had sank so low, the little dog finally got sick of it, or perhaps got an attack of conscious, went insane, and ran away.

The fragrance of Quality's French cologne filled the room as she got out of the shower and stood nude at the foot of the bed. Her flowing black hair draped her shoulders, covering her jutting nipples, which complimented her caramel skin and shapely small frame. From the foot of the bed, with thoughtful and caring eyes, she watched and we talked as I dressed for the evening. She was as loyal as whores come. It had been a year since I turned her out in New York City. She would often remind me that neither she, nor her family had ever forgotten the bag of skinny chickens and groceries that I had bought for her starving family on that cold wintry evening. She would never be a thief, but that didn't mean that she wouldn't steal.

Reader, when building a stable, one has to realize they won't all be thieves. Some had to be solid flat-backers. Some were jostlers, while others would be professional cannons. A master pimp utilizes a mentality parallel to that of a combat general in the Army. Some of his troops are cooks, some supply, some infantry, and some office workers. They all had a role. If a pimp is going to be successful, he must know his role. His crew must know theirs and play it well. Contrary to popular belief, pimps don't just send whores to work on street corners without a clue about what to do. The master pimp's movements are well thought out. He applies daily technical strategies to avoid his whores' arrest or detention and imminent dangers, while attaining as much cash as possible fast, fast, fast, often times in cities where he and his whores have never been before. He must have the logistics of a combat field marshal and the cunning of a military strategist.

The angry rain continued to pour as the doorbell began to ring. I hit the intercom. "Who is it?" I asked.

"It's some young pimping Jim Starr and I'm here for you," the sarcastic voice replied. I buzzed him up.

It's a strange thing about whores. Most often times when a whore chose, they would choose a nigger of lesser status, in a blatant attempt to drag your name through the mud and make you look bad. There was a knock at the door and I opened it. Before I ever opened the door, I already knew what it was. There was only one lose end in my business. It had to be Squirrel's new man. She had chosen, and he was here to serve me.

"Jim Starr," he arrogantly began, "I'm Mystery, Reno's cousin. Do you remember me?"

"No, I don't," I said coldly.

"I just stopped by to serve you and come to a proper understanding about that bitch," he said. "I'm here to lace your boots about that whore you've got that's missing," he excitedly continued.

"And what whore might that be?" I asked.

"The Mimi bitch," Mystery proudly announced, as if she were something special. "She's with me now. You know, she really likes the flavor of this young pimping," he continued. In the warmth of my home I smiled and took on his humorous entertainment. "Yeah, Jimi Starr, the Mimi bitch that use to be yours got with this young pimping late last night," Mystery proudly announced, sticking out his chest. Excitedly, he continued to speak, "She gave me this diamond watch and ring, $200, and a Mercedes Benz."

Mercedes Benz? My mind exploded!! I looked on the mantle over the fireplace. The keys were missing. This lousy bitch had stolen my car and had chosen with it. Up until this point, I had truly found this scenario and this fledgling pimp quite amusing.

"Wait a minute, little whore-hungry, nigger," I spat. "Let me pull your coat to something, pal; that Mercedes Benz belongs to me. Unless you're a car thief, you'll drop the keys on the table and leave my home immediately. That whore is not with me and hasn't been with me for a while. You don't owe me any news, brother. If I were you, I would accept that bitch as a blessing and a gift of the Game, and pimp on that out-of-pocket bitch hard and fast. Get a shit load of cash quick, because one thing is for sure, about that whore; she runs fast but she doesn't run long. If you're not an imposter and you're really pimping, boy, you can make that bitch pay you like a race horse, Secretariat, Citation, or Seattle Slew," I stated and then continued, "So you take that bitch and pimp, pal. Go with the blessings of The Game, little nigger, but leave my keys on the table," I said as I pointed my manicured hand toward the door.

Mystery reached into his pocket and hesitantly dropped the keys to the Mercedes on the table. He was slightly annoyed that I had taken his pimping lightly and had dismissed him from my premises, not to mention the fact that he was leaving with no Mercedes Benz and was still a walking pimp.

Although I had slighted him, I actually respected his pimping and took him seriously. I realized he was an upcoming, young pimp, trying to make a name for him. However, he would not make his reputation off of me, no not tonight anyway.

Slowly, the confused youngster walked towards the door. In mid-step he stopped and spun around and pointed his finger directly at me.

"Jimi Starr," he spat, "I believe you have holes in your game, and sooner or later, I'm going to find them. I'm going to reach into one of those holes and start pulling out whores until there's none left. I'm going to go outside now and campaign in front of your house," the little nigger spat.

"Being how it's raining, maybe it'll rain another one of your ex-whores on me," he growled sarcastically.

As the young, wannabe pimp exited the door, Reno entered laughing and said "Starr, I had to come by to see the expression on your face when that nigger told you that the skank whore had chosen him with your Mercedes. You know he's my turnout and my cousin and I'm looking out for him. I told him you didn't give a rat's ass about the bitch, some trick's cash, and jewelry. But I knew you would hit the roof about your car."

In all of my years of knowing Reno, he had always been strange, in a finicky kind of way. With all my perception, I could never tell whether he would show up in the embrace of friendship and brotherhood or with a baseball bat. My guess was that only time would tell.

In the dimly lit room, Quality and I lay in a passionate embrace, watching the shadows from the fireplace move across the wall. Branches of lightening danced through the sky, lighting up the horizon. Hail and icy rain shook the foundations of the house as they plummeted against the windowpanes. The cruel howling winds shook the house to its foundation. A flickering yellow flame burned low on the red embers as the grandfather clock struck 3:00 and began to chime. The phone rang, bringing a halt to Quality's quality time and an end to this romantic moment. I reached for the receiver.

"Speak," I said.

"Hello Jimi? It's me, Mimi." What could she possibly want now? I thought to myself. She continued. "I just want you to know I'm going to get you and I'm going to get that bitch!" She was screaming. "Nobody rejects me, nigger, no body! You allowed that bitch to clown me the other day and you put me out of your house, into the storm. Now I'm going to clown you. I took ten grand this evening and I'm going to give it to the first nigga I see."

"Bitch, you know I told you if you got your hands on some real money, to reach out and touch me. Where you at, baby?" I asked.

"The Hilton Hotel," she replied.

"I'll see you in 30 minutes," I said flatly.

"Don't let it be one minute more than that, or like I said, I'll give it to the first nigger I see," she said.

I hung up the phone, jumped into a suit, and headed across town. The rain continued to pour as I made my way through the city. Mimi was a chippy, out-of-pocket, degenerate motherfucker, but she was also a thief most capable of coming up with large amounts of cash at any time. It made no sense to let my personal feelings come between 10,000 smakeroos and me.

My windshield wipers seemed to be working over time as I circled the block for the third time. Out of nowhere, there she was, standing in the entranceway of the Hilton Hotel under the canopy in deep conversation with the doorman. Dry, she stood wide-legged in a white two-piece suit with red high-heel shoes. I pulled to the curb, blowing my horn. Running to the car, she attempted to dodge the pouring rain; she had no umbrella. Her long black hair blew in the harsh wind. Mimi was soaking wet by the time she entered the car. I pulled away from the curb, crossed the intersection, and headed for the freeway.

"I knew when I called you and told you I had ten grand you'd pull your dick out of that bitch and get out of bed," Mimi said.

"Bitch, my dick, my time, and my money all belong to me," I said. "Do you have something for me?" I asked as I zigged and zagged in and out of slush and traffic along the highway. I turned and looked at Mimi's disgusting face.
"Now reach me my money, bitch."

She placed her feet on the dashboard and pushed her arm up to what seemed like her elbow into her crotch and removed two funky one hundred dollar bills. It had become blatantly apparent that she had lied about the ten grand. She was a person who didn't respect herself and for whom I had no respect for at all.

"Jimi," she bitterly wept, shedding real tears like a baby, "I only lied about the money because you didn't want to see me, and to I wanted to get you out of bed and away from that man-stealing bitch. Jimi, as much money as I have given you, you still refuse to touch me, yet you could wine and dine and fuck that Quality bitch all night long," aggravated Mimi replied.

"This may be our last chance," Mimi cried. "Tell me that you need me. Tell me that you love me Jimi," she said as she looked into my eyes.

"You bull-dagging, shit-eating, dog dick-licking, incestuous, degenerate bitch, just the sound of your voice sickens me," I bitterly responded. "You want me to fuck you?" I asked. "Whore, you've got to be out of your mind," I continued. "You've been fucking the dog; I won't touch that." I arrogantly concluded.
My bitter rejection was too much for Mimi.

"Don't tell me you don't want me. Don't tell me you don't need me," she screamed. "It's your whores. It's Bianca and Quality and those other whores. Jimi, can't you see what they have done? They have turned you against me and destroyed our love," she sadly said. "If I had given you ten grand Jimi, would you have loved me then?"

I asked myself, what had I become? Was I selling my soul for money? "If I had given you ten grand Jimi, would you have loved me then?" She questioned. With ill intentions, I rocketed my Mercedes through the darkness and down the highway.

In a soft somber voice she whispered, "Jimi, tell me you don't love me."

Looking straight ahead into the storm and the darkness of the night I said, "Bitch, I do not even like you. You've never represented anything but a potential problem or a probable dollar bill to me, that's it and that's all." I viciously spat.

"Don't say that, Jimi. You know you don't mean it; you know you love me," she cried.

"Bitch, I tell you again, I don't even like you, and your degenerate mammy don't like you either," I growled.

She screamed, "Nigga, if I can't have you, no other whore will!" Suddenly she stopped crying. Turning, she looked at me with a cold, expressionless face and deceitful, larcenous eyes.

"Jimi," she venomously hissed, "If I can't have you, nobody can." I turned away from the windshield and slapped the shit out of her, instantly swelling her left eye.

"Are you threatening my life, you stinking bitch?" I snapped.

"No, I've tried that before and it doesn't work," she said. "What I'm doing, nigger," Mimi viciously spat, " is finishing your motherfucking career and ending your goddamned life," she continued. "Now that's scary," she sarcastically concluded.

I turned and slapped the shit out of her again.

"Oh yes, that's it! That's it, beat my ass, nigga, whip it good and proper!" She said, smiling, and clutching her puffed eye. "No, Jimi Starr, I'm not threatening your life, nigga; tonight I'm sending you to jail for murder," she screamed.

Hearing her disturbing words, I stared at her in disbelief.

"It's like I said, Jimi, if I can't have you, no whore can," Mimi hissed. With those words, she jerked her white jacket open, sending the buttons popping off onto the dashboard and the floor. She revealed her well-formed, jiggling breasts. She removed her jacket and threw it onto the rear seat of the car. Placing her back against the passenger door, she removed her skirt and sat nude, wearing nothing but her red spike-heeled shoes. Someone had already beaten her. She was bruised and welted from head to toe. I can only imagine that that little whore hungry nigger, Mystery, trying to establish himself as a full-fledged pimp, had dropped his gorilla hand and had really done a number on Mimi. By the time I fully realized what was truly going on, it was too late.

With her back turned to the door and a tormented, demon-like face, she snarled, "Jimi Starr, you have checked your last whore dollar. Nigger, you are going to the penitentiary for the rest of your life."

Mimi spread her legs wide apart, resting her red shoed foot on the dashboard, revealing her hairy mound and the two huge, odious, black caverns that had once been her famed and celebrated moneymakers. Wagging her tongue, she rolled her eyes back in her head, exposing only the whites and, in a eerie voice comparable to the creature in *The Exorcist* said, "Don't you want this any more, Jimi Starr?"

My Mercedes was hurdling down the highway when the crazed bitch opened the door. The chimes went off in my car and the interior lights came on. I felt and heard the rush and the roar of the wind and rain and the chill of the strong icy wind. I turned my head just in time to see her red high-heeled shoes roll out the door. In that instant, I heard the sounds of horns blowing and the screeching of wheels. I looked into the rearview mirror and saw an eighteen-wheeler jack knife around Mimi's nude, beaten body, lying on the rain soaked road in the center of the highway. In shock, I slammed on my brakes and swerved screeching to a stop. I couldn't believe it. That maniacal bitch had contemplated the inconceivable, done the unthinkable. The bitch had taken her own life, committing suicide. She had leaped head on from my speeding car into the on coming traffic just to implicate me. Who would believe me? I didn't murder the bitch. I had to get the fuck out of there! I had left the confines of my home and a solid whore just to come out in a thunderstorm to meet a tramp because I believed she had some money. There is and old pimp cliché that reads, "All money is not good money."

In conclusion and summation of this bizarre portion of my scenario, no, the deranged whore, Mimi, didn't die that night. That crazed suicidal bitch was too dirty to die from simply leaping out of a speeding car headfirst, during a thunderstorm, onto the highway and into the on coming traffic. What she did do that night was jump right the fuck out of my car and right the fuck out of my life. Her sexual depravity and mental demeanor were too volatile and too progressive for me to pimp on her any longer.

Finally, I realized that I was playing a game of immensely high stakes, a game that couldn't possibly be won. Mimi's life and my freedom hung in the turbulent balance. I had pimped on that deranged bitch as if there was no tomorrow, and gotten the best of her best. The wear and the tear of the Game, her many lovers, and not to mention her fetish for dog dick, had rapidly diminished her moneymaking capabilities. It was time for me to move on to some worthy and hopefully sane whore with the wisdom and prosperity of my pimping, and that's what exactly what the fuck I did.

Reno and Madrid

Gangster Brown, Jimi Starr, and Reno

Chapter 11

New York Mugging, California Style

Whistling winds blew and gloomy gray skies seemed to sit still as black clouds stirred over the face of the Manhattan horizon. I could not recall the warmth of the sun, nor it shining at all that entire day. From the filthy sidewalks, straight up into the heavens, gray and brown cement buildings, as if they were rooted to the pavement sprang up from beneath the curb and disappeared into the clouded blackness of the coming of winter's first snow thunderstorm.

The teary-eyed street preacher held a sign that read "Sinners Repent" as he stood on the corner of 42nd and 8th Avenue in front of the Port Authority. He preached the gospel of Jesus for the salvation of mankind. The wind roared in the distance; there was a shivering chill in the air. A seemingly never- ending multitude of cars of all shapes and sizes with deafening horns blew as they bottle-necked, congesting the intersection in the heart of the city, and as the taxi cabs added to the existing traffic tension, lining up in front of the Port of Authority. People swarmed from the landmark building, pouring into the street. In the doorways of businesses, drug peddlers and conmen peddled their wares or plied their craft. The billboard above Madison Square Garden read, "Love Your Brother." Big-rig eighteen-wheel trucks double-parked along 8th Avenue, unloading and loading as lines of merchants pushed opened racks of furs and clothing through the busy streets of the Times Square area. Hot dog vendors, perfume salesmen, and conmen lined the streets. The smell of roasted chestnuts was in the air. Horse-drawn carriages, carrying tourists, made their way down 6th Avenue towards Central Park. The horses left stacks of maneuver down the center of the picturesque street known as The Avenue of the Americas.

Butt naked whores in shake joints rhythmically shook their asses as tricks made their way in and out of the titty joints. In wide-eyed, voyeuristic fashion, they observed as the nude dancing whores practiced their craft.

The brisk wind blew the leaves from the bending trees in Central Park. There was a still chill in the air as the first flakes of winter's snow descended from the heavens onto the city they called New York, New York.

People of all nationalities, Blacks, Latinos, Italians, and Asians poured into and out of the subways.

The Manhattan sun was setting, pimps and whores began to line the avenues and side streets as if the work shift was changing. The squares were getting off work and the players were coming on. It was Friday night in the big city. Whores, with one thing in mind, began to line the avenues and side streets of the Times Square area. Most were scantily dressed, wearing revealing panties, bras, and fur coats. They wore opened-toed, spiked high-heeled shoes. They stood in suggestive position, making whore chatter while waving at cars as the wanton cunt-hungry tricks circled the block, searching for the girl of their dreams. Along the major avenues, like colorful peacocks, pimps cruised the corridors and side streets, dropping off their whores and checking their traps. Some players stood in groups in front of bars and stores, meddling passerby whores, talking loud about their latest conquest as horny trick passers by with stiff rods and pockets full of cash excitedly cruised the avenue and side streets calling from their open car windows, yelling, "Hey lady, how much?"

From the vantage point of elevated buildings and from behind closed curtains, young and old, sweaty faced, bug-eyed voyeurs frantically masturbated as they watched the semi-nude whores in doorways and cars, and through hotel windows, practicing their lewd and lascivious craft. The police sat parked at the curb, uncaring and unmoved by the common surroundings of the evening. In a Midtown Catholic church, nuns on bending knees prayed for the salvation of mankind.

At the intersection of 12th Avenue and 41st Street, a young Puerto Rican girl with thick black hair stood sheepishly, dumbfounded and unknowing, in the center of the block, in a red and white floral ankle-length dress that covered most of her body. She didn't have a clue of what to do, as veteran, street-smart whores psychologically spooked, intimidated and verbally vexed her as they intentionally blocked her while stealing her potential dates.

I had never laid eyes on this novice whore before in my life, but there was something about her at first glance, something chemical. I could feel it deep in my bones that before the night was out, this fledging whore would become mines. What I couldn't tell at first glance was that this particular whore would become the seventh Gabor, and that she would become a top-flight thief and a sticker, lasting for years to come and assisting in the ongoing quest of making me rich beyond my wildest dreams.

On any given night in New York City, there were one thousand whores practicing their lewd and lascivious crafts on the twelve major whore strolls in the borough of Manhattan. If you were pimping, it was your job to know each and every whore stroll and each and every whore, by face at any rate and anyway.

As always on the weekend, Midtown traffic was bumper to bumper. At the intersection of 8th Avenue onto 41st Street, in front of the Port Authority, busy and scantily dressed whores clad only in their underwear lined both sides of Whores' Row, waving at passing cars, hopeful of a chance of stopping a gullible trick with a fat wallet. Under the cover of darkness and all along 41st Street, in front of God and man, nude whores dated their tricks, sucking and fucking in cars and in darkened doorways. Notorious New York whores were infamous for turning one hundred dollar tricks in john's' cars and in residential and commercial doorways, as if it was legal and as if they had they had a license.

It was 12:00 midnight, Saturday morning as Buster, a personal friend of mine from Providence, Rhode Island, Kenny Diamond, my California homeboy, and I cruised the avenues and side streets of Manhattan, seeking to exercise our pimping on some fresh, young, unsuspecting, and naive whores. Gradually we made our way through the blowing horns and cumbersome congestion of the Times Square traffic. At the intersection of 39th and 11th Avenue, in the heart of Hell's Kitchen, I pulled to the curb. On any given night, there was always a large contingent of glamorous cross-country whores in this area. Around the clock cars like Cadillacs, Mercedes Benzes, and Rolls Royces, with out-of-state plates, caravanned throughout this area often, putting their work in. Well-dressed and well-to-do diamond-laden pimps campaigned for the affections and illicit funding from some willing young whore. The on going caravan of pimps and a endless parade of tricks made their way through the known flesh peddling corridors of the infamous New York whores. It was Friday night in the city. Some of the flamboyant and jewelry-laden pimps pulled to the curb, parked their cars, and walked the track on foot, pursuing whores of their desires, while others pimps profiled, posing beside their expensive and flashy automobiles.

New York Tee stood in the doorway of a vacant warehouse in the center of the block. Tee was a tall, dark-skinned, slender brother, who was exceedingly vain, and arrogant beyond belief. I had met him in Hollywood, California. Tee motioned my car to the curb.

Glamorous cross-country whores were everywhere sucking tricks, fucking tricks, and jacking them off. The scent of cash and excitement was in the air. The overhead streetlight flashed off and on as I got out of the car. New York Tee was an arrognt nigger who wanted to be Billy Dee.

"Jimi, what's up?" Tee asked as we shook hands and greeted. I eyed a confused beauty in a red and white dress as Kenny Diamond stepped from the car and pimped at a group of approaching whores and began his pimp antics, following them up the street. Under the bright overhead streetlight, New York Tee stared at his own image reflecting from the window of my Eldorado. He moved his head from side to side. Profiling, he adjusted his smile.

A young, long-legged, doll-faced brunette in a white halter-top and hot pants attempted to pass. New York Tee grabbed her and pulled her to him, startling her.

"Give me that money, you bitch. Women pay just to look at a pretty Black nigger like me," Tee exclaimed. He profiled and smiled, clutching her around the waist. Tee continued to make snide and obnoxious remarks as he vainly and routinely stared at his own image reflecting from the window of my customized Eldorado.

"New York Tee!" I snapped. "I am not Captain Save-A-Whore, nor am I Will Save A Bitch, but you're out of line. That woman's out here taking care of some man's business and you, pal, you're in direct violation of the Game." Tee fondled her breast and ass while smiling at his own image reflecting in the window. In narcissist fashion, he pulled her closer, profiling, moving his head from side to side occasionally adjusting his smile. Furious winds blew. The overhead streetlight flashed off and on, rattling entire buildings, blowing money- hungry whores and horny tricks up and down 11th Avenue.

I made eye- contact with the tender young beauty in the red and white dress. The veteran whores intimidated her and did not allow her to get a dime. It was obvious to the trained pimp's eye that she was a turnout and that she lacked confidence and the proper guidance about her craft.

In direct violation of the codes of the Game, Tee continued to embrace and fondle his captive white whore.

"Give me that money, whore. I told you, women pay just to look at a pretty nigga like me."

"I told you Tee to let that whore go. You're in direct violation of the Game," I said again.

"Jimi, you don't understand," New York Tee said. "This bitch is with that half-white nigger called Trick Baby. I'm not going to let a half-white nigger have a whore in the same town that I'm pimping in." New York Tee routinely made obnoxious statements about the nature of Trick Baby's origins and pedigree.

The overhead streetlights continued to flash off and on and as if in a parade; whores marched up and down the avenues, in and out of doorways, turning dates in cars, in doorways, and the sides of buildings.

In a dry tone, Tee said, "You cannot pay no white boy around here; you belong to me now, bitch. Now reach me my money, tramp." With that, Tee slapped the taste from the white girls mouth. New York Tee was cruising for a bruising.

Under the streetlight, I stepped to the turnout in the red and white dress. I stood directly in front of her blocking her retreat. She became my captive audience. However, I never touched her with my hands. If I couldn't stop a bitch with my mind or my mouth, I didn't need her.

"Hello, Doll Baby, how are you doing? It looks as if some of these old larceny- hearted whores out here this morning are giving you a hard time and not allowing you to make any money," I said in a concerned tone and continued as she turned her face away from me, attempting not to make eye contact and pretending that she wasn't listening. She stepped into the doorway of a closed business, attempting to avoid my mental and verbal advances. I stepped into the doorway behind her, preventing her from leaving.

"Where are you from, girlfriend?" I asked, flashing a diamond-toothed smile. She nervously looked around the doorway for an avenue of escape, determined not to speak.

"You have no need to be afraid of me," I said. "You need to be afraid of the man who sent you out here with no instructions. He couldn't possibly know what he was doing. An aspiring whorewith no instructions, representing a fake nigga's business could get murdered, in a town like this. It looks as if you could use a friend tonight," I continued. "Let me know when you're ready, Doll Baby," I concluded. I stepped out of the doorway, heading back to my car, allowing her the opportunity to escape.

From behind me I heard a warm and sensual voice say, "Right now I could really use a friend." I turned to greet a smiling face. It's not so much what you say, it's how you say it.

"Were you really going to let me go that easy?" She asked.

"Jimi Starr doesn't want anyone that doesn't want him," I said flatly.

Her eyes widened in surprise. "You're Jimi Starr?" she asked.

"In the flesh," I replied. Already having her attention after a few moments of conversation, I was able to move her to my car. Her name was Denise. She was from Youngstown, Ohio. She had been a shake dancer there. While dancing, she met a whore-hungry and crackhead pimp named Steve from Cincinnati, Ohio who brought her to New York City and turned her out. He had left her on 11th Avenue, one of the most vicious, cutthroat, and bloodthirsty tracks in America. In the process, she met me and Steve got trimmed for the bitch; the rest is history.

It was perpetrating mental midgets like this nigga Steve, who believed that they were pimping that made the Game a whole lot easier for a man like myself, a real pimp. His kind of nigga kept real live giants pimping in the Game.

There was an angry roar of thunder and a flash of lightening that lit up the horizon and the darkness like the morning sun as flurries of fresh white snow swept throughout the city.

At the mouth of the intersection, a speeding ambulance with lights flashing and siren screaming zigged and zagged, making its way through the congested traffic. The overhead streetlight shone down on the busy whores who jumped in and out of the johns' parked cars and chattered at passing tricks, pretended not to see the flamboyant pimps who caravanned and profiled in their flashy automobiles up and down the track.

A highly polished brown Fleetwood Brougham crept to a stop at the intersection of 41st Street and 11th Avenue as I sat parked at the curb in deep conversation and in mental pursuit of my newest conquest. The thunder roared in the distance as the brown Brougham pulled to the curb directly in front of me. The door swung open and out stepped a six-foot blonde, blue-eyed, and smiling nigger who could have passed for a white boy, who at one time may have had been the model or a double for the

Gerber baby. Looks can be deceiving. This white boy was a pimp inside and out. In a matter of seconds, New York Tee would become a witness, proof positive of Trick Baby's legitimacy.

New York Tee was still mauling and manhandling Trick Baby's woman as the half-white nigger stepped from his luxury car.

"Hey, how's it going Jimi?" Trick baby said in a smooth tone as he looked into my customized Cadillac. His collar was turned up and his hands were pushed deep into his pockets as the howling winds continued to blow, flapping his black overcoat and his blonde hair on the breeze.
"I have another ignorant fool to check this morning, man. That nigga, New York Tee, has disrespected me and put his hands on my bitch." He said in conclusion.

"Handle your business, baby," I replied as he turned and stepped away from my car.

"Bitch, was that half-white boy your man?" Tee growled as he pulled the terrified whore closer to him, jerking her around by the arm like a rag doll. "I'm your man now, bitch. I don't allow white boys to pimp in a town that I'm pimping in," Tee barked. It was the last thing Trick Baby allowed that foolish nigger to say.

Excitedly, Trick Baby shouted, "Hey nigga! Let go of my whore." Hail fell from the black skies and began to beat against the windowpanes. In a flash, with ill intentions and with one sudden motion, Trick Baby removed his previously concealed hand from his overcoat pocket, waved his hand across Tee's face and body. Then in the midst of the confusion, Trick Baby did a strange thing. He smiled, grabbed Tee's hand and shook it. With that, the smiling blue-eyed Trick Baby and his whore climbed into his well-polished brown Brougham and, with wheels screeching, sped away from the curb and into the black bleakness of the winter storm.

In all honesty, it happened just that quickly, but it changed New York Tee's life forever. The half-white nigger from Buffalo, NewYork, known as Speedy or Trick Baby, took his pearl-handled razor and cut New York Tee a new attitude, a new personality, a new asshole, and a complete new way of life. He all but cut New York Tee right out of the Game that night.

I want you to look at that nigger and never forget him or this night. This is what happens to niggers who put their hand s on other nigger's whores. Denise stared wide-eyed and in horror after witnessing Tee's misfortune.

New York Tee would never be a pretty boy again. As I pulled from the curb and into the traffic, New York Tee continued to methodically gaze at the reflection of his freshly altered image in the window of my customized Biarritz Eldorado. New York didn't initially realize that Trick Baby, with a straight razor, had cut the ball of his nose smooth off his face and placed it in the palm of his hand. New York Tee almost humorously stared at the peculiar looking fellow with a snout for a nose casting a reflection in the window of my customized Caddy.

Who is that peculiar looking fella in my reflection with a pig snout for a nose? I imagine he thought to himself. He took two or three steps and stopped to profile in a storefront window. It was at that point that reality had set in. He ran, screaming down 11th Avenue in horror, shock, and disbelief as he held his own nose in the palm of his hand. My shining two-toned customized Eldorado slowly pulled from the curb into the traffic. He was later rushed to Bellevue Hospital where they reattached his nose to his face with stitches that could have belonged to the Frankenstein monster. He was later transferred to the Bellevue Psychiatric ward. No, New York Tee would never ever be a pretty boy again.

Denise gave me a five-year run. Tee's misfortune assisted me in a lock down move for Denise.

Reader, case in point: If it doesn't belong to you, keep your hands off of it!

The snowstorm didn't make any difference. It was Friday night in the big city. People were everywhere; it seemed as if the wind blew them to their destinations. The angry breeze continued to blow and howl, the hail fell, and cars slid on the slick wet cobbled stones.

From my car stereo lively Latin jazz flowed as Buster, my new whore, and myself and I rolled slowly along Amsterdam Avenue, taking in the midnight sights as we headed uptown towards Harlem. I began to run the crash course of Jimi Starr's school of life and instant prosperity past my newfound strumpet.

"Listen up, Denise. You got yourself a new man with a new plan. I want you to forget all the bullshit that crackhead sucker has told you. Now listen to this; one can never be greater than one's own thoughts. If one thinks big and acts on that thought, ultimately, that person becomes big. On the contrary, if one has small thoughts and acts or doesn't act, they will be small. You must understand this: If a whore is to be successful, that whore must be reflective of her man's teachings. The student must diligently attempt to comprehend and master the master's teachings, with the understanding that the student can never be as great as the teacher because the teacher will never teach you all. Therefore, a woman is a reflection of her man through practicing his ideology. In being that reflection, she must embrace his teaching in thought and deed. A woman must understand that she, herself, receives fame and adulation along with her man."

In the midst of the bitter storm, I pulled to a stop and parked in front of Orie's, the Tailor's, on 125th and Lennox Avenue. Orie was, to my knowledge, the finest custom tailor in the borough of Harlem and most probably the United States. He had a wide variety of clients from politicians to entertainers and, without a doubt, a substantial number of pimps. The man was widely respected for his talents and known by all. Arrogantly, I rang the bell until the sleeping Orie opened the shop.

"Go away! The shop is closed and it's been closed for the last six hours!" He angrily yelled via the intercom. I rang the bell again and this time I really leaned on it.
"Who the hell is it ringing my mother-fucking doorbell at this ungodly time of night?" Orie angrily yelled into the intercom.

"Its me Orie, Jimi Starr," I said. "Sorry to disturb you at this time of night, but I need a small favor," I continued.

"Sure, Starr, not a problem," Orie replied, calming down.

"Can a pimp enter your place of business and come in out of the storm?" I asked.

Orie buzzed us into the famous custom tailor shop. Bolts of silks, mohair, linen, and other fine materials were in disarray throughout the large and popular tailor shop. The walls at the entrance of the shop were lined with autographed pictures of movie stars, entertainers, and famous politicians. In the tailoring work area, in the center of the shop, racks of finely tailored finished garments hung on wooden hangers. At the rear of the shop and in the basement was a parlor for VIP customers, complete with a bar. Buster Price and I sat on stools at the bar sipping from snifters of fine cognac.

Orie poured himself a drink, then looked across the bar and wearily spoke, "Jimi Starr, it's after midnight. I'm a 65-year-old man; I can't keep these kinds of hours anymore. What was the small favor you wanted from me?"

"Man, I'm really sorry about this inconvenience, Orie. All the stores are in the city are closed, which stops me from buying this new whore of mine a descent outfit, one that's worthy of her representing a man of my stature. I have been forced into a situation in which I have to improvise," I said. "I need you to cut Denise's ankle length dress off at the pelvis," I concluded.

"Sure, not a problem," Orie said as he stood Denise in front of the mirror. Through his thick bi-focal eyeglasses, he studied her curvaceous body. Orie took his scissors and professionally began to cut as the red and white floral cloth fell away from the dress to the floor, exposing Denise's hairy mound. Orie, the tailor, gasped, and his face twitched, and drool ran from his mouth and hung from his chin at the sight of Denise's well-toned golden ass and the incredible mound that could have been attached to the statue belonging to the Venus de Milo, inside of the Metropolitan Museum. Buster Price's eyes widened, as he choked and the fine cognac spurted from his mouth. Denise was slightly shocked herself and blushed with embarrassment as she looked into the mirror and said, "I didn't know I had it like that."

I smiled and zeroed in on this vision of loveliness. Yes, Denise had been truly blessed, I thought. If this fine, young Puerto Rican and fledgling whore wanted me, I was going to want her back. Unlike before with the nigga Steve, this time Denise had made a proper decision and she was now in the presence of a real Mack.

"How much do I owe you Orie?" I asked.

Orie's glasses were completely fogged. There was a peculiar rising in the front of his pants; I believe it was a hard-on.

"Jimi, you don't owe me anything for cutting this young lady's dress. As a matter of fact, I should be giving you something for that sneak peek I took," he said. "It's been a long time since old Orie has seen anything quite as lovely as Miss Denise, if I ever have," Orie continued. "You can do an old man's heart good by letting me spend some of my money with her," he concluded as he fished his wallet from his rear pocket, smiling at her, exposing his toothless pink gums.

When we pulled away from the shop on 125th Street into the snowstorm, Orie was standing in the doorway, sweating profusely, holding his rapidly beating heart. Orie had fallen head over hills in love with Denise's tender, young Puerto Rican pussy and had just become her faithful, unwavering trick for the rest of his life.

Denise's bright eyes shone; she had a smile from ear to ear, as I said, "I haven't known you for an hour and you are getting money and giving old men heart attacks," I said. "From this point on, your name is Zsa Zsa. Know that you are my woman now, and understand from this day forward; you are with a real live pimp. Zsa Zsa, if you stand up and whore for me, I will provide for you, I will protect you, and if fate deems it necessary, I will die for you," I continued. "If you cross me, bitch, I just might fire you. Do you accept my terms and conditions?" I asked.

"Yes," she confidently whispered.

"Now, this is what I want you to do and this is how I want you to do it," I concluded.

As I began to run my game plan past her novice ears, and not wanting to make the same mistake that the last nigga, Steve, had by sitting her down by herself without guidance. I had ridden through the entire area, searching for any one of my whores for the last thirty minutes with no results. When I didn't see them, I could only assume they were either in jail or busy, and hopefully it was the latter. It is a proven fact that a scary nigga will never have money. I decided to cast my fate to the wind and go for broke. I had faith in the words I had diligently whispered into Zsa Zsa's ears. I also had faith in my pimping. It was Friday night and I had to have my money. I double-checked to make sure Zsa Zsa had all my information. My gut intuition told me this bitch was a winner and would follow my instructions to the letter.

Strong winds wailed like banshees as I dropped Zsa Zsa off on Park Avenue and 29th Street in front of Smiler's Delicatessen. It is customary in the Game that the first money, whore money, is used to commemorate the occasion of a whore's choosing by having cocktails and snorting cocaine.

Buster and I headed for the Sugar Hill Area for some powder and some champagne. We pulled into an alley near the intersection of 110th and Amsterdam and parked. The icy hail fell as we eagerly and rapidly stepped from the heat of the customized Cadillac into the warmth of the affluent high-rise residential building. We were going to cop at the after-hours, our regular place on the third floor. The drug dealer's name was Rico. He was a likable little Colombian guy with a violent temper, not to mention an army of armed bodyguards and drug runners. For years, Rico and I had a special relationship. We had once shared a cell in an institution in California. I saved his life and stopped the sadistic, jailhouse butt-pirates from taking his manhood. He had never forgotten it. From that day on, we became brothers. Rico always, without fail, showed the colorful pimps and players of the Game the utmost respect. We respected him and he us. He always served pimps with the best product that money could possibly buy. Rico was widely rumored on the streets to be a known distributor for the Colombian drug cartel, and murderer.

When Buster and I stepped into the lobby, two Colombians with large bulges under their over coats, vigorously patted us down. Miniature palm trees and tropical plants, in large colorful ceramic pots lined the pastel painted walls of the foyer of the building. In the lobby of the building, the elevator's black doors slid open. Buster and I stepped in and the black elevator doors slid shut silently behind us. Inside the dimly lit elevator, there was two more Uzi-toting Latin bodyguards and another security camera. These two guards patted us down also and escorted us to the third floor. The black doors slid open, Buster and I exited, and the black doors silently slid closed behind us.

If there is anything good to be said about New York drug dealers, then I must commend them on their security measures. Inside the confines of their domain, you were definitely safe. No one could get hurt in one of these drug distribution points, unless it was the will of the dealer. If the Colombians even thought you were entertaining a foolish thought, they would murder you in cold blood. Please believe me when I tell you that they were not putting up with the foolishness of any ignorant nigger shit. This had to be the most secure building in New York City and, in my opinion, possibly the world. As we got out of the elevator on the third floor, the faint sound of a live jazz band met my ears. There where video cameras at both ends of the hallway. Rapidly we walked down the hall to Apartment 314. We stopped and knocked on the door. Slowly the apartment door opened to the lively after-hours session and a room jammed pack, full of excited, thrill -seeking, and chattering people. The live band played Freddie Hubbard's hit tune, "Red Clay." The music blared as the people danced, drank, and socialized. The Colombian drug cartel had turned the whole third floor into a huge after-hours for people who were handling big money politicians, entertainers, and of course polished pimps. It was Friday night in Manhattan, in the middle of a snow blizzard, and the after-hours was on full. Rico greeted us as we entered.

"Jimi Starr, *mi amigo*, it's always good to see you my friend." Rico greeted and continued, "What brings you into my establishment?" Rico asked.

"I'm here to celebrate and commemorate my good fortune in the Game," I answered.

"I see." Rico winked and said, holding his champagne glass high over his head. "*Mi amigo*, to your good health, and continued success in the Game, and to prosperity and good fortune with your new whore," he said smiling. "This one's on me, my friend," he concluded.

Rico signaled a cocktail waitress to clear us off a table directly in front of the band. The long- legged, big titied Latin cocktail waitress returned with a large bottle of Mum's champagne and a saucer containing a quarter of an ounce of Mother of Pearl cocaine. That particular moment could not have been any finer. Zsa Zsa was blown into the Game. I had Mum's champagne and Mother of Pearl cocaine, courtesy of the Colombian drug cartel. Before we left we had drunk champagne and, snorted cocaine with every corrupt, baby-kissing politician, in the city. Not to mention most probably most of the successful pimps on the eastern shore board.

Because of the notoriety of underworld establishments such as these, the patrons who were known to carry large amounts of cash were always at risk of becoming victims of a desperado gank artist or junkie stick-up kids once they stepped outside. Even Rico's crew couldn't protect the patrons once they had exited the buildings security.

It was 3:30 in the morning and the well-bundled underworld patrons continued to enter the building at 95th and Columbus, in the search of a drink, some powder, and a good time.

The momentum of the cruel and harsh winds blew unsecured trashcans and debris down Columbus Avenue. In the middle of a storm and directly across the street from the after-hours, a newspaper delivery truck screeched to a stop. The driver threw a bundle of papers into the doorway of a candy store and pulled away into the storm. Motionlessly, a freezing homeless person slept in the doorway. I wondered to myself if the frozen, motionless person was perhaps dead.

Buster and I wrapped our scarves around our necks, turned the collars up on our overcoats, and rapidly stepped into and through the bitter chill and falling snow of winter's first storm and the predawn darkness. My customized hog was parked at the curb, in the mouth of the alley. My hands were freezing as I unlocked and opened the door with the electric locks on the drivers panel. I opened the door for Buster. I started the car and warmed the engine.

In a curious and questioning tone of admiration, Buster spoke, "Jimi, why is it that without fail, when that racketeer Rico sees you, he treats you like royalty? That Colombian has really got his shit together," Buster said as he searched his own mind for an answer as to why. I never responded to the question. I smiled, turned on the radio, and drove into the bitter bleakness of the storm, heading towards Midtown and the whore stroll, my new whore, and my money.

While passing through the Hell's Kitchen Section of Manhattan and in the heart of Tin Pan Alley, at the intersection of 54th Street and 10th Avenue, I heard the rustling of moving cloths from the rear seat. I stared into my rear view mirror and saw a figure wearing a black ski mask and holding a pistol that appeared to be as long as my arm, aimed directly at Buster's head. This motherfucker had to have been in the rear seat when we returned to the car. Until this day, I've never figured out how this armed rogue got around my security system.

Buster sat stiff, rigid, and horrified as the masked gank artist pressed the automatic, blue steel pistol firmly to his head with one hand and held him around the neck with the other.

"Stop the car or I will blow the top of your buddy's head smooth the fuck off!" The gank artist coldly demanded. Slowly and cautiously, I pulled the car to the curb and parked.

"Now put your hands on the dashboard, nigga, and don't move," he said with a heavy Latin accent. There was something strangely familiar about his accented voice. The hair raised on the back of my neck as I realized the identity of the masked Latin desperado. It was the Uzi-toting Latin bouncer from the Big Dipper.

"You niggers keep looking straight ahead and put your hands on the dashboard or I'll blow your buddy's goddamn head off," he said. We complied as he continued, "Now, bitch-ass nigga's break yourselves, your money or your lives," the masked bandit demanded as he milked the jewelry from our fingers. I'll never forget the horrible pinging sound the gold chains made as they were jerked from my neck, breaking the catches. It turned out to be a good thing that I hadn't worn any major jewelry that evening. The masked bandit plucked Buster and me bare, as if we were chickens. In the front seat of my luxury car, Buster and I sat shivering from the cold. We were nude from our heads down to our toes in the car as the armed highjacker removed the keys from the ignition.

"If I didn't have to go someplace, and count the money that you niggas just gave me, and if I had more time, I'd give you two bitch-ass niggas the beating of your lives, then fuck the both of you up the ass," he growled. His bitter and stinging words added insult to injury. Opening the door, stepping from the rear seat to the curb, the masked bandit disappeared into the darkness of the storm.

Buster broke the silence, screaming, "Take me home to get my pistol! That punk motherfucker held a gun to my head and robbed me. I'm going to kill that pepper-belly mother fucker!" Buster continued as we hurriedly got dressed.

"Chill out, Buster. We don't want to be in a hurry and we don't want to make any mistakes," I said.

"Jimi, you're awfully calm for a nigga who just got robbed," Buster said.

"Buster, I guarantee we'll see that motherfucker again. I recognized his voice; I know who he is," I said. I removed the spare set of keys from under the seat and started the car. Buster and I both knew that, for right now, the Latin bandit was gone with his ill-gotten gains. He had slipped into the snowstorm and disappeared into the darkness of the city. Searching for him tonight in this storm would do no good. Frustrated, we headed for New Jersey.

In the distance, headlights twinkled like diamonds. I sat in the darkness watching a stream of seemingly never-ending cars make their way down the icy and wet FDR Drive. With my drapes drawn, I sat motionless, staring at the sleeping skyline of Manhattan and pondering the bleak blackness of this life that is known as the Game.

On the horizon, lightening flashed, giving light and definition to the night. I was depressed from the night's events. The unthinkable had happened; I had been robbed. Although, throughout the course of my career, there had been several attempts, this was the first and only time I had actually been robbed. Being a victim of a robbery brought me into a strange consciousness, putting me in touch with my own vulnerability and mortality. I can only imagine these feelings of being robbed were similar to those of a woman who had been raped and violated. Having something taken against your will presented you with feelings of insecurity, fear, vulnerability, and isolation. These were feelings that I definitely didn't like; nor could I hold onto these feelings, if I was going to continue to pimp.

Throughout my life and during the course of my colorful career, I have been shot no less than three times. I have been stabbed and left for dead, not to mention being poisoned by a crazed, enraged, and jealous whore. Each attempt on my life only made me physically stronger and mentally wiser, adding to the viciousness of my predatorial cunning and the depth of my suppressed and sadistic nature.

The clicking of my whores' high-heeled footsteps, and the gaiety of their laughter, with the first rays of brightness of the morning sun stirred me to consciousness. In my distraught frame of mind, I truly could not divulge to you whether or not I sat alone in the darkness for thirty minutes or three hours. What I did know for a fact was that I couldn't allow these whores to know that I had been robbed and that I was tripping. If a nigga was pimping, he had to be a god to his whores in an absolute kind of way, and gods don't get robbed, right?

The front door slowly opened and Zsa Zsa stepped through. I saw her smiling face as she entered the room. I had all but forgotten about this brand new whore because of the evening's events. Bianca, Boom Boom, and Suzie Q followed close behind. They all wore smiling faces. It was obvious that, financially, it had been a good night.

Young Dummy

Bianca laid completely ravished and panting as I stepped from the bed. My feet sank into the rich maroon shag carpet as I crossed the room and set a log onto the fire, my enlarged shadow reflected on the wall. From my panoramic view, snowflakes flew and drifted rhythmically across the Hudson as the traffic slowly bee-lined its way down the FDR Drive. The flames curled and licked the inner walls of the stone fireplace in my penthouse sanctuary. In the inner sanctuary of my boudoir, I found peace and harmony with Bianca, my lover. Returning to the bed, I gazed into Bianca's wanting and dedicated eyes. She was still burning up hot; her lust for me was insatiable. I remounted her and made love to her and fervently deep dicked her, loving her until we were both exhausted. She slipped into a deep sleep. Yes, when I fucked them, they stayed fucked.

Later, when we were both awake, I motioned Bianca to retrieve my briefcase from under the bed, and she did. I opened it and it was there. Fifty thousand dollars, the scrilla, the cash, the snaps, the reason why!! We counted it, we made loved in it, and then finally we slept in it. My mission was accomplished here. Closing my eyes, I slipped into a deep euphoric slumber. I began to think of the logistics of the long trip home. Careful planning had to be made to move the three cars, the penthouse full of fine French provincial furniture, my wardrobe, four whores, and not to mention my briefcase full of cash.

The first ray of winter's daylight shone through my windowpane as I began to stretch and yawn. The aroma of fresh roasted percolating coffee reached my slowly awakening nose. I could hear the sounds of clattering pots and pans from the kitchen as Bianca prepared my morning meal.

I reached under the king-size bed and pulled out my briefcase. I checked the contents. It was still there. I believed in Bianca without condition; however, I trusted no one, nigger nor bitch. In the distance, I heard the faint ringing of the phone. Moments later Bianca, wearing nothing but a white satin robe which was opened in the front, with no panties and sporting a pair of white high-heeled ostrich feathered house shoes, entered the room carrying my breakfast tray. She wore a smile on her face.

"Good morning, Daddy," she said, placing the tray gently across my lap. Bianca began giving me a brief on the events of the morning and the night before as I began to eat.

"All whores have checked in this morning. We are all present and accounted for. That new bitch you knocked may be a money getter, but I don't like her. That youngster Casanova, with the Malta-Canadian, called here five times this morning. You know, I broke that bitch two times last week for having your name in her mouth. She's been asking a lot of questions about you around the track. It won't be long before she chooses." Bianca continued on with the day's brief.

My mind reflected back to my first encounter with young Casanova who should have named himself Young Dummy. It was last summer in

Montreal, Canada. We happened to run into each other there. He was the nephew of two brothers, notorious Rolls Royce, limousine-driving pimps who were associates and homeboys of mine from Sacramento, California. On the strength of this, I allowed him to befriend me. Mistake!!! Shortly there after, he fell in Montreal on drug charges. Sales and possession is a serious issue in Canada. Through association and through no will of my own, I was pulled into a disgusting and unsavory scenario.

The stars twinkled in the predawn skies over Manhattan as Buster and I made our way through the hustling New York City streets. This was truly a city that never slept. At the intersection of 30th and Madison, an endless line of tricks frantically circled the block, desperate to sock it into the hot young cunt of one of the voluptuous whores who worked the red-light area. Petty drug pushers peddled their wares in the darkened doorways and hallways along the avenues and side streets.

At a phone booth in the center of the block in front of the Blarney Stone Bar, I saw him, the Puerto Rican stick-up man who had robbed us at gunpoint last night. It was almost too good to be true. I turned out the headlights on the Eldorado and skidded to a stop directly in front of him. I stepped from the car and approached him. He continued to speak on the phone as if I wasn't there, starring straight through me with larcenous eyes.

"I want to talk to you man about my money," I said sharply.

"What fucking money are you talking about, bitch-ass-nigger? Can't you see I'm on the phone?" He growled. "Now get your California candy-ass out of here and away from me before I kick it and stick my knife in it!"

"Sure pal," I stammered. "Please don't get angry. I only wanted to talk to you about my money man." The Latin stick-up kid grinned from ear to ear and believing he had punked me off, he turned to continue his telephone conversation. From his statement about the knife, I realized he didn't have a pistol. Opening the trunk of my car, I retrieved a bumper jack and returned.

He was still grinning when he said on the telephone, "I'm going to break that nigger from California. Sooner or later, I'm going to catch him right and take it all. That nigger's just dripping with jewelry; you'd think he was King Tutt."

"Hey fella," I said softly. He turned; he was still grinning when I swung the bumper jack, making contact with his face and knocked the smile right out of the center of his face. He gasped and cried out in pain and reached for his jaw, but his chin was no longer there. The blood flowed freely as he gurgled and broken teeth fell from the wide-open hole in his face that used to be his mouth. I swung the bumper jack again. With ill intentions, I was attempting to tear the top of his head off; I swung the bumper jack again. He threw his left arm up in an attempt to save his life. There was a horrible thud as the bumper jack shattered his left arm.

He screamed out like a bitch. "Yeeek!" With teeth still falling from his busted mouth he begged, "No kill me, Poppy! No kill me!" I used my instrument of destruction like an ax. Whomp! Whomp! Whomp! I chopped him down to the ground. In any other city in the world, the citizens would have been calling for the police, screaming bloody murder, but this was New York. Without looking, unconcerned couples that were bundled up cuddled, and continue to walk past, oblivious to my attempt at homicide. The horny tricks continued to circle the avenues in search of hot, young whores. Unceasing traffic made it's way down Madison Avenue. The Puerto Rican lay on his back on the street, crying in pain. His eyes rolled back in his head. I placed his right arm on the curb. With my size thirteen shoe, I stepped down on it. I heard a horrible snap as I broke his other arm and he rocked and wretched in pain. Sobbing for mercy, he lay in the streets with shattered arms as the blood gurgled from the broken orifice in his face that had once been his mouth. Buster sat in the car and coldly watched in silence. I stood over Puerto Rican Billy and pulled my dick from my pants. His eyes widened in horror as I pissed into the open hole in his face that had once been his mouth. The hot, golden urine splattered on his forehead as the mixture of piss and blood gurgled out his mouth, down his neck, and into the street. Buster sat in the car grimacing in disgust. I stood wide-legged over my victim's bruised, beaten, and broken body.

"Hey, Puerto Rican Billy," I said sarcastically as I milked the piss from my black dick, "you entertained the thought of robbing me?" I shook the last drop of piss from my dick into his horrified, bleeding and disfigured face.

"You pepper-belly punk, you never had a clue about what you were fucking with," I spat. "But now that you see that my dick gets harder than yours," I leaned over and POW! I slapped his bloody face, "Mother fucker, not only do I want my jewelry back, but I want yours, too." Pow! I slapped his bloody, deformed face again. He flinched and moaned in pain. "Bitch, give me that jewelry!" I demanded. Grabbing his shaking hand, I milked the jewelry from his terrified, trembling fingers. I shoved my large hands into his pockets.

"Mercy, Poppy, mercy. Please don't kill me, Poppy," he gurgled and whimpered through his broken jaw. I tore the pockets off of his pants. I removed the cash from his pockets, which he had stolen from Rico's drug runners.

I heard the sounds of pistols cocking behind me. From somewhere behind me and under the cover of the darkness, an authoritative voice called out, "Police! Freeze nigger!" My whole world flashed in front of me. At that precise moment, I believed I was headed to the pen for attempted murder. Again, in any other city in America, I would have, but this was New York. Baloney and Cheese, two of Manhattan's finest, slowly emerged from the darkness with pistols drawn. I stood over the brutally battered, piss-and-blood splattered body, with cash and jewelry in my hand.

It couldn't be much worse than this, I thought to myself, as the Puerto Rican gurgled, "Thank God, officers, that you're here. This nigger robbed me and tried to kill me. He took my cash and my jewelry and he urinated on me. Thank heavens you showed up when you did or he'd have killed me for sure," Billy gurgled. He continued, "This crazy nigger has broken my jaw, my arms, and quite possibly my leg. I can't get up. " I want this nigger arrested," he slurred, while lying on his back under the streetlights. The cop looked down at the badly bruised, battered, broken, and bloody victim.

With a heavy Irish accent, Red called out to his partner, "Hey, Shawn, this is Puerto Rican Billy, the drug seller and th notorious stick -up kid we've been looking for, turning the city upside down. This is the guy who has been robbing drug runners for the Colombian cartel. Rico's going to give us a reward for this one," the red headed detective concluded. Tears flowed freely from the swollen eye sockets of the Latin stick-up kid's recently twisted, and deformed face. In anguish, he gurgled his life's blood and moaned in agony.

"Puerto Rican Billy, this cash belongs to us," the officer said. "No doubt the jewelry belongs to this nigger who just attempted to kill you," the detective wisely deduced, "and you, Puerto Rican Billy, your ass belongs to Rico and the Colombian drug cartel. This moollie really did us a favor by catching and giving this hooligan stick-up kid, his propers," the red headed detective said. "I tell you what I'm going to do Mr. Pimp," Red said in his heavy Irish accent as his partner fished endless packages of dope from the inner pockets of Billy's coat. "Drop the cash on the ground, turn around, and get in your car. For the work you've done for us this evening, you can keep the jewelry. And Jimi Starr, I never thought you were a peeping Tom. We knew who you were the first time we saw you," the officer continued.

Smiling, he concluded, "Now never let us hear anything about this incident, and never let us see your dirty black nigger face again or everything you did here tonight to Puerto Rican Billy, we're going to do to your stinking black moolie ass." As instructed, I dropped the cash on the ground, stuffed the jewelry into my pockets and split.

An event like this could only happen in the city of New York. I turned on my headlights and pulled away from the scene. The horrified drug dealer turned stick-up kid laid on his back on the sidewalk sobbing, moaning, and uttering some incomprehensible gibberish about mercy. The two laughing sadistic and rogue detectives stood over that gapping hole that I had created and relieved themselves in the bruised, battered, broken, and deformed face of Puerto Rican Billy.

Tee Starr

Chapter 12

Portrait of a Prostitute

Some might call it fate, while others may attribute it to destiny. Be it the former most or the latter, I dedicate this chapter to the loving memory of Tee Starr, a top flight whore, and to the years of dedicated service and companionship that she gave to me. Tee Starr is a friend who will be sorely missed and her memory will never be forgotten.

She took to the Game like a duck takes to water. Lividly looking back on my life in retrospect, financially, I can only say I cannot recall a bad day to mind. It was the best of times. It was the worst of times. Like the leaves from the trees in an autumn breeze, as if by divine intervention, Tee drifted into my life. Her story went something like this:

After a severe, weeklong blizzard, the vicious and icy, razor sharp winds continued to howl. As a deeper chill fell over the small city of St. Paul, Minnesota, players with flashy automobiles lined both sides of the frozen streets, in front of the well-known after-hours spot. Inside the club, the huge black potbelly stove sent heat throughout the illegal, underworld establishment. Well-dressed, well-bundled players entered and exited the illicit, nightlife establishment. The music from the jukebox blared the blues as the pimps and whores, con men, dope dealers, and thieves paraded and profiled, and made joyful street chatter. The cruel bleakness of winter had rendered this event the only show in town. It was thirty minutes to midnight on New Year's Eve. The people of the night anxiously watched the clock in anticipation, awaiting the arrival of the New Year.

In a filthy room in the rear of the after-hours, Marie, a pregnant young Native American Indian woman, who was in labor; tied off and slipped a needle into her arm and coasted into a deep nod. She was born Theresa Iron Hors. Marie was one of three sisters known to be notorious Indian thieves. She gave her baby the name Theresa Iron Horse, though as she grew up, most people would call her Tee. It was the first day of the year and it was to be the first day in her eventful, short, and tragic life. When Tee was three years old, Marie was sentenced to three years in the state penitentiary for grand larceny. Baby Tee was left at the mercy of her Aunt Maggie, Marie's oldest sister. While there, Baby Tee was systematically beaten, rejected, psychologically abused, and locked in a dark closet. Tee lived her entire life longing for nothing more than her mother's love and acceptance.

The baby was returned to her mother Marie, after she was released from the pen, Marie took Tee back. However, Marie was addicted and continued to use narcotics. One night, on her knees in the bathroom, Marie cringed and retched into the toilet. Cold chills ran up and down her soaked spine. The beads of sweat rolled from her forehead and off her trembling lips. Her stomach knotted and her asshole quivered as she lost control of her rectum, squirting the pungent, steaming, watery feces from her asshole, down her thighs, dripping to her feet. The unmistakable odious, sour stench that only comes from an ill drug abuser's shit filled the room. Like the grease from a cold pork chop, the sticky, greasy sweat covered her body. She was cold. She was hot. She was cold again. She didn't know what she was, as the chill bumps covered the entirety of her cramping and aching body from head to toe. She was dope sick in the worst possible way. Frantically, she flipped through the pages of memory in her confused, tormented drug-hungry mind. She thought to herself, where could she beg, steal, or borrow the cost for a small fix? Whose dick could she suck? Who could she fuck? But she realized she couldn't do any of that; and that she was too ill, too weak. Besides, she would probably loose control of her bowels again and shit on the trick. Marie knew she had to find someone to do these things for her. The thought entered her mind, whose pussy could she sell?

From behind Marie, Tee's small voice said, "Mommy, are you all right?" With the eyes of a venomous serpent anticipating devouring it's prey, the mother turned and eyed the child. Reaching out, she pulled the child close.
Hugging Baby Tee, Marie whispered, "Yes, honey, Mommy's all right now."

Embracing young Theresa, Marie wickedly thought to herself, I'll call Uncle Mike. He's got dope and he's got cash. She thought back through the years; yes, Uncle Mike always did like kid pussy, Marie remembered. She frantically made the appropriate phone call for the narcotics and cash she so desperately needed.

"Hello, Uncle Mike? It's me, Marie. Do you still like them young? Man, do I have a treat for you." Within the hour, a white-haired, sweaty faced, potbellied Uncle Mike removed his dick from little Theresa's sticky mouth. Placing her small nude body in his lap, he buried himself inside her seven-year-old womb. Meanwhile, in the solitude of the bedroom, Marie removed the needle from her arm and slipped into a deep euphoric nod.

During Marie's narcotic-induced slumber, in the living room Uncle Mike laid young Tee down on the couch face first and on her belly and from behind her, Uncle Mike performed the ultimate degradation, he buried his bone deep in her seven year old butt, ruining her forever, ending any vestiges of innocence.

On a dark, star lit night, when Tee was 12 years old, she heard a car door shut in the driveway outside of her home. She heard the drug induced voice of her mother and two strange men. With her bedroom lights out, she stood behind the door and listened to the conversation in the next room.

"No! My girlfriend's not ugly," Marie said. "She simply wants to keep her identity a mystery. You see she is married to one of your co-workers at the factory. Her husband's a manager, to be precise, and she don't want her husband to know she's whoring around. Sure, my girlfriend's got some real good pussy. They tell me her pussy is so good, I've been thinking about getting some of it myself." The drunken men roared with laughter. Marie entered Tee's darkened room.

"Baby, Mommy needs you to do her another little favor," Marie said softly. "Mommy has some friends who want to meet you. I want you to be especially nice to them," she whispered. "Remember like always, keep the lights out. We don't want them to know how old you are." Tee nodded her head in acknowledgement, anything to keep her mother happy.

In the supposed and anticipated secrecy of darkness and in the confines of Tee's small room, her mother and the two playmates performed circus acts and made freak love. "Oooh weee! Oooh weee!" The giant, Black, bald-headed trick moaned and groaned in sexual delight; unable to hold his joy he cried out, "Lord, my Lord, sweet Jesus!" The trick wept and cried, tears then screamed and blew his wad in complete ecstasy.

"Damn, this is some good pussy," the giant Black man sobbed.

"Is that pussy everything I told you that it was?" Marie demanded. In the trick's curiosity and excitement over Tee's tiny adolescent pussy, and his puzzlement over which co-worker's wife he was fucking, the giant, Black, bald-headed trick turned on the light. His face filled with unexplained horror, then shock, and then disbelief. Raising his hand, he pointed at Tee.

He screamed to the top of his lungs, "She's just a little girl! That's why she has no tities. Junkie bitch, this is your baby!" Marie sat up in the bed nude and wide-eyed, as Tee attempted to cover herself with the bedspread, not knowing what to expect.

In complete disgust, the trick continued to scream, "You crossed me into fucking a baby, you disgusting tramp!" He balled his fists and rushed across the room. The two tricks beat and stomped Marie into convulsions, rendering her unconscious.

And so it was, in the winter of the year six years later, in the city of Spokane, Washington, the stage was set for all practical intents and purposes for the entrance of Tee into my life. On a brisk and wintry evening, the winds of fate blew Theresa Iron Horse into my life.

Over the years, the narcotics had begun to deteriorate the once beautiful Marie, as she systematically and methodically manipulated her one and only daughter to deeper levels of degradation. As I've mentioned before in this novel, street people have their own code of conduct, rules, and regulations on ethical and moral standards.

Reader, when and if a perspective woman ceases to take care of her man's business and engages in conversation or communication with another player, she becomes what is known in the Game as "out of pocket." This term most adequately describes the woman who has disrespected the player whose company she is in, as well as her own man, whom she is supposed to be representing, where upon the player whose company she is in, has the supreme right to demand compensation in the form of financial restitution, by means of any and all cash the woman may possess or jewelry, or anything else she may poses of value, up to and including sex.

However, reader, only a whore-hungry, degenerate pimp would demand sexual favors from another man's woman. Where is the constructive purpose in letting a whore have you when you don't have the whore? The prospective player also has the right to place the out-of-pocket whore under what is termed in the Game as "pimp's arrest," placing her in custody until her disrespected man comes to claim her. At this point, the whore's disrespected man will generally verbally and physically abuse the whore for her illicit behavior.

Spokane

There was a crippling chill in the air, and snow fell on the Garden State of New Jersey. The Checker cab took the LaGuardia Airport exit and made its way through the slushy cumbersome traffic. There were two Checker cabs packed solid with trunks and suitcases. I tipped the skycap and he began to place the seemingly endless rows of luggage on the conveyer belt. I was flying into Spokane, Washington. It was a medium-size city with a small-town atmosphere in the great Northwest. It was a place that I was well dug into. It was a place of personal and spiritual retreat. It was a place that I called home. Bianca and my crew had left New York, New York two weeks before me. Manhattan Mike had reluctantly and bitterly accepted his new found position as my driver, with the stipulation that he could hold on to that no money-getting bitch, Shirley. Mike had left New York two weeks prior with the moving van containing most of my household items and personal belongings.

I have traveled to New York many times over the years. In all of my travels, I have found no other place like it. As the holy city of Mecca is to Islam, so is Manhattan is to pimps, whores, and other players of the Game. If a pimp is really pimping, he must make the pilgrimage to Manhattan at least once during the course of his career. Manhattan is the island of twelve million inhabitants with twelve million dreams and they're all on fast forward. It is the city that never sleeps. It has eleven major whore strolls and, on any given night, no less than one thousand whores practice their craft on the streets of New York City. Manhattan's intense sights and sounds and it's multitudes of people and fast cash create and generate the atmosphere and ambiance for the true player that is nothing short of a spiritual experience in the land of good and plenty, making it the city so nice they named it twice, New York, New York.

It was a cold and brisk wintry evening. It was my second night home and my first night out since my return to Spokane. Snow banks lined the streets, as scantily dressed whores practiced their illicit craft of survival. The howling wind blew, exposing more than one bare bottom. Manhattan Mike swung into the parking lot of the China Gate Bar and Lounge, a popular downtown hangout. The lot was full of cars with out of state plates as we got out of the car. With gloved hands, I buttoned my cashmere coat and wrapped my scarf around my neck. Mike and I briskly stepped from the lot into the bar, and into an atmosphere of music, dancing, and general street chatter.

A shining disco ball hung from the ceiling of the dance room floor. Young local wannabe whores jiggled and bounced their bottoms rhythmically to the music, hoping to arouse the attention of a cross-country pimp. The drug dealers sat in the darkened corners of the lounge, selling narcotics as if they had a license. Colorful and immaculately dressed pimps lined the bar with an air of arrogance, cunning, and vanity, and with the hopes of adding one of these fine, young, big-booty whores to their stable.

"Jimi Starr," a familiar voice called out. "How long have you been back in town, baby?" It was Rickaché, a one time cross-country pimp who had seen better days, with his hands cupped, as if in prayer and a tear in his eye.

Rickach'e attempted to put the beg on me. "Do you think you could loan a pimp $20?" He humbly asked.

"Rick, I'm here tonight because I once loaned a nigger some money. I don't loan money anymore."

"I feel you," he said. "Well then, can you buy an old pimp pal a drink?" He continued.

"If you're pimping, Rick, you can buy yourself a drink, and if you can't, you're not pimping." Mike and I laughed and continued to walk to the bar.

Young Casanova sat at the bar, viewing into the overhead mirror. He watched my every move. Casanova was a brown-skinned, big-boned, longhaired youngster whom I had once helped out of a jam in Montreal, Canada. He continued to view me through the overhead mirror, making no attempt to greet or acknowledge me. With confidence and poise, I pulled up a stool next to Casanova and engaged him in conversation by way of the overhead mirror.

"Remy in a snifter," I said to the long-legged, fat-bottomed and big-titied barmaid. Mike sat down on my left side. "Make it two," I told the barmaid.

Returning my eyes to the mirror, focusing on Casanova, calmly I said, "It seems we have a slight discrepancy about that $3,000.00 I fronted you in Montreal. That discrepancy being, you forgot to pay me." Casanova said nothing. I said coldly, "You borrowed my money and left town without saying good-bye. That was another country, that was one year ago, and that was 3,000 miles away from here. But you still owe me my money."

Taking his eyes from the mirror, Casanova swiftly spun around on his stool and, with glaring bloodshot red eyes, began to snarl through his rotting yellow teeth, "Jimi, I'm not going to give you a dime!" he growled.

I pushed my gloved hand deep inside my pocket and wrapped it around my trusted blue steel friend, just in case Casanova got silly. I was prepared to blow the top of his head off. Mike saw me push my hand into my pocket and, hearing the conversation, grabbed my arm, locking my gloved hand into my pocket, quite possibly preventing a homicide.

Whispering, Mike said, "Let's keep it pimping, fellas."

Regaining my composure, I continued to speak, "When you took that fall in Montreal and called me in need of help, I extended the favor. Never for a moment did I believe it would come to this." Taking my gloved hand from my pocket, I picked up the snifter from the bar. I held my glass high in the air and placed my other hand on my hip.

"Bar maid," I said firmly, "give every pimp in the house a drink on Jimi Starr. Oh, give this sucker-ass nigger a glass of milk." The street players laughed at my light humor.

From the darkest corner in the room, Rickaché screamed, "Pimps in the house!" He rushed to the bar with someone else's dirty and empty glass. Putting my focus back on Casanova, I stood eye-to-eye and toe to-toe with him.

"If I don't get it from you, I'll get it from your bitch," I said sarcastically.

"That bitch ain't never paid nobody but me," he replied. "She loves me," he said proudly, sticking out his chest. Boy, was he a sucker! I thought to myself. "No one else can have her, not even you, Starr," he responded.

Looking into his eyes, I spoke these words; "There was never a horse that couldn't be rode and never a cowboy that couldn't be thrown." Casanova turned and left the club. Little did he know that hi whore Dawn had attempted to choose me twice in New York, but because of my personal ties with Casanova's family, I had spared him. I would spare him no more. Friendship is one thing, but pimping is another.

The music continued to play, as did the chatter of the intoxicated players. By now the drug dealers, practicing their trade from the darkened corners of the room, should have been rich as their thin customers rushed from the darkened corners to the parking lot and back again. Meanwhile, the fat booty dancers continued to jiggle and gyrate their bottoms in the hopes of being discovered and promoted by some cross-county pimp that evening.

It was at that point that she walked in and stood beside me. Her wavy jet-black hair flowed halfway down her back. She had almond-shaped dark eyes and a body that could have been sculpted by Michelangelo. There was for some reason an air of warmth and innocence about her, to this day, for some reason; I'm not able to explain.

Someone cursed from the darkest corner of the room. I knew that voice. They called him Wild Bill. He was the most bloodthirsty drug dealer in the city of Spokane and quite possibly in the state of Washington. His eyes shot daggers at me from across the room. I returned his angry glare. What in the fuck is his problem? I wondered. Pocahontas, the young Indian princess and I made eye contact. She smiled and quickly looked away.

With my suave and debonair demeanor, I approached the princess and spoke, "Excuse me," I said, looking deep into her almond-shaped eyes, which were like shimmering pools of black reflective water, "I'm Jimi," I said softly.

Giggling, she replied, "I know who you are, and I also know you're a pimp. My dad told me. He also told me that pimps are liars and prone to violence, and not to talk to pimps." She smiled and turned her head away.

"That was real clever of your dad, telling you not to talk to pimps and all," I replied. "However, when he told you not to speak, did he instruct you not to listen? I want you to know one thing for a surety and a certainty, darling. Before I'd harm one hair on your glamorous head, I'd cut my arm off at the shoulder," I continued. With those words she turned and swooned, stepping from her seat she staggered towards me.

"Who is your dad anyway?" I asked. With her dainty hand she pointed across the room and said, "That's him over there."

It was Wild Bill, who now was no longer shooting daggers with his eyes, but meat cleavers. I wanted no more scenes tonight. I pulled a gold pen from my pocket, and on a napkin wrote my number and placed it in her hand. When we touched, she shuddered and gasped; in later times Tee would confess she had achieved an orgasm. Smiling, I rose from my seat and left the China Gate.

International Shiloh Chicago

In silence, Manhattan Mike and I rolled along the tree-lined streets of the business area. In somber meditation, I pondered the course of my future and my finances. We made our way through the icy streets. My long black Cadillac came to a stop at the intersection of Sprague and Division Streets. Through my tinted windows, I sat and watched young wannabe whores practicing their craft.

One of them whispered and pointed, "That's Jimi Starr, the pimp." Over the years, I had become notarized in the Black underworld.

There was a nest of junkies standing around a burning trashcan, attempting to stay warm. Mike parked and I got out of the car to enter the store. In a flash, he burst forth from the nest of the junkies. It was a crackhead hype that was filthy and raggedy, an older version of International Shiloh. With outstretched arms, he attempted to embrace me. With an extended arm, I placed my palm firmly on his chest, stopping his advancement. His mouth moved like a scene from a Japanese movie, exposing his only two black and decaying teeth. His eyes were blood red and his pupils were faded and beady as they were bucked in disbelief. From his decaying, junkie mouth escaped an odious stench, which smelled like shit. The Game has an ugly ending when you don't play fair.

Shiloh began to stutter, "Ji-Ji-Jimi Starr, you dirty pi-pi-pimp!" I stepped back, reaching under my shirt, putting my hand firmly on my pistol.

"Ji-Ji-Jimi," he said, "these scandalous mo-motherfuckers don't believe I know you baby, and they don't believe that old Shiloh once was pimping." He concluded.

Taking my hand from under my coat, looking into his eyes with contempt and disgust, I sarcastically replied, "That's because you don't know me nigger, and for the records, you were never a pimp. You were a stick-up kid, a robber, and maybe even a pimp's flunkey, but a pimp? Hell no, nigger!" Shiloh dropped his head, turned around, and rejoined his friends standing around the burning trashcan. Turning, I briskly walked into the grocery store, reflecting on the past.

My mind flipped through the script and dialogue of years gone by. Oh yes, Shiloh Chicago, how well do I remember, you. He had once been a colorful character, the court jester, a clowning would-be pimp, a trusted associate and ally of many. Early in the Game, he had claimed the pimping as his life style and professed it as his way of life for a goodly amount of time. He had received some degree of success and notoriety. His humor and spirit assisted him up the social ladder. In time he was accepted and befriended by many of the underworld elite. In retrospect this was a big mistake. Admittedly, he had flare, yet many things were lacking from his flow and the quality of his character. Somehow, we all overlooked his faults. However, time exposed his inabilities, and divulged the fact that Shiloh was not a true Mack. After that, Shiloh became the doorman, body guard, and driver for many a dope dealers and pimps, and then one day, realizing within himself that he was no a pimp, without warning, he removed his mask and revealed his true self. Shiloh Chicago was a stick-up kid and worse.

Incestuous Twins

The stop-and-go traffic made it's way along Paradise Boulevard. It was a warm and beautiful mid-spring morning as I cruised past the entrance of Paradise Park. Slowly, we made our way down the three-lane boulevard. Tired, red-eyed, and provocativelydressed whores still lined the avenue of illicit passion from the previous evening.

If at all possible, a pimp always rode in the lane closest to the curb. This made it easier to talk to prospective whores and to receive our money. For this reason, this lane was called "the eating or the feeding lane." We cruised along the lane as I read and weeded out the true whores from the fakes. Perhaps another one of these lost and confused stragglers was in search of the truth this morning. Mentally, I scanned the on-hand inventory of Whores' row. There wasn't a real whore amongst them. I continued through the stop-and-go traffic, down the boulevard towards Shiloh's hotel.

I can honestly say I cannot recall her name. So as not to have to call her "bitch," I will call her Laura. Over the years, I have possessed scores of whores. The eternal gods of the Game know I have forgotten so many.

She was a young, redheaded, cum freak out of Denver, Colorado and a whore extraordinaire. She did it all. There was no job too big or no job too small. She made money as if she had a printing press. She claimed to be with some nigger named International Shiloh. I had checked her trap for the last three nights. The third time had been the charm; she chose. We pulled into the parking lot of the El Rancho Motel. Bedazzled and lustful whores cast their eyes to the ground or looked away, some perhaps hoping they would be the lucky one. It was well known in pimp circles that I did not accept non-productive whores. I got out of the car as curious pimps and players nodded in recognition and pulled their whores closer, holding them tight as Laura and I made our way through the parking lot and down the motel corridor. Some pimps scratched their heads or sighed in relief, glad I wasn't there for them. We stopped in front of Room 211 and I knocked on the door.

"Who-who-who is it?" Someone stammered from inside.

Firmly and confidently I replied, "Open the door, nigger, it's pimping." Slowly the door swung open to the repulsive view of a pigsty, and the most unlikely candidate to pimp a whore that I had ever seen in my life. He was a dark-skinned fellow with a super-nervous twitch in his face and shoulders. He had three yellow rotting teeth, beady bloodshot eyes, and wild, thick black hair that hung to his shoulders. The room was a shambles. Rancid food and dirty clothes were everywhere. This snaggle-tooth nigger could have passed for anything but a pimp. I found it of little wonder or consequence that he had blown this choice, young, moneymaking white girl.

"Shiloh?" I questioned.
"Yeah, yeah," he stuttered, as his face and shoulders began to twitch, making him appear to be doing some kind of jitterbug dance.

"I'm Jimi Starr," I said.

"I know who you are, baby," he replied. "What I don't know is why you are here with my whore." He questioned. I looked into his beady bloodshot eyes.

"Shiloh, you don't have a whore. I'm here to let you know that the whore you sent to work last night is mine now. She broke herself this morning and had the good sense to follow her money. You're no longer pimping, pal." At just that point, there was a knock at the door.

"Check out time," a demanding voice said from behind the door.

Shiloh rolled his bloodshot eyes toward the ceiling. Tears streaked his unwashed face as his eyes and shoulders began to twitch and his mouth began to quiver, "Da-da-damn, baby, she was the last one," he stammered. Yep, this nigger's got some kind of nervous disorder, I thought to myself.

"I can't let you have her, Jimi Starr," he said. "If I do, I won't be able to pay my rent. I'll be homeless and hungry, baby."

With that statement he frowned, turned, and rushed towards his bed. Unbeknownst to me, under the scattered trash, a .38 blue steel revolver laid on his bed.

"He's got a gun!" Laura shrieked.

Calmly, I pushed my hand under the jacket of my two-piece walking suit. "That's too bad Shiloh," I somberly said. "I was so hoping we could be friends and handle this distasteful situation like gentlemen. Unfortunately, you want to see me drop my gangster hand."

Calmly and softly I whispered, "Shiloh, if you want to talk to Jesus, it's okay with me, I've got his number. Pal, you're about to die behind a bitch that is no longer yours and who no longer wants you."

He froze in his steps. His beady, red eyes followed my movements.

"Wait a minute, wait a minute, baby, don't shoot," he shrieked. "I was just testing you to see if you were really pimping. If you got the whore," he said, " then you got me too, Jimi Starr." He sighed, "I ain't got no dough, no hoe, and no where on earth to go, and the rent man's at my door. If I can't be a good pimp, then let me be a driver and the flunky for a great one," he pleaded. "I don't eat much and I don't take up much space," Shiloh continued. .

" Jimi, I'll eat when you eat. I'll sleep when you sleep. I'll go when you tell me to go," he concluded.

Ten minutes later Laura, my new whore, and I were sitting in the rear seat of my customized Cadillac as Shiloh, my new protégé, pulled from the motel parking lot into the street, chauffeuring us through the city.

Looking into the rear view mirror, Shiloh asked, "Jimi Starr, I've got to ask you just one thing, baby. Do you really have a pistol?"

I glared into the reflection of his beady bloodshot eyes. "If you were to have taken one more step, pal, you would not have been here now to ask me that question," I coldly and dryly replied. This was my first encounter with Shiloh and the beginning of our strange acquaintance.

Time flew, as did my crew and my reputation, too. Shiloh had become a constant and curious companion. We traveled up and down the West Coast. We played the major whore strolls in the big cities. On a dark spring night, in the city of Oakland, California we left the Fox Lounge into the night air. A crescent moon and stars sat high in the midnight sky lighting up the darkness.

"Jimi," Shiloh stuttered, "I can't seem to keep a whore. Every time I catch a bitch, some good-looking, polished or high-powered pimp comes along and knocks me off. So I've sent for a whore that ain't going to ever leave me. Sh-sh-she's been in lo-lo-love with me all of her li-life," he stammered.

The jumbo jet had already arrived and begun unloading passengers. As we entered the busy Oakland International Airport, passengers excitedly exited and boarded flights. They scurried about, going and coming to and from destinations all over the world.

"Flight 15 from Ft. Lauderdale, Florida has arrived and is unloading at Gate 12," a friendly female voice announced over the public announcement system as Shiloh and I made our way through the crowds of people entering and exiting the building. Shiloh and I were walking side by side through the busy airport corridor when Ann walked into view for the first time. Shocked beyond belief, I froze in my unsuspecting and disbelieving footsteps. Shiloh's face lit up, exposing his pink gums and his only three yellow and decaying teeth.

"Ba-ba-baby," he stammered. Opening his arms, he embraced her. My mind reeled as I went back on my heels; dazed I witnessed their unholy reunion. In a lover's embrace, they stood in the center of the airport with their faces and shoulders twitching. As they embraced each other, they appeared to be doing some kind of lover's jitterbug dance. The tears welled in Shiloh's bloodshot eyes.

"Ji-Ji-Jimi, this is Ann, my woman," he stammered. "What do you think, baby?"

Ann reached out to shake my hand. Smiling, she exposed six yellow and rotting teeth. I shook my head in disbelief. Her face and shoulders twitched nervously.

"I-I-I heard about what you did for my boo. I-I-I just want to thank you personally, Mr. Jimi Starr, for looking out for my ma-ma-man," Ann stuttered.

"What do you think about my woman, Jimi?" Shiloh proudly inquired.

"This bitch looks like she could be your sister pal," I replied, disgustedly.

He was still grinning with tears in his bloodshot eyes when he said, sticking out his chest as he proudly announced, "That's because she is. She is my twin sister. Ann is also my woman and has been all her life.

"Jimi, you don't understand. I got to pi-pi-pimp, man. This whore is my woman and I'm her man. I will claim this bitch in front of God, man, and everybody. Jimi, Ann and I were both spawned and sprung from the same nut sack and fell out of the same Black mammy's ass. Jimi Starr, I'm going to pi-pi-pimp this hoe or die."

I whispered, "Shiloh, if I were you, I wouldn't tell anyone else that Ann is your sister. Personally, I think you ought to be ashamed of yourself, nigger. That's what I think." I concluded. I can only imagine any and everything was conceivable in the swamps of the Florida Everglades. But there was a name in the big city for what he and that peculiar-looking whore were doing. It's called incest, and I think it's wrong.

My sleek, customized Biarritz Eldorado missiled its way down the deserted Nevada highway. I opened my briefcase and began to count my receipts.

Shiloh, the court clown, looking through the rearview mirror, stuttered while curiously questioning, "Starchild, how much you got there? I didn't know you had it like that. Damn, you are really pimpin'!!"

We exited Interstate 10 to Tropicana Boulevard, and onto the Las Vegas Strip.

Stopping at a red light on Las Vegas Boulevard, Shiloh continued, "Jimi, you doin' way too much. I drove your car all the way here from Oakland. I didn't know you had it like that. If I had that kind of money, I could pimp again." The light changed and we sped through the intersection.

"Let this pimpin' through," he said as we zigzagged through the traffic. Smiling, Shiloh revealed his only two decaying teeth.

The sleek Eldorado pulled to the curb in front of The Moulin Rouge Hotel and Casino on the west side of Las Vegas. Dropping Shiloh off, I sped away from the curb. In the last few minutes of our trip, Shiloh had raised some disturbing thoughts in my head. Was it possible that Shiloh was a jacker or perhaps even worse? The man had no bitch other than his sister and no legitimate hustle. He had been too curious about my briefcase of cash. The hair rose on the back of my neck and the words of a deceased pimp pal rang out in my mind echoing, "Jimi Starr, trust no one, nigger nor bitch!" Out of all my mental attributes, my intuition and perception were the keenest. I made a mental note to beware of that degenerate nigger. We had been on the highway for twelve hours from San Francisco to Las Vegas. I was hungry, wanted to shower, and I wanted some much-needed sleep. In the cool darkness of the desert night, I headed for home.

The sweltering dessert heat was unbearable. The temperature was one hundred ten degrees and it was well after midnight. While in San Francisco, I had met and turned out Theresa. It was a classic knock, one for the books. For Theresa, it had been graduation day from Saint Grace's High School, a Catholic educational institution. Proudly she left the school and the graduation festivities in her blue cap and gown, with her diploma still in hand. Theresa's long shapely legs and flowing black hair caught my attention. She had the look of the future in her eyes, and was filled with dreams of a better tomorrow. She didn't realize it then, but it was my dreams and my future that she dreaming of.

I was smiling, with my window down, and my hair blowing in the breeze. Eagerly, she stood on the steps of the high school waiting for a ride. I pulled to the curb, flashing my thirty-two white and sparkling teeth as I introduced myself. I congratulated the schoolgirl on her academic achievements, and offered her a ride.

Mischievously, she smiled and said, "I really shouldn't. My mother has always told me to never talk or accept rides with strangers, but there's something about your smile that tells me I can trust you. Sure," she said and hopped into my customized hog.

"What was your name again?" She asked as I pulled from the curb into the traffic.

"Jimi Starr," I replied.

"What kind of work do you do?"

"Pimp whores," I said flatly as I placed my foot on the accelerator and headed towards the freeway.

In retrospect, perhaps Theresa should have listened to her mother and not talked to or accepted a ride from strangers. In the short span of 24 hours, Theresa had been transformed from an innocent schoolgirl to a street whore in training who sold pussy in truck stops in three states; California, Arizona, and Nevada, on the road to Las Vegas. Hard to believe, but true. Jimi Starr pimped like that.

Melodic jazz tones floated through my desert home as I got out of the gold-ivory fixture shower and stepped onto the plush red bathroom carpet and toweled myself dry. After I get dressed, I'm going to get that fine turn out to the track and get my pimping in, I thought to myself.

I stepped into the living room; Shiloh stood in the middle of the living room floor with his arm extended and a pistol in his hand. He spoke calmly and without stuttering, believing he had me in check. Brougham Slim, Shiloh's drug-addicted co-conspirator, frantically ransacked my apartment, searching for my cash and jewels.

I glanced around the room. Theresa sat nude in a chair near the sliding glass door. Dazed, wide-eyed, and horrified; she had been scared shitless. Her clothes were torn and scattered throughout the room. Semen dripped from her chin.

"Jimi, I kissed this bitch while you were in the shower; she and I became real good friends. Niggers like me don't get a chance to kiss pretty girls like this every day. I got to kiss them when and where I can."

Shiloh had traveled from San Francisco to Las Vegas with us. Theresa, believing Shiloh to be a friend, foolishly opened the door to a robbery and a possible homicide.

Shiloh placed his hand on his hip and sternly said these words, "Starchild, I'm a nigga who plays many games. I've always told you that I was down for the money. I'm here tonight to lighten your load. Jimi, I hear you been doing too much. I'm here to play the stick-up game or the murder game; it's up to you. Personally, I would prefer to play the latter. It's your move."

Brougham Slim, Shiloh's tall, lanky, drug addicted co-conspirator, frantically ransacked my apartment, searching for my cash and jewels. I stood in the middle of the living room floor, expressionless. Suddenly, I began to smile because of their humor and their buffoonery; I wasn't going to give them shit!

In utter sarcasm Shiloh spat, "When I'm through robbing you for your cash and jewels, I'm going to knock that smile right off your face. I'm going to give you the ass-whipping of your smug, motherfuckin' life, ni-ni-nigger. I'm going to beat you up real bad playboy, until you look like me," he smiled exposing his three and only rotting teeth. My mind reeled as I realized that Shiloh was a murderous jacker!

Cocking the pistol he snapped, "Now give me all of the cash and your jewels, nigga," he said wagging his tongue and rolling his eyes back in his head. He could have been a stand-in for the monster in the movie, *The Exorcist*. Throwing both my arms in the air, "Sure," I said. "I don't want any problems with you guys." I complied in submissive fashion. "I've got the cash right in here."

I turned and they allowed me to enter the kitchen. Whether they came to rob me or whether they came to kill me, I'll never know. I only knew for a surety that I wasn't going to give them anything. Stepping into the kitchen, I reached into a kitchen drawer.

"It's right in here," I said. Reaching in and grabbing my pistol, I turned around slowly with a .357 nickel plated magnum in my hand.

"Nigger," I growled, "this is what I call an equalizer. Now, snaggletooth motherfucker, which one of you bitch-ass niggers wants it first?" I growled. Brougham's eyes almost leaped from his head, he ran from my apartment, slamming the door behind him. Shiloh dropped the blue steel pistol to the floor. Cupping his hands, he began to plead and stutter, "You-you-you know I didn't really mean it, baby. I was just bull shiting with you, baby."

"Get out of my house, tramp nigger, and never let me see your poot-butt stuttering ass again, or I'll do the world a favor and blow your punk mother-fucking brains out," I concluded.

Leaping and screaming as if his ass and his immortal soul were on fire, Shiloh ran towards the door screaming, "Don't shoot, don't kill me, Jimi! Can't you take a joke? I was just bull shitting with you, baby."

He opened and slammed the door behind him. I could hear the soles of his shoes as they rapidly slapped the sidewalk, running away from my apartment. I heard the door of their car open and shut and his tires screech and race away from the curb, and into the warm blackness of the desert night.

Years later, snow flurries fell in Spokane as I rapidly stepped from the store into the sub-zero chill towards the sleek black Cadillac parked at the curb. Oh yes, only how well do I remember you, International Shiloh! The trash can fire was still burning, but Shiloh and his curb creature friends were gone.

Limo Driver, Madrid, JC, Jimi Starr, RC, JB, Reno, and Rosebudd

Mack Sheldon

Chapter 13

It Takes a Thief

Snowflakes drifted down to the ground and the furnace blasted as the weatherman on the television news reported that it was ten degrees below zero. I removed the two small bells from the birdcage and pinned them to the inside pockets of my coat. Quality and Suzie Q watched and listened in elation as I began to speak.

"When you can do this, then you will be able to get your man some real money. To elevate in the Game and in stature, understand that you must perfect your craft," I said.

At that point, with my middle finger, forefinger, and thumb, I gingerly slid my hand into the inside pocket of the coat and retrieved a watch and a money pouch without ringing the bells. Excitedly, the eager girls looked on in awe. Slowly, I returned the watch and the pouch to the inner pocket of my overcoat. The bells never rang. If I hadn't been such a devastating pimp, I most probably would have been one of the most spectacular thief who ever lived.

"Not everyone cannot do this," I said confidently, "it takes a thief. When you girls can do this, perhaps you will be capable of taking care of me in the style and fashion into which I have become accustomed."

Suzie Q, with her thumb, forefinger, and middle finger tried time and time again. The bells from the birdcage rang from November until the snow thawed in April. True thievery was not for everyone. Some whores were exactly just that, flat backing, dick-sucking whores and nothing else.

Two intoxicated Indian Native girls shrieked and laughed as I pulled to the curb and entered the liquor store. As I got out of the car, they began to chant and dance around me. Smiling, I pressed past, thinking to myself, obviously they have had too much firewater. The older looking of the two stopped and stood in front of me, preventing my advance to the store. She raised her dress above her hips, exposing her nudity, and began jiggling her thighs and licked her lips.

With a deep and gruff American Indian voice she said, "Whiskey, whiskey mister. You buy me whiskey, I do what you want," she said and began laughing. With that, she lifted her skirt and pointed down to her bare pussy. Damn, this must be why it is against the law to sell alcohol to Indians.

The Great Northwest was truly a pimp's paradise, full of white girls and Native Indians. I sidestepped young Pocahontas without responding and entered the store. As I entered, a grinning, elderly, toothless white man left the store, carrying a large bottle of whiskey in a brown paper bag. When I left the store, the two Indian girls were sitting in a pickup truck with the grinning, toothless old white man. They passed the bottle back and forth. The old man threw his head back. He was still grinning. For a moment, one of the young girl's head disappeared from sight and then it began to bob up and down.

I headed toward the intersection of Sprague and Division Avenue. Looking into my rearview mirror, I saw the lights flashing on three police cruisers just before they zoomed past. They slammed on their brakes in the middle of the block, jack-knifing on the icy asphalt as they slid to a stop. In the distance, I saw a white police van slide to the curb. The cops jumped from the van in pursuit of the fleeing whores on foot into the darkness of alleyways and down dimly lit side streets, attempting to obstruct them from practicing their illicit craft. Horny tricks continued to ride throughout the red light district, hot to sock it into the cunt and taste the juices of a glamorous, young street vixen. The whores continued to practice their craft, kneeling on the side of cars, out of their pursuer's view. Stopping the lust-hungry tricks on the side streets, the whores entered their cars and rode away. Others waved down tricks from darkened doorways. Yes, the police got a few whores, but the majority of whores got away.

Unbeknownst to me, Quality and Suzie Q saw my yellow Mercedes parked at the curb. Seeking to escape the long arm of the law and under the cover of darkness, they kneeled and walked along the row of cars, just out of sight from the police. There was a knock at my window. Looking out into the night, I saw no one. I returned my attention to the police activity across the street. Again, there was a knock.

Suzie Q spoke in a little girl's country voice, "Down here," she said. "Quick, let us in, the police are sweeping whores."

Firmly I snapped, "I don't give a fuck if they're picking up whores or not. Now listen up, dizzy-ass bitch, the police are out here tonight taking care of their business. They're locking motherfuckers up; that's what police do. I sent you whoring tonight to sell pussy because that's what I do; that's my business. And you came to work tonight to sell pussy because that's what you do; that's your business."

Looking down at their kneeling, shivering frames and studying their immediate mindset I spoke, "You see, everybody has a job to do, so you whores go do yours. Don't ever approach me like this again. I'm not a rest haven for spooked whores. Bitch, I'm pimping for real! Now whore, bitch, or go bitch, the decision is yours."

Quality looked up teary-eyed, still kneeling, then turned and duck-walked away. I lit a cigarette and pulled from the curb and continued to ride along Sprague Avenue. I slowly rolled along Sprague Avenue, in search of Dawn, young Dummy's six-foot tall mulatto. In the ice and snow, shivering and dutiful busy whores ducked in and out of cars and darkened doorways. That was when Dawn stepped from an all-night coffee shop, carrying a cup of hot coffee. Pulling to the curb, I let down my window. She looked at me and lit up like a Christmas tree.

"Get in quick, the police are rolling," I said. Without another word and with a grin from ear to ear, she rushed the car, got in, and shut the door.

"We had better get you away from here fast. We don't want you to go to jail," do we I concluded.

When a pimp is trying to have a whore, often times they will belittle or berate the pimp whose whore he is trying to have. I knew that what this whore needed was to feel good about herself. She already felt bad enough about Young Dummy. It wasn't long before I realized the truth about my beliefs.

"Jimi," she said softly as we pulled from the curb, "twice before I have been out-of-pocket with you. You accepted my money, but you didn't accept me. You made me feel insecure about my talents, myself, and who I was. Your actions made me question the man I was with and his talents, Jimi." She said with her voice cracking, "I'm a good whore. What I don't have is a good man." Reaching deep into her thighs, she produced a rubber containing a thick rolls of bills. "I've been saving this money to escape."

Keeping my eyes on anything but the money, I continued to drive.

Leaning over, I opened my glove compartment and spoke with confidence, "If that's for me, drop it in there." Dawn adhered to the course of her destiny and her new man's request. I leaned over again, closing the glove compartment containing the dick rubber with a tightly packed roll of bills. It was the first installment of many, and the start of a beautiful relationship. I looked into her eyes as I held her face in my hands.

"Dawn," I whispered softly, "the third time is the charm." We rode into the black darkness of the cold wintry night. Some might call it fate or divine intervention, but somehow I knew that with this woman, my future would be as bright as the sun.

Easy Money

I took a deep look into her smiling face and twinkling hazel eyes. I winked, returned a smile, and pulled into the traffic. Dawn stood six feet tall. Sh was a slender blonde mulatto; she was articulate, well mannerable, and intelligent. I felt that with the proper enhancement and management of her skills, I could develop her into one of the all-time greats. Somewhere along the way, she had met Casanova, whom I always referred to as Young Dummy, who obviously convinced her that he knew a better way. This fine young whore had attempted twice to choose me, but out of respect for Casanova, believing we had some kind of friendship, I had passed. It was unknown to Casanova that I had broken her twice, sending her back to him empty handed. The third time was the charm.

The shadows of lovers moved against the walls. Red and yellow flames lit the inner sanctum of the brick fireplace. Three inches of snow fell that night as we lay in the warmth of my romantic boudoir. Dawn studiously listened as we lay together and I discussed my concerns about her future. Dawn was not a tramp by any means. She was simply just a woman who respected and enjoyed her profession and who by some strange twist of fate, chanced into Young Dummy. Dawn broke the silence of this romantic moment when she blurted these words from her mouth, "Casanova is a junkie." She placed her hand on her mouth as if she couldn't keep the words from escaping her lips and repeated her statement, "Casanova is a junkie. I came home last night and found that nigger nodded out with a needle still in his arm. Jimi," she said, "Casanova is on dope."

In the dim light from the fireplace, she lay nude beside me. My suspicions were confirmed, Casanova wouldn't be getting this one back. I watched Dawn quiver, as she lay nude and panting beside me. I had been blessed at birth. When I fucked them, they stayed fucked.

I summed up the situation without speaking. So Casanova was a junkie, that explains that nigger's attitude and the reality of what had happened to my $3,000.

My thoughts reflected back over the year past to Montreal, Canada. I focused on the initial phone call that brought me into this distasteful and unwarranted situation. The phone rang. It was Casanova; he was boohooing, crying like a real live bitch.

"Jimi," he excitedly cried, "I'm in jail. I was busted last night for possession of narcotics with the intent to sale," he sobbed. In the background, I could hear the voices and the catcalls being made by passing inmates.

"Hey, Blackie, you're going to be mine all night long," a muffled voice said.

"Sweetheart, you're too pretty to die," the voice of another horny inmate cried out.

During this conversation, Casanova never let on that the Canadian butt-hole surfers had already fondled and rode his junkie ass to a stand still.

"Jimi, the police took all my money. I truly need your help," Casanova pleaded. "You know my family, Jimi. I'm good for it," he whimpered.

I responded, "You're in a most unfortunate situation, pal, but I don't lend money." Somewhere in the background, I heard someone blow Casanova a kiss.

"Oh God," he screamed. "Jimi, these white boys want to fuck me. Help me, please!"

They say that Black ass has long been a notorious delicacy among the white prison inmates in the French-Canadian penal institutions. Against my better judgment, I decided to assist.

"You will never be sorry, Jimi Starr," Casanova cried and sobbed like a bitch. That was the phone call that had led to this current situation.

The heater blared as Mike and I sat with the engine running. I watched the icy snowflakes drift gently from the sky to the ground. With a tear-streaked face, Casanova raced from the Canadian holding facility. Trembling, with the buttons torn from his shirt and his arms folded across his chest, he left the building and dashed through the parking lot as if he were an endangered animal running for his life, with his hunters in close pursuit. His right eye was black and his lip was busted. He was visibly shaking as he attempted to light a cigarette. There were several large and small passion marks on his neck and on his chest. In retrospect I thought, perhaps I was a little late with the rescue move. It was blatantly apparent that last night, the other inmates had forcibly convinced Casanova to play the role of Juliet. His long shoulder-length hair had been displaced. As he raced through the parking lot, his ass jiggled like jelly, making a squishing sound as he sat down in the car seat.

"Get me away from here, quick!" He said. Whew! His breath reeked with the unmistakable and odious stench of human shit and dirty dick dust. The tears flowed freely from his eyes and he trembled as if he had the palsy. Whew! The foul stench from his mouth was almost unbearable. Those jailhouse white boys had done some terrible things to him last night. Slowly I pulled from the lot and onto the street.

There was an eerie silence that rested on the three of us as the customized Cadillac made its way through the traffic congestion of the city. What do you say to a Black man who has been gang raped, used like a woman? I dropped young Casanova off at his hotel. Tomorrow, we would all leave for New York and forget this situation ever happened.

Cautiously, we made our way through the ice-slick streets of the city. Angrily, Mike broke the silence saying, "Those jailhouse white boys put a terrible fucking on that man. They gang-raped him. That nigger could hardly walk. He has been ruined. He's definitely never going be the same again." Little did I know at that time how true Mike's words were.

I looked past Dawn and towards the flurries of snow that drifted past the window onto the streets below. It had to be close to freezing outside. The Game had an ugly ending when it wasn't played fair. Casanova's betrayal of my friendship caused me to break his back, crippling him in the Game. This was true retribution. Casanova was on dope, he was broke, and it was below zero. Yes, this scenario was definitely going to be interesting. I dialed Casanova's room and placed the phone on intercom.

"Yeah, it's young Casanova. Speak," he said confidently.

"It's your old pal. It's the pimping nigger. You do remember pimping," I said slyly. "Damn, it's cold outside tonight, Casanova. Did that whore make it home tonight?" I asked.

"Listen nigger, why are you questioning me about my whore? She was at home hours ago with my money, nigger," he viciously spat. I brought the cat and mouse game to an abrupt halt.

"Nigger," I said, "not only are you a thief, but also you are a liar. You see, Casanova, a couple of hours ago, I broke Dawn and she chose me. So, you are lying brother, unless that whore has an identical twin. I just called to inform you that your card has been removed from the pimp file."

"My card removed from the pimp file? What do you mean?" He curiously inquired.

"I mean, nigger, you ain't pimping no more, and nigger, know for a surety, from this day forth, you have been relieved from any and all ties with Dawn." The line went silent. "Casanova, are you still there?" I asked.

He excitedly stuttered, "Jimi Starr, I don't believe anything you are saying. If she's there, let me hear it from her."

"Oh, so you want to hear it from the bitch, huh? Sure guy," I agreed.

"Umm," she moaned from somewhere deep in her throat. In a sultry, euphoric tone, "It's true Casanova, I've chosen Jimi Starr. You're whoreless, nigga," she said.

In the heat of the moment, I buried my bone deep in her butt. I socked dick to her like I was a nineteen-year-old stiff-dick boy.

"Ahh," she cried, then gasped and moaned in excitement while Casanova begged and pleaded over the phone intercom.

"Please Dawn, I'll change. Please Dawn, I love you, I'm sorry baby," Casanova cried. This nigger was a sucker and a chump and didn't have a pimp bone in his entire body. The ride on Dawn's behind was so smooth; I could have sworn I was in the back seat of a stretch limousine.

I was almost moved to compassion; Casanova sounded as if he were crying real tears when he showed himself for the true despicable junkie that he really was.

"Dawn, I'm going to be sick. Just leave and get some more money and come home." With this statement, he had exposed himself and she realized that he really didn't care.

"Fuck you!" Dawn viciously snapped. "Go get your own money with that pussy those white boys made for you in that Canadian jailhouse, nigger!" With that, she pushed the button on the intercom phone, ending the phone call.

"You're about to see the Game like you've never seen it before," I said. "You're about to experience some drug-free, top-flight pimping with a real man. Out with the old and in with the new. A brand new man with a brand new plan," I continued. We made love until we passed out.

Two weeks had passed and the snow was still falling. My crew of whores laughed and talked in gaiety as we rolled through the tree-lined, snow-drifted streets of Spokane. Tee had taken to whoring like a duck takes to water. She was getting money hand over fist. I knew that as long as I stayed in town, I would experience problems with her family. She knew she had to have my money every day. At Sprague and Division, the shinny black Brougham came to a stop at the signal light. We saw a ragged, drug-starved, young Casanova forging through the thawing snow. He was in search of a straggler or an outlaw whore that he could rob to support his drug habit. Cringing at the sight, Dawn scooted closer to me. Casanova angrily veered into the passing Brougham window.

With rage and contempt and through larcenous blood-shot eyes, he glared, shook his freezing fists in the air as he yelled, "Hey, come back here with my whore! I'm going to kick your ass, Starr!" I pulled Dawn closer to me. I flashed Casanova a conniving smile as Dawn kissed me tenderly on the cheek. My crew of whores and I slowly rolled through the intersection and the skid row section of town, Casanova's newfound haunt.

From the rear seat, Chop Chop said, "Damn, that nigger sure fell to pieces quick."

The whores continued to make small talk about last night's events as we rolled along Sprague. From my rearview mirror, I watched Casanova get smaller and smaller until he disappeared. This nigger's some kind of nut, I thought to myself. He had lost his pride and self-respect. One thing for sure, until he regained his pride and dignity, he would never pimp again.

While driving along the frosty, tree-lined streets, I listened to the whores' joyful chatter. Chop Chop was a Korean turn out whom I had acquired during my latest stay in Spokane, Washington.

Playfully I asked her, "Why do they call you Chop Chop?" With her cute Asian accent, she wittingly replied, "If you fuck around with this pussy, you will cum real quick, chop-chop." The whores and I roared with laughter at her response.

Away from the glitz, glamour, and antics of the Game, I enjoyed the privacy of my home. As I entered the confines of my bedroom sanctuary, Bianca sat on the side of the bed. She was breastfeeding my new son.

The sun was setting on the day and on my stay in Spokane. I took in the view of the snow capped mountains and frosty countryside from my bedroom window. Bianca and I watched the red sun set on the icy, snow-capped mountains and the thawing snow that covered the rooftops of houses as the smoke rose from the chimneys. The lush, frost-covered greenery that filled the valley and surrounded the sleeping hollow town was almost too beautiful for words. I had found peace here. It was my home away from home. It was a secure place of solitude and sanctuary for rebuilding and educating my new crew. But I longed for those warm California nights and the cool Pacific Ocean breeze.

The knock on the bedroom door and the sound of Bianca's voice aroused me from my much-needed slumber. Dawn lay sleeping nude beside me.

"Jimi," Bianca whispered excitedly, "Casanova's at the front door. He says he's been beaten up really bad."

Nude, I stepped from the bed. Bianca handed me the green silk robe from the chair. I rushed to the front door to assist a pimp supposedly in distress. I removed the chain and opened the front door just in time enough to see Casanova slide down the wall and fall face first into a snowdrift in the walkway. It was out of legitimate concern for his health and safety that I helped him up and assisted him into my home. Sitting him on the sofa, I turned to the bar to pour him a stiff drink to help to revitalize him. Hearing the rustling of clothes and the click of a revolver behind me, I turned to find myself face to face with blue steel .357 magnum that was cocked and aimed directly at the center of my forehead.

"I knew eventually I would get you Jimi Starr. I can be smart too. Heh, heh, heh, heh," Casanova mumbled and ranted some form of lunatic gibberish.
"You see, nigger, you're not so smart after all," he said grinning. "You made me look small in front of my woman and everybody else. Now, Jimi Starr," he said, "I'm going to make you look small. You made a mockery out of me, then you stole my woman from me, and for that, Jimi, I'm going to beat your ass with my pistol before I take my whore out of here."

I realized that out of my concern for Casanova's health and safety, I had placed my household and myself in a precarious situation. I looked deep into his eyes. Yep, it was just as I thought; this nigger was crazier than a sack full of shit-house rats. I knew I could show no fear.

"You say you're going to beat my ass with a pistol? Nigger, you're not going to do a goddamn thing here this morning except perhaps make me kill you. All whores here in this house belong to me," I growled.

With his pistol in his outstretched hand, his red eyes bugged, and his contorted face could have belonged to a demon. He said, "Nigger, you're right. I don't have a whore here." With that, he crossed his blood-shot eyes and began to waggle his tongue and coldly and methodically recanted chanting these words as he did a little dance, "Nigger, I'm going to shoot you, I'm going to kill the bitch, and then I'm going to kill myself."

Egads, sweet Jesus!! I thought. This nigger is possessed. I looked deeper into his runny, blood-shot eyes. Yikes! There wasn't anybody home. This nigger was totally insane! Was this going to be the end of my life? Casanova swung the pistol with all his might, attempting to tear the head off of my body. In that moment, my entire life flashed before me. Hell, no! I refuse to die because some perpetrator who couldn't accept the Game for what it was, cop and blow.

With the speed of lightning, I stepped into Casanova and grabbed the pistol. As we struggled, my mind flashed on my sweet mama, Bianca, and my newborn son. No, not like this, not now. During the struggle with Casanova, the belt of my money-green silk robe fell to the floor. Looking down, his blood-shot eyes widened and bugged in alarm and disbelief. He raised his brow. His lips quivered and his mouth fell wide open. His face filled with an unbelievable and unexplainable horror and then rage. He still held the pistol with one hand, with his opposite hand he pointed his finger, he gritted his teeth as his eyes stared in total and complete disbelief at my genitalia.

Stammering, he screamed at the top of his lungs, realizing Dawn was lost and ruined forever. "Did you use that? Have you been using that on my Dawn, nigger?" In that instant, he became empowered with the super-human strength of a mad man. With a phenomenal burst of power, he jerked the pistol away from me.

"I'm going to hurt you real bad, Jimi Starr. Did you put that in my bitch, nigger," he asked. I stared coldly into his bugged blood-shot orbs.

"No, fool, I put it in my bitch! You don't have a bitch, Casanova. The Game is cop and blow, and you had blown that whore long before I showed up and long before she had left you. You were a fake from the beginning. You didn't have any business with a real whore anyway. As I told you before, I'll tell you again, the Game is cop and blow, Casanova; no whore comes to stay, nigger, they come to pay. They come through the front door searching for a way out of the back door," I spat.

Bianca and Dawn stood at the top of the stairs. They had overheard the dramatic entirety of this distasteful situation. At gunpoint, Casanova demanded that I call Dawn down the stairs.

"Sure guy, not a problem. Hey, Dawn, come here, someone wants to talk to you," I called out.

"Hell, no! That nigger's crazy! It's every man for himself!" Dawn screamed. With that, she rushed to a bedroom window and attempted to pull it up. The screeching sound of the snow against the window alerted Casanova of her impending escape. With pistol still in hand, he rushed up the stairs. Unbeknown to me, neighbors had earlier seen Casanova lurking outside my household with a pistol. I thanked God they had called the police. As Casanova rushed up the stairs, I retrieved my robe and rushed towards the front door.

Opening the door and stepping over the threshold into the icy snow, I ran headlong into the police. At that point, I heard two gunshots behind me.

I cringed in fear at the thought of what must have happened. "Oh, God!!" I screamed. He has shot Bianca and my precious, innocent baby, "I thought".

The police stormed past me into my house and up the stairs, tackling and handcuffing the mad man. This situation had gotten totally out of hand. The pressures of Casanova being a whoreless nigger and addicted to narcotics, roaming the streets in sub-zero temperatures, compounded with the fact that he wasn't a real pimp anyhow had driven him over the edge. At best, he was a well-paid boyfriend on drugs and a plaything for whores, but he didn't have one pimp bone in his entire body. His realization of this fact rendered him in a state of psychological dementia and almost cost me my life. The Game is not for everybody.

The police ransacked my finely, furnished home. I walked to the top of the stairs expecting to see the unbelievable and praying to God that I was wrong. Bianca stood at the top of the stairs, holding my newborn son. Casanova had thrown the pistol under the bed and tried to hide in the closet. Spokane's Finest had retrieved the pistol and found him in the closet where upon they gave him the ass whipping of his miserable life.
Casanova lay faced down handcuffed, vehemently sobbing, "Jimi, tell them I didn't do it. Please, tell them I didn't do it."

I looked past him into the bedroom and the vision that I saw sent chills up and down my spine, raising the hairs on the back of my neck. The once-beautiful Dawn lay motionless, appearing to be lifeless, with blood running from a gash in the side of her skull produced by a bullet from Casanova's blue steel .357 magnum. Blood oozed into her once silky, golden, straw-blonde hair. What a waste of flesh," I thought to myself. The paramedics came up the stairs.

"Oh, please, please, please!" Casanova wept and wailed, shedding tears like a bitch as the reality of life imprisonment and those big dicks in his mouth and his ass came back to mind. Perhaps, even the harsh reality of the gas chamber had begun to set in.

"Jimi," he cried as the tears flowed like water from his blood-shot, guilt-filled eyes. "I didn't do it, Jimi. Tell them I didn't do it," Casanova boo-hood and sobbed. With snot running down his face, he pitifully looked up from the floor, attempting to make eye contact with me hoping for sympathy.

"Nigger," I spat, "I believe perhaps you are truly out of your mind." With the investigative deduction of Sherlock Holmes, I made this statement as the police officers stood by and took notes.

"There was nobody here, Casanova, except you and me. So if you didn't do it, that means I did. Officer," I said firmly, "this man broke into my home, he threatened my life, and the life of my family. He assaulted me with a pistol, and then he murdered sweet, innocent Dawn."

Casanova was still wailing like a baby when he looked into my eyes with astonishment. If he could read minds, he'd know. He knew I was attempting to send him to the penitentiary for the rest of the day. I was going to get rid of his perpetrating junkie ass for all times. Casanova looked up as his eyes rolled back into his head. He had regained his sanity and he knew his life was all over. I looked at the officer who stood by writing the charges.

"Sir, this nigger has killed a white woman. Take him and punish him to the fullest extent of the law," I said sharply. The grumbling, angered, red-faced police officers beat and stomped Casanova's boo-hooing, begging, fat ass all the way down the stairs and, out the front door, stuffing his torn, worn, battered and broken body into the police car. I heard Casanova pleading, screaming the words "Mercy, mercy!" just before the police car door shut and the police sped away.

How could that ignorant nigger think those redneck police were going to show him any kind of mercy after he had shot a white woman in the head? All of my life I've always found it amazing how a good old-fashioned ass-whipping, administered by the proper authorities, did wonders for restoring the sanity to the otherwise criminally insane.

Farewell to Manhattan Mike

Shadows moved against the walls of the dimly lit room. Red and yellow flames danced inside the fireplace, sending warmth throughout the room. The soothing sounds of melodic jazz filled the air. Today was the third straight day of winter's harsh and final snowstorm over the city of Spokane.

Mike and I sat playing cards as he waited for a phone call from Shirley, his whore. She had been unable to make bail and had been in jail for the past five days. I had been in the great Northwest for the last four months, allowing Bianca to heal, while cultivating and stimulating my crew of young, sexy whores. I was well rested and my crew of whores had been street tested. It had been pimps up and whores down throughout the cruel, sub-zero winter climate. It was springtime in California and I was headed home. The time was right for my crew of whores to make their Hollywood debut.

The snow was falling and the wind was howling when I heard the doorbell ring.

"Who is it?" Mike asked.

"It's me, your ex-whore, you punk, whoreless, motherfucking nigga!" The voice on the other side of the door screamed. It was Shirley. Surprised Mike opened the front door. She rushed into the room removing her winter coat and growling. She stood gloveless, facing the fireplace, rubbing and warming her hands.
"Yeah, that's right Mike, you're a whoreless nigga," she concluded.

"Don't say that, baby. You know you don't mean it," Mike pleadingly whimpered as he put on a front, trying to look hard to save face.

What a cunt-hungry sucker Mike was. He had been utterly pussy-whipped, I mentally concluded.

"I want to know why I didn't get out when Jimi Starr's whores got out of jail. They were bailed out within an hour after being arrested. Nigger, I served five days. Oh yeah, Mister Manhattan Mike, you're whoreless all right, nigga," Shirley growled sarcastically.

Mike dropped his head, whimpering as if he were a puppy who had pissed on his master's new carpet.
"Oh, baby, please don't talk to me like this. You know I don't have any money," he concluded.

"Nigger, you should have gotten it from him," Shirley barked as she pointed at me.

It was all that I could stand. I couldn't take anymore. This vile vagabond bitch had taken my kindness and charity for weakness.

"Listen up, worthless, punk, broke-ass bitch, you didn't get out on jail with my whores because you're not my whore. And as far as you leaving this man and finding a pimp, a real pimp wouldn't have you, you stinky vagabond bitch! You are the sorriest whore on the planet, and the sorriest, skank tramp that the Game has ever spawned," I viciously continued. "You lousy bitch! You mean about as much to a real pimp as pussy means to a faggot." Flatly I concluded, "You worthless mother fucker; you don't have any value at all. And as far as you leaving here, you no-good tramp, if you had any pride or dignity, you wouldn't be here in the first place. Now get your shit and get the fuck out of my house."

She and Mike both looked at each other, shocked and wide-eyed. Insulted, she gasped, "Daddy, are you going to let this arrogant nigger talk to me like that?"

For whatever the reason, she was attempting to get Mike an ass whipping. The look in Mike's eyes told me that he was searching the bottom of his soul for courage.

"Don't hold that thought too long Mike, or I'll have to charge you for it," I said harshly.

Snarling, Shirley said, "Daddy, you're always telling me that you're the one who has all the sense." Now the dirty bitch had reversed the script, she was trying to play me against Mike. Shirley continued, "If you're half the man that you say you are, Daddy, you will give Jimi Starr the ass-whipping of his life for the way he has talked to me this evening," she bitterly spat.

It was easier for her to attempt to find fault with my crew of whores and myself than to accept the harsh reality that she and Mike possessed sub-par survival skills. Shirley truly was a larceny-hearted strumpet who relished in toying with Mike's mind, pushing him to the limit and then beyond.

"Mike, if you're not going to protect me from this nigga, at least take me back to New York where you got me from," she said in a dry and final tone.

My crew of flat-backing and thieving whores had long psychologically intimidated Shirley. She felt inferior because of her lack of skills and her own inability to compete with real whores. She wanted to get away to any place so she could feel better about herself and continue to convince Manhattan Mike that she was something that she wasn't.

Mike stood in the middle of the floor, his chest heaving. He glared at me with clinched fists, which resembled two huge hams. As well as I had attempted to treat Mike, our friendship had soured and this scenario had gone bad fast.

Believing she had done something clever, Shirley commanded, "Let's get out of here, Mike!"

"Yes, why don't we," Mike angrily agreed.

"Looks like we're all of one accord," I responded. "But you must get the fuck out of here tonight," I said smugly. I removed Shirley's damp winter coat from the back of the chair and handed it to her. The brisk and howling wind blew as I walked to the front door, turned the doorknob, and opened the door. The flakes of cold white snow and the chill from the icy winds rushed into the room.

"Hey Starr," Mike said. As he realized their fate, he attempted to smile. "I think we'll leave tomorrow or after the storm let's up; it's ten degrees above zero out there," he humbly implied.

"I know, it's ten degrees above zero Mike, but you're going to leave my house right now, nigga," I concluded. I motioned with my finger towards the door. I was overwhelmed with a philosophical thought; a dog will eat the crumbs that fall from the master's table, though the master has fed and taken care of that dog, the same dog will bite the master. When a dog attempts to bite the hand that feeds it, it is a definite sign that the relationship between dog and master has gone bad.

"What about all my things?" Shirley pushed past Mike back into the warmth of my home. Bianca emerged from what had once been their bedroom. She carried in her hand one shopping bag containing all of Mike and Shirley's worldly possessions.

"Jimi, I cannot believe you're really going to do this," Mike said. Chill bumps as big as golf balls covered their entire bodies.

"Farewell, Manhattan Mike," I said as I slammed my door, behind them. From the vantage point of my window, I watched Manhattan Mike and Shirley vanish into the bleak darkness of the freezing wintry snow.

Filmore Slim

Gangster Brown

Chapter 14

Pretty Boy Floyd

A gentleman pimp is a true artist, and daily he sets about his craft to sharpen his mental skills through his colorful suave charm and being predatorily cunning. He possesses and controls his whores with superior psychological wit. He gets paid because he always has the right answer at just the right time. He must know the innermost thoughts of his whore, even before she herself does and respond accordingly.

Reader, contrary to popular belief, pimps don't get paid for fucking, they get paid for thinking. If a pimp is really pimping, he doesn't even need a dick, pimping is a game of psychological prowess. It is very much the mental game. Through creativity, imagination, and charm, the pimp uses the collective minds of his whores as if they were a canvas on which he creates his masterpieces of illusions. His mental portraits are as vividly colorful as a Picasso, as deeply intriguing as any Van Gough, as bold as a sculpture created by Michael Angelo, as totally full-filling as any Rembrandt. To a real pimp, pimping is an art form, and not everyone can do it. There are a multitude of titles and positions in the Black underworld. But there is none as coveted or desired or celebrated as the pimp. Because of its stature, glamour, notoriety, and esteem, there are many who would don the mask of the pimp, and like a chameleon masquerading, assume the identity of something they neither know nor understand. The story I am about to tell you is true. The names have been changed to protect the innocent.

It was a brisk winter predawn morning in Berkeley, California, as the Cadillacs and Mercedes lined both sides of San Pablo Avenue in front of the Black Knight After-Hours. Well-dressed people of the night entered and left this well-known after-hours hot spot. Two giant smiling doormen greeted the patrons. At the curb, the doors of a vintage black Rolls Royce opened. Like a scene out of a Hollywood movie, out stepped six gorgeous white girls, followed by a light-skinned black man, that was of medium height and build. He wore a pair of black and white shoes, gay wool slacks, white shirt, and a black sports coat. There was always a white carnation in his lapel. Excluding the fact that this fellow had no personality or skills, he was a carbon copy of Billy Dee Williams.

In the interest of discretion, let's call this character Pretty Boy Floyd. He had been a billboard model for a now defunct liquor company and a part-time bit actor. He was an actor caught up in the glitz and glamour of the Game, and now decided to act like he was pimping. Floyd looked like a pimp. He sounded like a pimp, but Floyd was a pimp by no means. But as long as he realized he was just acting, he was OK.

He seated his ladies and swaggered his way over to the VIP section, which was always corded off by blue velvet ropes for top-flight players and their entourages. Floyd, with his keen features and naturally wavy hair, profiled and smiled at the cocktail waitress. "It will be white wine for me," Floyd smoothly said. "The ladies won't be having anything this evening," he continued and then he seated himself at our table.

The musicians were really jazzing it up. There were five of us at the table when Floyd had pulled up a chair with his bottom whore in tow. The Black Knight was on full as we lounged sipping cognac and passing the tray of powdered cocaine. Pretty Boy Floyd was a freak and a pig for snorting powder, especially other people's cocaine. It seemed, even though Floyd had six hookers, he never managed to have any money. The real truth was that Pretty Boy Floyd was a perpetrator, a fake, a fraud, and a phony, not to mention he didn't have a pimp bone in his entire body.

"Hey, Wayne, pass me that powder," Floyd said. Wayne hesitated and reluctantly pushed the tray towards Floyd, who immediately took a one-on-one, repacked his quill, and pushed it towards his whore's nose. Wayne simultaneously slapped the quill from Floyd's hand and away from Floyd's whore's eager and awaiting nose. Then, with an air of heated sarcasm, Wayne began to read Floyd's pedigree.

Wayne angrily spat, "Bitch-as-nigga, you ain't no pimp! You're a rest haven for whores. How could you feed your bitch my powder? Where's your pride? Where's your dignity? You're a baby sitter, nigga! You couldn't even buy your own whores a drink."

Wayne took a snort of cocaine as he regained his composure, then looked Floyd straight in the eyes, pointed directly at Floyd's whores and calmly said, "Nigger, those are lookers, not hookers. This is a classic case of the blind leading the blind. You're a soft shoe motherfucking perpetrator. The very next time I see you and those whores, nigga, I'm going to take them and give them the true instructions and the proper direction of a real pimp." Wayne snidely remarked.

Floyd jumped up and tried to mumble some sucker shit. The two giant bouncers pushed their way through the crowd. I gave them the nod. They grabbed Floyd, kicked him in the ass, threw him over the blue velvet rope, and beat his ass all the way out the door.

Floyd yelled, "Wayne, you're going to get yours, motherfucker!" as the giant doorman buried his foot deep in his perpetrating ass. "I'll never forget this!" Floyd screamed. "You disrespected my manhood, and for this, you will pay!" Little did Floyd know that he had made a drastic and terrible mistake in threatening Insane Wayne.

The House of Newbill

I sat in the barber's chair as Ace, the barber and owner of the renowned establishment known as The House of Newbill, began to put the finishing touches on my hair. Ace, an older, medium-built, brown-complexioned gentlemen with shoulder-length perm white hair, spoke in his gruff voice over the rhythmic music wailing from the jukebox and the constant chattering of pimps, whores, beauticians, and thieves in the shop, "You see there baby, I made you so pretty that just a pimple on your ass would make the average nigger a Sunday face."

Ace was well versed in the Game. I stood and looked in the mirror as my reflection glared back at me. It was true. I was one fine motherfucker. I stood six foot four, and my weight was two hundred and five pounds of absolute man, and I knew that my purpose in life was to pimp or die, and I had no intentions of dying. For me, it had to be whore money or no money at all! I glanced at myself again. My hair was whipped to perfection; every hair was in place. My long nails had been manicured. I wore a maroon suit and maroon shoes to match, and the creases in my slacks were almost sharp enough to cut you.

In the rear of the shop, I heard a commotion. It was an old guerilla pimp called Honey Bear. He had been living on his reputation of his being a fool for a long time, but this time he had intimidated an aspiring, young player. We'll call him Bowdy.

"Now go over in the corner young, bitch-ass nigger, and sit down until you're spoke to," the Bear roared.

Young Bowdy dropped his head and turned away as if to step to the corner. The Bear grinned, believing he had punked the youngster off. Suddenly Bowdy, reaching under his coat, spun around and produced a pistol, a .357 magnum to be exact, and slapped the grill right out of the Bear's mouth. The Bear's blood and broken teeth went flying everywhere.

"Oh no, don't kill me!" the Bear cried, building the youngster's confidence, adding momentum to his own ass whipping.

The enraged youngster mercilessly and cowboy style pistol-whipped the one time bully, Honey Bear, into complete and utter submission.

"Don't ever let me hear you call yourself the Bear again, bitch ass nigga. You're not even a bear cub," Bowdy excitedly yelled.

The youngster kicked the Bear in the mouth, head, and the ass, sending the one-time bully scurrying and scooting across the floor on his hands and knees, his eyes searched the once intimidated faces in the room for help, however he found none.

"Oh no, please don't kill me," the Bear cried. "Don't hurt me no more!" The Bear cried.

I glared at the pitiful, raggedy mouth, boo-hooing and sobbing hulk who cringed and cried on the floor like a fat baby, who that had just a few moments ago been the legendary Honey Bear. For years, the Bear had been living on his reputation as a dope dealing, gorilla pimp, and a goddamn fool. Now he didn't even have that.

Ace looked at me, winked, and shrugged his shoulders. We all knew that what the Bear had gotten had been a long time coming. I returned my attention to the mirror and straightened my pimp attire as if nothing had happened. I popped my collar and calmly strolled out of the shop and onto Divisadero Street, shutting the door behind me. My customized, maroon and white Eldorado awaited me.

My dear Reader, I had my own giants to kill, but unlike the youngster Bowdy, I would destroy my giants with my mind.

Perpetratorss

The antique grandfather clock struck six and began to chime. Wayne stood proudly in the center of my living room floor. He wore a white silk two-piece walking suit and matching alligator shoes. Tonight, he was show casing Sue Ella and her new full-length white mink coat. Sue Ella turned, modeling and striking provocative poses.

Wayne and I sat on the couch snorting cocaine and sipping cognac while enjoying Sue Ella's small fashion show. Wayne began to speak, "Jimi, I feel real good about this bitch. I call her Sweet Sue Ella. She'll do whatever I tell her. Take that coat off and let Daddy see," Wayne said as he lustfully licked his lips.

Wayne was perhaps one of the best pimps I had ever known; he was also one of the biggest cum freaks I have come to know over the years. On the plush maroon carpet in the center of the living room floor, Sue Ella opened and dropped the white mink coat to the floor and stood nude in her silver spike-high heeled shoes. Her silky brunette hair hung well below her shoulders. Pink nipples jutted forth from her firm milky white breasts.

"Jimi, I'm a white girl's pimp," Wayne proudly said. "One black-ass bitch ain't worth three dead black-ass flies with their wings plucked," he continued. "Sue Ella, I want you to go to work and get my money. When you get off this morning, baby, I'm going to take you home and fuck you real good."

Picking up her white full-length fur coat, she headed towards the door. This would be the last time Wayne would see Sweet Sue Ella for a long time.

In my boudoir, I sat as the melodic sound of comforting jazz drifted through my sanctuary. All alone, I enjoyed myself. Throughout my entire life, I have always been my own best company. The phone rang, ending my moment of solitude. It was Pretty Boy Floyd.

"Hey what's happening Jimi, is your pal Wayne around?" Floyd nervously asked.

"Why would you call my house, disrupting my peace, asking for someone that doesn't live here? If you want Wayne, call him at his house," I spat.

"Jimi, when you see Wayne, tell him that I knocked him for that Sue Ella bitch," Floyd said.

"I'm not a messenger nor the F. B. I. You're going to have to bring the news to him yourself, if you're really pimping," I replied.

Knowing the kind of coward he truly was, Floyd did not have the heart, nor the nerve. He would never serve Insane Wayne.

"Floyd listen, you know you can talk to me," I deceivingly said. "Did you get any money?" I asked.

"Uh, no," he replied.

"You can't serve a nigger if you haven't received any money," I said. "Did you stick your dick in that man's whore?" I asked.

"Uh, well..." Pretty Boy began to stammer.

"Did you stick your dick in her?" I asked again.

"Yes, yes," he confessed. "I fucked her. What do you think my chances are with Wayne?" he questioned.

"Well, Pretty Boy, if it was anybody but you and any bitch other than Sue Ella," I said before continuing, "for running interference in Wayne's business and stopping his money, he would most probably beat your ass real good. But for trying to serve him with no money and for sticking your dick in his prize white girl, Floyd, I'm quite certain Wayne is going to murder you," I said calmly. "Floyd, do you believe in God?" I asked.

"Yes," he responded.

"Then perhaps you should consider calling a priest, because whenever or wherever Wayne sees you, nigger, you will surely die. If you are true to the Game, the Game will be true to you. If you violate the Game, the same game will violate you, Floyd," I said. "Obviously, nigger, you've done something wrong," I concluded.

In fear for his life and in the hopes of pimp super-stardom, Pretty Boy Floyd gathered his crew of non-productive, cocaine freak white girls. He headed south for Hollywood to elude Wayne and test his pimp skills. Later

Floyd would come to the realization that he didn't have any real whores and he possessed no pimp skills at all. After three or four mentally grueling and humiliating weeks in Los Angeles, Floyd returned to San Francisco.

Meanwhile, Insane Wayne went on a witch-hunt, intimidating and mentally vexing and terrorizing anyone who knew Floyd or perhaps his whereabouts, scouring San Francisco and most of the West Coast in search of Pretty Boy Floyd and his runaway whore, Sweet Sue Ella. The hook Wayne used to keep it pimping was the theft of the full-length white mink coat.

Pretty Boy Floyd returned to San Francisco and his date with destiny. He worked the back streets and alleyways, deep inside the bowels of the ghetto. Fearing for his life, he became a complete paranoid, seeing Wayne in every shadow. He would awake from his sleep sweating and screaming like a racist white woman on a plantation who was being raped by a dirty black, blue-gummed nigger slave with a deformed dick. Floyd had forgotten The Pimp's Creed, if he ever knew it. The Creed states, "If you whore for me, I will die for you." Because of rampant, negative rumors of Pretty Boy's blatant cowardice circulating through the Black underworld, Floyd ultimately blew his six white girls to pimps of renown who didn't bother to notify him, primarily because they neither respected nor recognized him as a pimp.

Floyd's vivid dream of pimp super-stardom was over. His crew of bleached-blonde, fly-by-night, cocaine fiend whores had flown the coop. The only one left was Sweet Sue Ella.

From the ocean, a thick white fog rolled over the city as Pretty Boy Floyd left the after-hours. With his hands pushed deep inside the pockets of his over coat, he walked briskly through the darkness. The wheels of the Fleetwood Brougham screeched to a stop. The front door and trunk flew open simultaneously.

"Hello, Floyd, do you need a ride?" the cold and cruel voice asked. Floyd stopped, unable to believe his ears, forced to believe his eyes. He stood gazing down both barrels of Insane Wayne's .357 magnums. Sue Ella lay nude in the trunk of the car. She had been bound and gagged and was covered only by the white full-length mink coat. Her muffled screams escaped into the openness of the fog and the predawn darkness. Wayne stepped from the car with his pistols in his hands, escorting Pretty Boy Floyd to the trunk of the car. Sue Ella and Floyd looked into each other's horrified eyes, realizing it was the time of retribution.

"Please don't kill me!" Pretty Boy Floyd screamed as he rolled his eyes up towards the heavens, dropping to his knees and cupping his hands as if to pray. "I aint nopimp man," Floyd shrieked, "I do not want to die. I'm an actor and a model. I never intended for this situation to get this twisted. I want to live," he cried as the tears rolled freely over the keen features of his photogenic face. "I just wanted some fast cash and notoriety, that's all. Please don't kill me," he pleaded.

Wayne flashed a maniacal grin. "You're not going to die, pal. I'm not going to kill you. I know you're not a pimp," he coldly said. "Unfortunate for you, you will never model or act again," Wayne cruelly interjected and began to viciously whip Floyd with both pistols, knocking the teeth from his mouth and savagely beating him about the head and shoulders, horribly deforming Pretty Boy Floyd forever.

Frisco Slim

Roaring thunder rang... the gong of darkness... howling winds blew as black clouds rolled against the midnight skies revealing a huge, full yellow moon close enough to reach out and touch. Branches of lightning danced in the heavens, lighting up the horizon like the sun. The distant roaring thunder accented the riveting hail and pouring rain. The blue Fleetwood Cadillac slowly made it's way through the city. It was like a scene from a horror movie. I looked into the rearview mirror. The lightning flashed. There he was, my mentor, Frisco Slim. Wavy shoulder length hair, brown-skinned, tall and slender, keen features with a boyish gold-tooth smile. He had been murdered or found dead on many occasions, but there he was, the Epitome of Evil. Some say he was in excess of 80 years old, but he appeared to be 25 years old. I can only say for sure, that he took many a young girl's virtue and youth. He sat in the fullness of the excellence of his morbidity. He possessed the youthful facial features of a young Chinese boy and a heart that was black and cold as ice.

Born and raised in the Deep South, he acquired an air of Dixie land sophistication and wanted to be recognized as a Southern gentleman. In his rough Southern drawl, he began to speak.
"Jimi," he said, "you have been a friend and a protégé to me for years. In that time, we have had many conversations, and I have explained to you many things. You have been my star pupil. I have given you the knowledge I would have given a son. I have nurtured you as if you were my own."

No matter where I was in the country, no matter how busy I may have been, I always managed to stay in contact. Frisco Slim was the Godfather of pimpdom.

Frisco continued, "Jimi, the 'pimp' is the most celebrated, renowned, elite, and coveted title in the world. We are also among one of the most hated. Why? The average male slaves and toils his life away. He lavishes his woman with cash, jewels, homes, and furs, all for the promise or for the hopes of a shot at her stinking, once-a-month-bleeding pussy. The woman accumulates these gifts and, at her leisure, makes a freak and a dog out of him. And in return, he cannot wait to bow down and waddle his face in her ass. The true pimp is a real man. He has the con and psychology on women, while they toil and slave their lives away and they lavish him with cash, jewels, and cars. This is the exact opposite of a woman's philosophy on men, and the very reason we are rejected and despised by the masses of society. So it only stands to reason that in the black underworld, the pimp would be the champion. Toast to the Game. Many thieves try to pimp. Many drug dealers try to pimp, and conmen too. These perpetrators may receive results for a while, but in the end, they all fall off penniless, allowing vicious, larceny-hearted whores to make freaks and dogs out of them. In order to be a real, live, top-flight pimp, you must first be a natural, and Jimi, you're the best natural I've ever seen."

My mind raced back through my vividly colorful past. After all these years, Slim was still remarkably well preserved. The years hadn't changed the fact that Frisco Slim was an institution and is a gentleman pimp in every sense of the word. He was a living legend, and the last word in pimping.

The rain beat almost rhythmically against the windowpane. I stood in the foyer of 2020 Fell Street. I heard an upstairs door shut as I shook out my tailor made London Fog and placed it over my arm. Suddenly Lulu, Slim's giggly teenage daughter, appeared at the top of the stairs. She was medium height, petite, and brown-skinned with shoulder-length hair. She wore a black halter-top and stretch pants. On her feet, she sported a pair of black spike high heels. In her hand, she carried a black-fringed umbrella. I thought to myself, her exposure to Slim's whores couldn't have been good for her. It was blatantly obvious that she had but one desire. Lulu wanted to be somebody's whore, but little did I know she wanted to be mine.

Playfully and smoothly I said, "Hello, school girl," thinking to myself, schoolgirl pussy. I stepped to the side, making room for her to pass. She stopped in front of me.

She shyly looked up into my eyes and said, "Jimi, does this look like the body of a school girl?" Frisco would have a nigger murdered or worse for pimping at this fine, young, wannabe whore, I thought.

"Shhh," I said sharply as I began to caution her, "somebody might hear you."

In her giggly voice, half-laughing she said, "I'm a woman in every sense of the word, and I'm going to be your whore."

"I need whores, not girlfriends," I snapped. "Don't talk to me anymore unless you have me some whore money." Her words sent me back on my heels, not out of fear, but out of respect for Slim.

She continued, "I've already told Daddy about us."

Angrily I replied, "What fuckin' us are you talking about, you dizzy little bitch? Now get your hot, young ass out of here and go on to school."

She stepped back, exhaled, and looked down at the bulge in my pants and hungrily licked her lips.
Flatly she said, "Tomorrow is my birthday. I'll be 18 years old, a woman, and I'm going to be your whore." With that, she turned and sassily switched out the door. Whew, I thought to myself, somebody's been fucking that little bitch. In retrospect, I had no idea how right I was.

From the foyer, I started towards the top of the stairs. Slim stood there with a faraway look in his eyes, "Starr, I want to talk to you," he softly said. He turned and walked into his penthouse apartment. I innocently followed him. He sat down in his big, black, leather easy chair and said, "My darling daughter, Lulu, has a crush on you."

Then he dropped his head sorrowfully and softly spoke, "you know, Lulu's momma ran off with some nigger when she was just a baby. I've been a father and my whores have been a mother to her ever since. Now Starr, my baby tells me that she wants to be with you."

He continued, "Lulu's mother was a thoroughbred whore and her father is a blue-blood pimp. I've taken care of her all her life because she is my daughter of my lineage and part of my pedigree. Jimi Starr, tomorrow Lulu will be eighteen years old, and I've never denied her anything that she has wanted. Now she tells me she wants to be your whore." He stopped, took a snort of cocaine from a saucer on the glass table and continued. "Jimi, I'm going to give you my daughter, however, I want you to promise me something."

"Sure, Slim," I responded, almost unable to accept his expressed commitment and dedication to the game.

Taking another snort of cocaine, he nervously leaned closer to me and whispered, "Jimi, Lulu can neither read nor write. Jimi, to my knowledge, you have never lied to me. I want you to promise me that you will allow her to at least finish high school."

Damn, I thought to myself. That fine motherfucker can't read or write. In Slim's zealousness for pimping whores, he had completely forgotten to send that fine, young bitch to school. In my opinion, she wasn't slow by any means. She simply wasn't educated in the conventional sense. That explains that yellow bus that's been picking that bitch up.

The showering rain beat against the windowpane. Slim appeared nervous as I stood and prepared to leave his penthouse apartment. I took a snort of cocaine from the saucer on the glass table.

"Oh, Starr, there's one more thing I want you to realize," he said as his face began to quiver, "my darling daughter Lulu is a pathological liar. You cannot believe any two words that she puts together, especially about me." With that, I left his apartment.

The sleek Eldorado glided through the rain-slick streets of San Francisco. The customized luxury car glided to a stop at the intersection of Geary and Jones, in the heart of Whore's Row, in the infamous Tenderloin area.

It was the day after Lulu's eighteenth birthday when I turned her out. From the window of my Eldorado, excitedly she watched the whores run to and from cars, to doorways and back again. I had been preparing for.this moment for the last forty-eight hours. Having no other ambitions or desires, she had been preparing herself for this moment for a lifetime.

This was the moment of truth! She stared from the window of my parked car and excitedly began to speak, waving at passerby whores. "Hey, Mary," she shouted from my opened window, "how have you been doing? I haven't seen you in a long time. Yeah, uh-huh, that's right, I'm a whore now," she smiled in pride, threw her head back, raising her firm, young breasts. "Yeah whore, I done went and chose myself a pimp; yeah, Jimi Starr. I know you knew it was coming."

My mind reeled. Lulu was not only illiterate, but in this moment, I realized that she was ignorant beyond belief, beyond my wildest expectations. If a woman like this was to fall into the hands of the police, this kind of illiteracy could cost a nigger his prized freedom. I had to get rid of this bitch and get rid of her quick. I sat and watched and listened in astonishment and disbelief. It seemed as if she knew every pimp and every whore in the city of San Francisco.

She yelled at the top of her lungs to a junkie pimp walking down the streets, "Hey, Pretty Paul, it's me, Little Lulu, Frisco's daughter!" Whore-hungry and dope sick, the junkie stopped and puked, then wiped his mouth on the sleeve of his tattered coat. This off-brand nigger poked his head in my window and flashed his decaying grill. The odious stench of puke and perhaps even shit escaped his rotten mouth.

"Hello baby, do I know you?" the junkie leaned over into the car and asked.

"I'm Frisco's daughter, Lulu. You remember me?" she shrieked excitedly, looking for acceptance.

I pulled my pistol from under the seat and stared at the ptrid junkie. "Back up out of here you disrespectful junkie motherfucker!" I barked.

"I'll see you later, baby," Pretty Paul said. "Your man is not too friendly." As the junkie pulled his face from my open window he mumbled, "this nigga's got an attitude." In stooped, bent over, junkie fashion, he scurried across the street, disappearing into the darkness of the night and then falling rain.

I quickly analyzed the situation. All Lulu's life, Frisco's whores had been her friends. She knew every pimp and every whore who had come into her father's house or had made his acquaintance. In some sick, twisted way, she wanted to be a whore because that's what every woman she had ever known was. Growing up with a father that was a pimp, made it difficult for her to know anything else. She knew to be accepted as a whore, she had to have a pimp. I looked at Lulu, realizing for a surety and a certainly that she would never be a top-flight whore. It didn't matter who her father was or what her mother did; she was her own person. My gut feeling told me that she wasn't worth three dead, black, shit-eating flies with their wings plucked. I opened the car door. Like an anxious puppy in a pet store, Lulu leaped from the car onto the curb, shaking her tail and looking for acceptance. She danced around the outside of a gang of chattering whores.

"Hey, I'm Little Lulu, Frisco's daughter and Jimi Starr's whore," she excitedly yapped.

Some say never look a gift horse in the mouth. I say anytime you think you're getting a deal; you get fucked. I pulled away from the curb and made my way towards Divisadero Street, the club, and a much needed cold, relaxing cocktail.

China

There was not a cloud in the sky. It was a rare and clear San Francisco day. In a city where there was normally smog and fog, there was none.

Like Julius Caesar in ancient Rome, I had returned home to my native California, victorious. I was nigger-rich and had more whores and money than I knew what to do with. For a nigger who pimped whores, it just didn't get any better than this. How was I to know that things were just about to get a whole lot better?
From the vantage point of my penthouse suite, Darling Don Dupree, Big Dave, and I gazed at the overview of the city, discussing my cross-country campaign.

The doorbell rang, interrupting our conversation. It was Ivy Starr. Ivy was a barker at a Broadway shake joint, a young would-be and wannabe pimp. I had told him, in a previous conversation, that if he ever got a whore, I would show him the ups and downs and turn arounds of the Game. Big Dave buzzed him into the building.

Big Dave, my personal valet and bodyguard, showed Ivy Starr and his lady friend in. Darling Don Dupree, a long time personal pimp pal of mine, and I took in the San Francisco panoramic view. Dupree was tall, slender, and brown-skinned, with shoulder-length wavy hair. I trusted him implicitly. If I was ever in a life-and-death situation, I had no doubt Dupree had my back.

Big Dave had once been the personal bodyguard of Filmore Slim. Big Dave stood 6' 6" and weighed 345 pounds. He was a blue-black giant and had a scowling face only a mother could love. Big Dave motioned my visitors into the room. I turned from my view of the city.

"What's up, Cuz?" had already cleared my mouth when I saw her for the first time. Look what the gods of the Game have sent me to feast upon, I thought. She was a Chinese doll. My mind entered a fog. The cash register went off in my head as chronologically I began to riffle through hundreds of thousands of dollars. Oh yes, yes most indeed, I must have this fine young bitch.

"Am I pimpin' yet Jimi, am I pimpin'?" I heard Ivy say, snapping me from my mental euphoria. I smiled widely and shook his hand, leading him into the next room, separating him from his would-be whore.

"Am I pimping yet Jimi, am I pimpin'? Ivy excitedly asked.

"Mischievously I asked, "Do you really want to pimp Ivy?"

"Yeah Jimi, I want to pimp so bad I can taste it," he replied.

"Ivy, do you trust me?" I asked.

"Sure Jimi Starr, you know I trust you," Ivy answered.

"If you truly want to learn how to pimp, then you must do everything I tell you," I said.

"OK." Ivy replied.

"You must first let that bitch know that you are the one in charge. I want you to go out there and knock that bitch down on the floor and put your foot on her neck, just to let her know you're the boss. Slap her around a little bit and then send her in here to me. Then I'll interview her in private to see if she really likes you and truly wants to be your whore. Who knows, she may not be qualified. A good pimp needs a good whore, especially when he's just getting started," I said.

This man wanted to pimp so badly; he did exactly what I had instructed. He left the room; I heard a slap, a thud, and a crash, and Ivy yelling at the top of his lungs that he was her man and that she should obey him. I heard her gagging when he put his size-twelve foot on her throat and began to slap her around. He sent his bitch, China, crawling to me on her hands and knees into my personal boudoir. Who was I not to accept her? The Game is to be sold, not told. It was niggers like Ivy who assisted in keeping pimps like me pimping

Like a battered Chinese doll, she crawled to my feet sobbing. With my index finger over my lips I softly said, "Shhh," whispering her to silence.

Wide-eyed, she stared into my face with an expression of terror, speaking softly. "Will you help me?" She asked.

Responding to her question, I replied, "That nigga, Ivy, is motherfucking crazy. He always has been, you know?"

"Why did he do that to me?" she whispered.

Pretending to rationalize I said, "Ivy did it because he's crazy, bitch." I looked deep into her confused eyes, penetrating her soul.
Shaking my head I began, "China, you must understand, Ivy's totally and completely insane."

Excitedly she whispered, "I didn't know that nigger was crazy; I'm scared."

With my fingers shaking and held to my mouth, I echoed recanting her response. "Baby, I'm scared, too."

In the living room, Dupree was giving young Ivy Starr Act II of this short, "How to Knock a Bitch" skit. Ivy would come into the room, waving a baseball bat in her face, demanding that she suck and fuck Big Dave's deformed dick to prove her loyalty and the fact that she was his woman in the name of the Game.

China clutched me around my knees, pressing her crying face against my peter, sobbing. From her position of inferiority and my position of superiority, the average guy would have probably stuck his dick in her head. But not me; I was really pimping. The way you catch them is the way you hold them, she was sobbing. I looked down on this fine, young Asian bitch whimpering at my feet. Her fingers were lit with diamonds. On her back, she wore a black diamond mink coat. This bitch was jazzy. This bitch was hip; she was fly, but this bitch was not a whore; at any rate, not yet.

No self-respecting, straight up and down pimp would allow a whore to have the luxury of diamonds and furs unless she had earned them under his tutelage and his program, and this nigger didn't even have a program. When she first walked through the door, at first sight, I knew I would play this lame buster out of the bitch and have her for my own. I also knew, at first glance, that she was some form of thief or jostler that I supposed still had money. For a surety, if she still had a mink, still had diamonds, she still had cash.

Sobbing with her face pressed against my crotch, she whimpered, "Please save me."

I said, "Listen up baby and let me tell you something. Darling, that nigger is crazy as a Crocker sack full of shit-house rats! Anybody who tries to run past interference with him is cruising for a bruising. Why, it's even possible that crazy nigger might even slaughter them. Sweetheart, for the kind of protection you need, you're going to have to reach deep down in your bosom and break yourself, or face the fate of fucking and sucking Big Dave. Break yourself, bitch, and become my whore."

She realized I wasn't going to buy the poor abused bitch bit, and the inevitability of crazed Ivy beating her to death was all but imminent. "Now reach down in your tities and break yourself quick and while you're at it, give me that jewelry too, bitch," I said. She sat back on her knees and looked up at me in puzzlement while reaching into her bra.

"I'm a booster Jimi, not a whore" she began. "I've never paid a man before. I met that ignorant nigga in a bar; I thought it would be fun. This day has turned into a complete nightmare." China produced a wad of bills from her bosom.

Just then, the door flew open and there stood Ivy waving a baseball bat over his head with his eyes bucked and gritting his teeth. Dupree had coached him well. He looked like a huge, Black Roman gladiator with an ax.

"I choose to be with you," Ivy saw and heard China say. She reached out with the money. He recognized the cross and snapped. I took the money in hand.

Ivy, swinging his bat and frothing at the mouth, began to cross the room. Screaming, "You lousy motherfucker! You've disrespected me, clowned me, and crossed me in front of my woman. The ass-whipping I had intended for her, now I'm going to give it to you!"

Waving the bat above his head, he raced across the room. It was going to be close. I reached for my pistol. Dave stormed into the room behind Ivy with a hugh, black sap in hand.

Waving his bat, Ivy raced towards me yelling, "I'm going to kill you, you dirty pimp bastard!" he viciously screamed.

Pow! Ivy saw stars, small moons, and planets, and slumped to the floor. Yes, the lights had been turned out on young Ivy. Big Dave, the bodyguard, had planted his sap deep into the back of his head.

I turned to China as Ivy fell wide-eyed and unconscious to the carpeted floor. I stripped the mink from her back and milked the diamonds from her fingers. She was mine now. This situation had gotten a little out of hand, because a pimp never knows what a sucker motherfucker might do. I only knew I had to have that bitch. As for me, I was going to keep it pimping.

For a long time after that, Ivy Starr would return nightly to my building, put his hand on his hip, and with the other hand, count every brick on the face of my building. I had stated earlier, Ivy was a Broadway barker. Yes, Ivy was still barking, except now he was barking at the moon.

Often times in the Game, you will find suckers and busters passing themselves off as pimps, only to find out that when their game is tested, they will either go get a pistol and make a complete punk out of themselves and threaten to kill you and the bitch, or start crying real tears, asking the pimp to please let her go and begging the bitch not to leave them, telling her if she leaves them, they will lose their minds and kill themselves.

In this act or statement, this perpetrator makes a complete dick-in-the-booty faggot out of himself. The inept perpetrator, in his attempted participation at masquerading as a pimp, now acknowledges his true self for the fake that he really is.

My dear Reader, the pimping is a way of life. It is a complete life style, it is a frame of mind, and it is in fact the spirit of a mindset that is often imitated; however, it cannot be duplicated. Either you have the spirit of the mindset and you're truly pimping, or you're a perpetrating fake, giving the Game a black eye.

What unknown power would lead a sober woman to perpetually have sex with a countless number of unknown degenerate participants, performing vile illicit acts over a long or short period of time, only to turn around and give the earnings of her hard earned labor to another at the end of the evening? You, yourself, can ponder the question or you can call for the assistance of educated intellectuals; psychiatrists, sociologists, and criminologists, the answer will always be the same: A pimp.

Red

It had been five years ago; however, I remember as if it were yesterday. Red had been a college coed when my pimp pal, Insane Wayne, had been chipping with her. She had aspirations to be a schoolteacher. It was her first year away from home at college. She probably should have listened to her mother's advice and not talked to smooth strangers in fancy cars, but she didn't. Her failure to listen to her mother's sound advice ultimately cost her. She lost her freedom, not to mention the sanctity of her sanity.

It started, somehow, while out on a night on the town with Wayne, a pimp and a celebrated thief, in his own right. Red lost her rent money from the secured confines of her purse. Wayne was more than happy to lend her the money back, with exorbitant interest and a shot of that fine, young, half-breed Latin pussy. When she couldn't repay the loan, he introduced Red to hardcore gorilla tactics and gangstered her into the fast sheets and the street game.

I was slowly drifting back from a deep, warm, and comfortable slumber and it seemed that as always, it had been a good night. As I regained consciousness, I tenderly embraced Bianca, my velvet lover. She was a carbon copy of a young Gladys Knight. I stroked her firm young body. This woman was something special; from the moment I first laid eyes on her. There was an instant chemistry between us, which was not just sexual. This was spiritual. Somewhere in the distance, I heard Wayne's voice and then a knock at the door. I motioned Bianca to the door. She stepped from the bed into my leather house shoes. Covering herself with my silk robe, she crossed the room and opened the door. Wayne stepped through the door grinning, with a newspaper in his hand and a used and confused Red behind him.

"Jimi, you lazy one black whore-having motherfucker," he said jokingly, "you just can't seem to keep your dick out of that black bitch. I feel so sad for you, having only one whore and all."

"Nigger!" I snapped, "You feel sad for me? How come, nigger, because I'm rich or because I have one of the coldest thieves in the country?"

"No, no, Jimi, that's not what I mean," he said. "Jimi, I have seven white whores. I'm pimpin' man, I mean really pimpin' and you have one black bitch. Nigga, I might have to stop fuckin' with you. You know, one is next to none."

Bianca paid no attention to our pimp antics. She sat on the end of the bed, making small talk with Wayne's latest conquest. Wayne threw the newspaper on the bed.

"Here, nigga, check out the Help Wanted Section of the daily paper 'cause a nigga with one whore ain't no pimp."

We both laughed. We were long-time friends. I knew him well and I sensed that he was up to something.

Wayne smugly adjusted his attire, stuck out his chest, and walked to the window.

"Yes, it looks like rain. While you were sleeping this morning, it rained this half-breed bitch on me," he said pointing to Red. "You know, I don't fuck with nothing but white girls. Bianca and Jimi, this is Red, my new whore."

"Wayne, where did you get this baby?" I said playfully.

Grinning he replied, "She's a college kid that owes me money. She couldn't pay, so I made a whore out of her."

I was well familiarized with his morbid nature and sense of humor. He walked to the foot of the bed where Red was sitting. Reaching down, he pulled her close to him. He placed his hands on both sides of her cheeks and looked deep into her confused eyes. Knowing his arrogant nature and his vanity, I received his next statement as commonplace. But it rocked her world forever.

"Jimi, one live black bitch ain't worth three dead white ones. There is nothing a black bitch can do for me." Pulling her closer, he kissed her lips, and stepped back and said in an elevated tone, "Take her Jimi Starr, take her quick. I'm a white whore's pimp. Give me $500 and take this half-Black bitch out of my sight," he said. His morbid, sadistic nature, along with his vanity and arrogance, compounded with the events of the day, just happened to be more than her mind could take. Her eyes rolled back in her head. She fell straight back. Her head struck the floor. When she awoke, it was a done deal.

Reader, to go from college coed and aspiring teacher to prostitute, to common slave, all in one 24-hour span, was enough to overwhelm any one person. The deal was renegotiated. The price was cut in half. You cannot receive that kind of paper for an unconscious bitch. It became one of the best negotiations of my career and the beginning of Wayne's undoing. For $250, Red gave me a five-year run, during which time she elevated in whoredom, becoming one of the most notorious and productive whores in America.

In later times, as Insane Wayne's pimpdom began to decay and his prized whores began to take wing and fly by night, he would return in the fullness of his brilliance and the coyness of his cunning, trying to recapture the moment which they once had, only to find his persona had been poisoned and that his throat had been cut. The reflection here is that a real pimp never knows where the next whore is coming from, and that pimping is one thing, friendship is another.

Jimi Starr

Rosebudd Bitterdose

Chapter 15

The Oops Game

From out of the darkness and from somewhere in the distance, a ship's horn bellowed as the cool fog rolled over the sleeping city of San Francisco. Honey Boy, Bay City Fats' personal confidant, and I made our way through the city to the red light section at Geary and Powell. In the early morning predawn hours, the illicit ladies of the night showcased in furs and evening gowns, parading as if they had a license.

While stopped at a signal light, Honey Boy nervously said, "Jimi, I'm going to tell you a story. I want you to remember it always. I do not know how you will accept it. But I want you to know the story I'm going to tell you is true."

With the urgency of his words, I sat back and listened attentively. This sad and revealing story is the truth, the whole truth, and nothing but the truth. However, the names have been changed to protect the innocent and the dead.

It was on his seventeenth birthday when he boarded a coach in Fresno, California. On his tall, thin, blue-black frame, he wore an oversized black suit and a pair of black Stacey Adams shoes. He carried an extra pair of shoes under his right arm, wrapped in brown paper and bound in twine. It was a warm evening in the autumn of the year. The leaves of the trees drifted gently on the breeze to the ground as he boarded the Greyhound coach with the destination sign that read, "San Francisco Express".

At that period in his life, his friends and family called himself Johnny-O. He was full of wanton desires and lust, aspiring to be a pimp in the big city like his father, Goldie, before him. He longed for his own shot at the big time of fame and fortune in the big city.

Farm animals, farm houses, and fence poles flashed by the window as the roaring gray dog belched black smoke from its overhead pipes into the clear blue sky as the bus rolled along the highway. Honey Boy watched the poor suckers labor in the fields and in their sweating toil, working their lives away. He thought to himself as he sat and ate the lunch prepared by his grandmother, fried chicken and fresh picked oranges. He fantasized about his fortune and fate as a top-flight pimp in the big city. He had visions of the Game, flashy Cadillac's, diamond rings, and sweet-smelling, long-legged whores in mini skirts. In his visions, he wore diamond rings, solid gold watches, and tailored-made suits.

"Now go get my money whores," he would say as they left the fantasy Cadillac in his mind. "Don't make me have to beat your ass this morning, bitch!" That little red head always talks back, he thought to himself. For some reason, he could never get past this point.

His vision ended as the Greyhound bus made it's way down the highway to the city and towards the destiny and fate of Johnny-O. The coach made it's way through the congested downtown traffic, towards the terminal at Seventh and Market Street. The red sunset covered the horizon as the lone Greyhound bus made its way through the drug-infested sections of the city and past the multitudes of homeless and starving persons living in the streets.

There was an announcement that stated, "The 7:30 Express from Fresno has arrived on time at Gate 7." The anxious, wide-eyed passengers, searching for friends and loved ones, scurried to the front of the bus. At the gate, sailors were reunited with their sweethearts. Mexican migrant farm workers were reunited with their loved ones. Little old men were met and embraced by little old ladies, but there was no one to meet and greet Johnny-O. Alone, he stepped out of the coach and stepped into a cruel, cold, and uncaring   San Francisco and the Game. Alone, he made his way through the crowded terminal as people rushed to different gates for different destinations and in and out of the main entrance. Little did he know, from this day forward, his life would never be the same again.

Inside the bus terminal, two seasoned pimps, Filmore Slim and Bay City Fats, sat at the shoeshine stand. Like vultures, in true voyeuristic fashion, they observed the patrons of the bus terminal in search of a scrumptious young runaway or tasty, young, would-be whores, or just some unsuspecting victim to fall prey to the Game. Johnny-O stopped and bought a pack of Kool cigarettes at the concession stand in the center of the platform area. Reaching into his pocket, Johnny-O removed the twenty-five dollars his grandmother had given him. Curious and conniving eyes from every corner of the room studied his every move. From somewhere behind him, a slum player eyed his tiny bankroll.

"Hey, player, can I interest you in some fine jewelry?" The slum hustler inquired, flashing a gold watch and diamond ring that shone like the sun. Seeing his dream jewelry, Johnny-O lusted earnestly as his mind exploded.

It was part of his vision. There they were, his diamond watch and ring, but he knew he couldn't afford them.

"Excuse me pal, I'm Johnny-O. I just blew into the city, whoreless. I'm going to be a famous pimp in this town. When I get rich, I'll look you up and buy some of that gold and jewels," Johnny replied. Shrugging his shoulders, Johnny-O turned to walk away.

"Listen up, young pimp," the slum hustler said. "I dig your style, so I tell you what we're going to do. One thing you've got to realize," the slum hustler continued, " if you're going to pimp in this town or any other town, a pimp has got to have pimp things. So give me that cash you got and you can pay me the rest later."

Moments later, Johnny-O stepped from the bus station into the streets, strutting in his black oversized suit. On his smooth, thin, blue-black face, he wore a grin from ear to ear. Under his right arm, he carried a pair of Stacey Adams shoes bound in brown wrapping paper and twine. His pockets were empty. The slum player had separated him from his cash. On his left hand, he sported a gold watch and diamond ring that shone like the sun. He did a Mack's stroll towards the Tenderloin, the red light area, and towards his destiny and ultimate fate.

He strolled through the downtown streets of San Francisco as the red sunset disappeared and was replaced by the darkness of the night. The overhead streetlights became the sun, showing him the way. Grinning, he made his way through the crowds of homeless people and the drug-infested streets. Though he was exhausted from his journey from Fresno to San Francisco, he relentlessly pounded the streets of the red light area in search of whores. Tonight was going to be his night, he thought to himself. In his over-sized suit, grinning and strolling, he pounded the pavement. He had no cash and nowhere to sleep. Aggressively, he attempted to speak to every whore and wannabe whore or any female eight to eighty who came within range. Finally, 72 hours later, with his feet swollen like loaves of bread, his shoes no longer fitted his feet. He staggered to a stop in Union Square, a park in the heart of the city. He was cold, he was tired, and he was hungry. He hadn't eaten a thing in three days. He did not possess a Chinese nickel nor a Canadian dime. He hadn't caught a whore and couldn't get a girlfriend; pimping wasn't as easy as he thought. Unable to catch a stray and couldn't find a runaway. Things had begun to look real grim to him. Putting aside all pride, he curled up on a park bench and placed the pair of Stacey Adams shoes bound in brown wrapping paper and twine under his head, falling fast asleep. The heels of his feet had been rubbed raw from his Stacey Adam's Shoes.

The sun came up and went down. He awoke just in time to see the back of a transient walking away. Johnny-O sat up on the bench only to find that his pockets had been turned inside out. Looking at his bare hand, he realized the passing transient had stolen his diamond watch and the ring that shone like the sun. Penniless, smelling the aroma of food in the air, he stumbled from the park. Then he tiptoed three blocks. He finally came to a stop on Leavenworth Street in front of the infamous underworld bar and restaurant known as The Exodus. In his innocence, grinning with sore, swollen feet, he hobbled by what seemed like hundreds of streetwalkers and multitudes of homeless people. His oversized suit hung from his thin blue-black frame. Little did he know that many of the drug-filled derelicts who lined the streets or sat in the doorways who were comatose, waddling in puddles of their own piss, had once aspired to be pimps too, only to find out much later that pimping wasn't for everybody, and that all are called, but few are chosen. With this realization, they had arrived in the land of broken dreams.

The crack of a cue ball sounded as Johnny-O entered the dimly lit room. He flinched at the sound and sat down at the bar behind an empty glass. A variety of street hustlers stood around holding up the walls. Whores giggled and wiggled their asses, sliding in and out of the booths. The old blues song, "I Pity the Fool," blasted from the jukebox.

"Last call for alcohol," the gray-haired bartender said. "What will you be having, buddy?" he asked Johnny-O as he removed the empty glass from the bar.

Penniless, hungry, and thirsty, Johnny-O grinned at the gray-haired bartender, "I'd like a glass of water, please." The wide-eyed gray hair bartender looked across the bar, observing Johnny-O's over-sized black suit. For the first time, he noticed the shoes sitting on the counter wrapped in brown paper and bound with twine.

"To enter this establishment, you must buy a cocktail or a meal. This bar is for paying customers," he barked. "Now get out before I kick you in your grinning, derelict ass." A silence fell over the crowded bar. Johnny-O stood and gathered his belongings.

A gruff voice spoke from behind him in the dimly lit bar room. "He's with me." Johnny-O turned and stood face to face with Bay City Fats. He recognized him as one of the two pimps who had sat at the shoeshine stand in the bus station.

"Now give him whatever he's having and put it on my tab," Bay City ordered.

Johnny-O made eye contact with Bay City. "I'd rather have something to eat," he shamefully whispered. Johnny-O's, blue-black face grinned at the bartender. He was glad to have made a possible new frend in Bay City Fats.

Bay City continued in a Southern drawl, "You know that was no way to address a customer, especially an aspiring pimp." Bay City elevated his voice, drawing attention to himself. "If I ever hear you've been talking to my friends like that again, I'm going to come back here, buy this building, kick you in the ass, and then I'm going to fire you." The patrons laughed at Bay City Fats' attempt to be amusing. The clock on the wall read 2:00 a.m. The bartender poured his last legal drink of the day.

A medium-built, brown-skinned pimp with thick wavy hair, wearing a two-piece royal blue, tailored-made suit and a matching pair of alligator boots climbed up on the bar and said, "Give every pimp in the house a round on Peppy LePew." He hesitated momentarily, taking a snort of cocaine from a hundred dollar bill he had left sitting on the bar and then continued, "and give every sucker a glass of milk."

The swinging doors of the infamous nightspot swung open. Excitedly, a well-dressed player entered the room and stood next to Bay City and Johnny-O. He roared, "Has anyone of you niggers seen my whore?" Complete silence fell over the patronage of the bar as the well-dressed man stared at his reflection on the mirrored walls. As he gazed, he straightened the wrinkles from his attire and placed a scowl on his smooth, pampered face.

The man began to repeat himself, "I said have any of you niggers seen that chippy-ass whore of mine?" At that point he did a strange thing, he smiled and pushed his hand deep into his coat pocket, exposing the imprint of a pistol. Damn, he's got a gun, Johnny-O thought to himself.

"When I see that bitch, I'm going to flat-blast her ass!"

Bay City flashed a wide grin and pointed towards the men's toilet and in his unique Southern drawl he said, "When she saw you come in, the dirty tramp ran into the restroom. She's been around here out-of-pocket with some young Hollywood pimp all night long."

"I'm going to murder that tramp bitch and that nigger, too!" the stranger snarled and stormed towards the restroom, kicking the door open and slamming it behind him. He crashed the trashcan into the mirror, cutting his hand.
He roared, "Chippy-ass, out of-pocket bitch, where's my money? Bitch, I'm going to murder you!" he spat. Eerie blood curdling screams, thuds, and screeches escaped from behind the door of the rancid shithouse.

"Don't kill me, Charlie Brown! Don't murder your out-of-pocket bitch!"

From behind the bar, the bartender shouted, "Don't kill the whore in here, Charlie Brown. Take that whore outside and kill her!"

The patrons roared with laughter. Johnny-O looked into Bay City's cold, uncaring eyes as Peppy continued to walk the bar, proclaiming the gospel of the Game. Charlie Brown left the putrid restroom and stood at the bar. He took a handkerchief from his pocket and wiped the sweat from his face and the blood from his cut hand.

Johnny-O turned to Bay City Fats and Filmore Slim and spoke in a low frantic tone, "Oh my God, did he kill that woman? We can't just sit here and do nothing."

Filmore grinned and stated, "If you're smart, young man, you'll leave this bar and leave this city tonight. The Game ain't for everybody. You ain't going to make it through the night."

Bay City's face quivered and in a sinister tone he replied, "Johnny-O, I don't know if that nigga killed the bitch or not. Why don't you go to the shithouse and check for the whore's miserable corpse."

With his hands on his hips, Peppy jumped on top of the bar. "It's time for the pimping to separate the macaroni from the spaghetti this morning. There are niggers in the presence of the gospel of the Game this morning that are perpetrators. There are niggers that have been accepting money under false pretenses. I don't have to tell you who you are, because you know who you are," Peppy preached. Peppy walked the length of the bar. While walking, he stopped now and again and with a quill, took deep snorts of cocaine from a hundred dollar bill.

Johnny-O returned from the restroom and sat next to Bay City and stared in fascination. "I checked the shithouse and she wasn't there." Bay City turned and placed his hand on Johnny-O's shoulder and began to whisper the ins and outs of the Game.

"That nigger there is Charlie Brown, one of the most dangerous niggers in the Game. He was a hell of a Mack. We go way back. He was my celly in the pen, but one night, when no one was looking, somebody got to him. They made a bitch out of him. He's been a nut every since. He's a schizophrenic pimp. He's a pimp and he's his own whore. The bitch you heard getting murdered in the toilet, that was him. Every now and then the out-of-pocket whore in him gets lose and will give a young pimp some money. But the pimp in him will make him check that bitch and bust that ass."

Peppy, walked the bar, reading the pedigrees of all. He kicked the empty glasses, sending them shattering to the floor. He gave acclaim and adulation to the prominent, the rich, and the famous. With the tongue of a serpent, he verbally lashed and psychologically intimidated those of less renown. Smooth and colorful pimps huddled close within an earshot. The dutiful whores nonchalantly took in Peppy's antics as he strolled along the top of the bar, preaching the "Gospel of the Game" and in the all mighty dollar, we trust.

The music blared from the jukebox as the gaiety of street players and the pimp antics continued. "Remember what I told you," Filmore reiterated, "Nigga, you ain't no pimp. Leave this town and get away from the Game tonight while you still can; that nigga you're trying to befriend ain't no man." Fats flashed Filmore a knowing smile. Johnny-O paid no attention to Filmore. This was going to be his night. He was determined to pimp. Johnny-O had visions of the little red head and that crew of whores in his mind as the door of the bar swung open and slammed shut behind Bay City Fats and Johnny-O, sealing the newfound friendship as they left the bar into the fog and sobering chill of predawn night.

Bay City Fats' car screeched away from the curb and into the sparse early traffic. He grinned and fantasized as they zigzagged through the whore-line streets of the downtown red light area. As they rolled through the red light area, Bay City began to smile and speak in a gold-tooth Southern drawl.

"You know pal, Johnny-O ain't no name for a real pimp. That's the name of a second-story boy, a burglar. So this morning, I'm going to do something for you. I'm giving you a new moniker; the name will be Honey Boy. I've watched you pound the streets for the last part of the week in search of a whore. I've watched you sleep on park benches and in the back seats of abandoned cars. Yeah, I've been watching you; your dedication is to be commended. Anyone who wants to pimp that bad has got to be legitimate." Bay City continued, "If you're broke right now, as I'm sure you are, and in need of some quick cash and a place to stay, you can come and do odd jobs for me until you catch a bitch just to keep some money in your pocket."

"Man, you must be reading my mind," Honey Boy said. "I've been pounding the pavement for what seems like forever. I have not had a bath or a good night's sleep since I hit town three days ago. Sure, I could use a few dollars Bay City; I could stand something to eat, too." The two men both laughed at Honey Boy's expressed wit.

"You know kid, I kind of like you. You remind me of a celly of mine in the joint." Bay City leaned closer to Honey Boy and spoke in a whisper. "A pimp should always have food in his belly and stay rested and freshly dressed. If you cannot say these things about yourself, you're not pimping, pal. No disrespect intended, but until you clean yourself up and catch a whore, you just might want to consider being my personal valet and understudy."

Bay City continued, "The job doesn't pay much, but you get free room and board and first hand knowledge of the Game. Who knows, after you've proven yourself trustworthy, I might even give you a whore. I can trust you, right, pal?" Bay City asked.

"Sure Bay City," Honey Boy anxiously replied.

"I got a strange feeling we're going to have lots of secrets," Bay City replied.

Having heard those words, Honey Boy was sold. The young novice sat elated and mesmerized at the thought of his newfound friend and his new moniker. Along with the events of the evening, he began to feel the effects of the raw cocaine. He watched the effects of the overhead streetlights shining down on Bay City's jewelry, causing red and yellow flecks. Honey Boy continued to grin, unable to speak; his mind was spinning. Bay City reached into his pocket and produced a small bottle of pills.

"Friend, you're a little too high. Here, take one of these," Bay City said, with his boyish face, Chinese eyes, and a sinister gold-tooth smile. Honey Boy took the pills, and Bay City got out of the car to talk to a turnout hooker on whore's row. Honey Boy drifted into dreamland, not realizing that he had just been handed a date-rape drug. Honey Boy thought to himself, to learn the Game from a master is what he had always wanted, getting the Game first hand. In his newfound friend, he believed he would achieve the knowledge and the inside track to the Game. As his new world began to spin and the lights began to dim and dark clouds filled his mind, he slipped into a deep and euphoric slumber.

POW!! Honey Boy saw stars and was rudely awakened from his drug-induced slumber. .

"Nigger, do you know who I am?" POW!! Fats slapped the shit out of Honey Boy like he was a common street tramp. POW!! "Nigger, do you know what I'll do to you?" Through slit eyes and snarling through his teeth, he spoke. "Nigger, I'm Bay City Fats. I'm God Almighty. Look here, nigger, I told you I was going to put you to work so you could have a little money in your pockets, but you're starting out ass-backwards. Now you're in debt, nigger. It seems you've pissed on that little black suit and all over the fine Corinthian leather in my customized Cadillac car, nigger. I'm going to take the cost of the damages to my fine automobile out of your ass."

Honey Boy cringed in fear and shame. His mind was cloudy. He couldn't understand what was happening to him. He couldn't understand how or why he had lost control of his bladder, pissing on his only suit and the leather seats of the fine automobile of his newfound friend.

He could not understand why he had pissed on himself. He couldn't understand why he couldn't stay awake. He couldn't understand why his newfound friend was treating him like this and why was he talking to him like he was a woman. In later times, he would come to know that the pills Bay City had given him had rendered him unconscious and had caused him to loose control of his bladder.

Bay City sat behind the wheel in his garage and pointed his long, manicured finger towards the door, "Now get your pissy ass in the house and get out of those nasty clothes," he barked.

Steam filled the room, fogging the mirrors. Bay City stepped from the shower onto the plush red carpets. After drying himself, he took a towel to wipe the mist from the mirror. He liked what he saw. He flashed a gold-tooth smile to himself. His mind drifted back into years gone by as he reminisced on his many conquests over young unsuspecting victims in confinement. His mind drifted back to the penitentiary; the birthplace of his bizarre habits and lust for young fat-butt boys. Aroused, he unconsciously touched himself. In a flash and on the canvas of his mind, he began to paint, reliving each and every vivid detail, and tonight his unwilling and unsuspecting victim was going to be his newfound friend, Honey Boy. Bay City Fats was a fart knocker.

Bay City stepped from the bathroom. In a drug-induced stupor, Honey Boy lay semiconscious and nude on the bed. Bay City fondled Honey Boy's butt.

"Hey, wait a minute, man," Honey Boy slurred, "I don't fuck around like that."

"Look here, little buddy, while I was in the pen, I acquired some strange tastes. If we're going to be friends, we're going to have to help each other out. Honey Boy, I know you're broke, that's why I'm giving you this $100 bill," Bay City said. In his hand, Honey Boy clutched the hundred dollar bill tightly.

"Now that I've done something for you, I want you to do something for me," Bay City continued.

Honey Boy, knowing what Bay City wanted, tried to get up and run, but he had no coordination.

"I want you to let me get behind you," Bay City said.

Crying out, "Please don't do this to me, man!" Honey Boy slurred as he unsuccessfully tried to escape.

"Look here brother, being how you feel so strongly about your manhood, I'll make you a compromise. So I will tell you what I will do, being how this is your first time and we're friends and all. As opposed to me busting your ass, I'll just put some Vaseline in the crack of your ass and slide my dick back and forth between the cheeks," Bay City said.

Oh God, I must be dreaming, Honey Boy thought to himself. Drugged and having no control over his legs, Honey Boy agreed to the inevitable.

"Ok Fats, please man, just don't stick it in there."

Bay City began to move and grind rhythmically in the crack of Honey Boy's ass. Bay City lined himself up with Honey Boy's puckered butt hole.

Honey Boy pleaded, "Please don't hurt me, man. Promise me you won't put it in there."

"No, I won't put it in there, pal," Bay City said as the saliva from his mouth rolled on to the bare, blue-black back of his unwilling victim.
"Oops, oops, oops," Bay City said as he violated Honey Boy, penetrating him and bringing an end to his innocence and his once aspired career forever.

Honey Boy became Bay City's kept boy and personal confidant. He would never be allowed to have a whore for any extended period of time, simply because he was Bay City's whore. A covenant of silence had been kept between Bay City Fats and Honey Boy for twenty years until now.

"Whatever you do, Jimi, never get high and fall out at Bay City's, and God forbid you should ever get broke and have to stay with Bay City for any period of time. If you do, you are definitely going to come up short. Bay City Fats fuck his friends," Honey Boy said. This story couldn't possibly be true, I thought to myself. But over a period of time and further analysis, I have reconsidered my decision.

The showering rains ran down the windowpanes of the sleek Eldorado, as the cruel howling icy winds seemed to push people and automobiles towards their destinations. I sat in silence, unable to speak.
Honey Boy's revealing words had shaken my world to the quick.

"Jimi, you know my health has been bad for sometime now. The years of drug and alcohol abuse, not to mention Bay City's deformed black dick, has put me on the dialysis machine. Jimi, the doctor's prognosis doesn't look good. I simply wanted someone, somewhere, a friend to know the truth about the life of Honey Boy. Now that you know the truth, I hope you don't think any less of me."

Two weeks later, Honey Boy died from kidney failure. I suppose this story could be considered his dying proclamation. In all my years of close acquaintance with Bay City Fats and Honey Boy, I had never asked the nature of their relationship. I simply saw two friends who were obviously very close. My mind reeled from the truth of Honey Boy's dual and horrible reality.

The angry rain and hail fell, splattering and plummeting the buildings, streets, and cars on Whore's Row. I pulled to the curb at Geary and Taylor Street. A young pimp left the restaurant in the rain and entered a Rolls Royce parked directly across the street from where I was parked. Drenched and shivering whores, standing in the doorways of closed businesses, waved at cars as the chilling rain and hail fell from the black skies and onto the city. Lulu sat in the window of the Pine Crest Restaurant with a group of whores who belonged to the young Rolls Royce-driving Mack called Solo. His whores were putting serious work in on little Lulu, attempting to take her home to him. From the car and through the pouring rain, we sat and watched Lulu's wannabe whore antics and her fast moving mouth. Like a puppy, she was chasing her own tail, searching for acceptance.

She pointed towards the car, still yapping like a puppy, "I'm little Lulu, Jimi Starr's woman, and Frisco Slim is my daddy." The group of whores left the restaurant into the pouring rain with Lulu in tow.

Seeing my car, she made a beeline straight towards to me. Horny tricks blew their horns as she made her way across the wet and windy whore-lined street to the car. Even in this wet weather, Lulu was attractive. Although she was a novice to whoredom, she commanded attention from tricks and players alike. She had short, thick, black, wavy hair, hazel eyes, a beautiful slender body, and a great personality. But for all her attributes, Lulu was dumber than dirt. Lulu didn't have a brain. In all innocence, without her even knowing, her mouth could send the non-thinking pimp directly to the penitentiary. That fact alone sent chills up and down my spine, and along with my newly acquired knowledge of Bay City's booty fetish, prompted me to give Lulu and Bay City some space.

Solo pulled along side of my customized Cadillac and rolled down his window. "If you had been five minutes later, Jimi Starr, you'd be one whore shorter," he said smiling. "It looks like I'll be paying you a visit real soon."

I flashed a diamond-tooth smile. "A lose bitch is like a lose tooth, it's got to be pulled," I replied as I pulled forward and away from the curb into the darkness of night, the traffic, and the falling rain. Little did Solo know how desperately I wanted to dump Lulu's dumb ass.

Filmore Slim

Sheila

Chapter 16

California Dreaming

It was a warm and vibrant, beautiful, sunny Hollywood afternoon, and it was good to be home. From my balcony, I watched the sprawling traffic crawl along Sunset Blvd.

New York had been good to me, much better than I had been to myself. She, the pea-green bitch, had blessed me with a suitcase full of cash, a Mercedes Benz, a Cadillac, and three new whores. Unfortunately, she had also cursed me with a drug habit. Yes, I had gotten a bite out of the Apple, but no one told me that the Apple had teeth; it had also taken a bite out of me.

Red glided into the room. She was my number two whore. This fine young thing had but one purpose in life, one will, and one desire. This was to serve me and keep me happy.

Reader, I tell you for a surety and a certainty, at that point, I had seven whores and the lifestyle of some form of royalty, surpassing the lifestyle of a rock star. However, I was faced with an ever-present situation. A master or career pimp, during the course of a twenty-year career, may acquire two or three women qualified to be his bottom or main woman. My current and ongoing dilemma was that the gods of the Game had blessed me with three young, attractive, intelligent whores, whom all desired to hold the title and position of bottom woman and all during the same period of time.

Red sexily swayed into the room. She was half-Black, half-Latin. She stood 5 feet 5 inches with exceptionally long, thick, black hair. The shade of her almond-shaped eyes was close to black. She had the body of a Greek goddess. We stood on the balcony and took in the view together. I stood behind her with my arms around her waist. It was truly a romantic moment.

"Jimi," she said softly as she pressed into my body, "do you see the hill over there that says 'Hollywood,' and all the houses and all the cars and people on that hill?" Where is this whore going with this? I thought to myself.

"Jimi, my pussy and my asshole are sore and puckered. I think I must have sucked and fucked each and everyone of those people last night. It's been more than a month since you've paid me any attention. When are you going to give me a little time? I make just as much money as anyone else around here."

It was time for me to go into action. She was testing me to see what she could get away with. She continued, "I'm 20 years old. I make a minimum of $500 a day on my back. Please don't even think about my thieving abilities. When I steal something, the sky is the limit."

Red was a good whore, but she always had a bad mouth. She had gotten a little too salty with the presentation of her credentials. "I can have any nigger I want," she began. I caught her in mid-sentence and from her waist, I spun her around on her heels and, with a lightning flash, I knocked her down to the balcony floor.

"Bitch, don't you ever speak to me in that tone or manner!" I spat. Her dress had risen above her waist when she hit the balcony floor. She lay sprawled out and wide-legged. I looked down at her hairy slit. Yes, it was sore and puckered all right.

Real pimps don't show emotion. It is virtually impossible to read them. I stared down at her expressionless. She gasped, placing her hands to her mouth in astonishment. I stared down at her with authority. Reaching down, I slapped the shit out of her again. The look in her startled eyes let me know that she didn't know if I was going to kiss her or kill her.

"Listen up dizzy bitch, you can not come into my life thinking because you give me two or three dollars you can make demands on me or my dick and my time," I barked. "I have six other motherfuckers just like you. And as far as you threatening me about giving my money away, bitch, let me help you," I growled.

I walked to the coffee table and picked up her trap. One of a pimp's best assets is his ability to think at lightning speed and act it out on the spot. I returned to the balcony, fanning her trap in my diamond-encrusted hand.

"No, Jimi!" she screamed. I cast her trap to the wind. The cash floated away on the breeze. She dropped her head and whimpered, "I let a trick fuck me in the ass for that money." I stood on the balcony, watching the money drift from view.

Red was one of the original Gabors and a good whore, but she always had a rotten mouth. Every now and then, I had to slap her in it. This had been a costly lesson; however, I didn't think she would try me again soon.

She was aspiring to be a schoolteacher when she met my pimp pal, Wayne, and he began chipping with her. However, a pimp has got to keep his whores off balance; they must never know what he's thinking and the whore must never be allowed to think that she can orchestrate or dictate because she made money. It was a valuable lesson, yes, but the proof is in the pudding. I had that whore for five years, but in latter times, she experienced mental problems. However, she never did that again, not with me anyway.

In the exclusive Hilltop area above the city of Los Angeles, California stood a huge aging white sign that read 'Hollywood'. The cliff-hanging homes of Hollywood executives and movie stars and wannabes dotted the hillside. Somewhere in the City of Angels, aspiring actors practice their parts for upcoming roles in the movies.

Sluggishly, the Friday evening traffic made it's way along the Harbor and Hollywood freeways. The tourists with maps to the homes of the stars circled through the neighborhoods of Hollywood, Brentwood, and Beverly Hills in search of a star walking down the avenues or perhaps riding down the boulevards in their luxury car.

On the hillside, glass windows twinkled like diamonds as the golden sun began to set in the red sky. The whores began to sprinkle the streets. Some stood in provocative possess while passing tourists and would-be tricks made catcalls or pulled to the curb and yelled through their windows, "How much, lady?" only to pull away, wheels screeching, upon the lady of the night's approach. Curious tricks circle the block trying to get a glimpse of a whore resembling Marilyn Monroe or some other movie star.

Behind the closed doors of sleazy hotel rooms, upcoming young pimps and down-on their-luck veteran pimps ran their last minute instructions past their whores in hopes of a safe and prosperous night.

Red and I stopped at the corner of Sunset and Wilcox. Parking, we entered South Town, a well-known soul food restaurant, for a meal, some conversation, and some quality time before her Friday night out on the town.

"Jimi, I just want to thank you for spending some time with me. You never seem to have any time for me lately, you know, with your other girls and all. And then there's Bianca's new baby," she said. Red had finally said it. There it was. That's what this scene is really all about, I thought to myself.

"Perhaps if I had your child, I could get a little more of your time and a little more of that dick, too," she sarcastically interjected.

I reflected back to the beginning. Red had once been Bianca's protégé. Bianca had trained, counseled, and personally guided Red through her early days in whoredom. Once Red had acquired the skill, she fast became Bianca's primary rival, desiring for the greater portion of the lion's share of the attention and dick. What had started out as a friendship and camaraderie, ended in a vicious rivalry between the two women.

In the average master pimp's lifetime, if he was blessed, he might receive two or three women who were qualified to be his bottom woman. Red proposed to ascend to the mountaintop.

"Perhaps if you pulled your dick out of Bianca's ass long enough, you'd realize there's another pussy that needs fucking around here, nigger! I want my money's worth! I paid for that dick and I want it!" she yelled at the top of her lungs as she stormed from the restaurant into the streets.

Screaming and crying, she stood in the doorway and said, "I'm going to get your money! Maybe then I can get fucked! Maybe then I can get my baby too!"

This bitch had lost her mind, I thought to myself. The waiter who set our table stood near by, speechless.

Hearing the commotion and seeing Red storm out, he shrugged his shoulders and spoke, "Hey, what's up guy?"

"I really don't know," I said. "Stress or PMS, I guess."

Red had been crying and acting strange all day long, ever since Bianca had her baby in Spokane. At that time, I simply believed she was upset. I realize now she had a nervous breakdown.

Red stepped into the streets and into the unknown dangers of the Hollywood night in the hopes of whoring up on or stealing enough cash to get my attention. She stood on the corner of Sunset and La Brea.

A bald, elderly, intoxicated gentlemen stumbled from a nearby bar to his Mercedes parked at the curb on Sunset Boulevard. Unbeknownst to him, he was staggering into harm's way. Red suggestively stood on the corner waving at passing cars. She truly had beautiful legs and a rare body that stood out in a crowd, one that could have been sculpted by Michelangelo.

"Hey, would you like some company?" Red said to her intoxicated balding admirer.

"Well, I don't know. How much?" the balding gentleman asked as he looked at her long shapely legs and her firm, tender young ass. She looked into his eyes. There was something very familiar about him. In the darkness of a doorway, she rubbed her body close to his. The sweet scent of her sex and expensive French cologne drove the horny trick wild. He pulled his swipe out of his pants and began to frantically masturbate. His hips gyrated as he humped his invisible lover.

She felt the wad of cash in his right front pocket. She observed his gold Rolex watch and a solitaire two-karat diamond ring. The bright lights and flashing neon signs lit up the boulevard. The elderly intoxicated trick stood in a nearby doorway drooling as he frantically socked it into the wind. The headlights from approaching traffic shone through the sheer fabric of Red's evening dress, revealing private spaces and forbidden places.

From the concealed darkness of the doorway, the bald passionate trick called out to her, "Hey, pretty lady, I've got all the money you could ever need, more than you could possibly ever want." The degenerate television star reached into his pocket with his free hand. He produced a large roll of bills and, peeling off a hundred dollar bill, he placed it into her hand. "Now tell me who loves you baby," the Hollywood star slurred as he stood in the darkness of the doorway with his pants down to his ankles, holding his massive well-beaten penis in his hand.

The famous trick then said, "I've been a naughty and very bad boy. Now can an old man get a spanking or what?" He was smiling, as if he could be your brother or next-door neighbor with a lollypop hanging from his mouth.

He whispered into her ear, "I'm of Greek descent and I like to play rough. Now can you handle it or what?" the famous trick asked.

"Boy, can I!" Red excitedly replied. In the doorway, she began to fondle and massage his swollen swipe.

"I would like a little sample before I take you to my home in the hills. Can you give me what I want?" He asked firmly.

"Boy, you bet I can," she said as they stepped further back into the darkness of the already concealed doorway.

"I want you to give it to me really good. Don't cut me any slack because I'm a star. I want you to treat me as if I were someone you were really angry with. I want my money's worth," the movie star said. The bald star had unknowingly staggered into harm's way as he foolishly followed Red into the darkness.

"I like it rough,"the trick said.

"Good!" Red whispered as she spun with a roundhouse kick, striking him in the neck, dropping the trick to the ground. Surprised, the trick looked up from the ground wide-eyed.

Red spoke softly, "Oh, did I hurt you, honey?"

"That was nice," the masochistic trick said. "Give me more like that. I've been a very bad boy." With a martial arts kick, Red buried her spike high heel into his shoulder as he tried to stand. The trick's eyes lit up with excitement.

"That's it! That's it!" he said excitedly. "Now pretend that I'm someone you're very angry with and give me my money's worth," he demanded.

The movie star trick had not realized and did not know of Red's current psychological state, and the fact that she was a brown belt in Kung Fu and was a one time former kick-boxer. She did a series of thrusts and kicks to his ribs and head, tacking his breath away. The trick dropped face-first to the ground.

"Stop, stop, you're going to kill me!" The trick said excitedly.

"That's the point; I'm trying to kill you, motherfucker!" She began to plummet his face with lefts and rights. She beat his face bloody, bruising her own hands in the process. The famous trick lay on his back semiconscious.

"You've never sucked my pussy before, Jimi!" Red was shouting. Oh, but you're going to suck it tonight, nigger!"

Oh my goodness, the dazed trick thought as he pissed on himself. I have picked up a straight nut. I am going to die tonight!

Red removed her panties and sat on the trick's face. "Suck my pussy, suck it, Jimi, or I'll beat you to death!" she growled.

In a desperate attempt to stay alive, the terrified trick frantically licked and sucked as the deranged whore rode his battered and bloody face, banging his head on the ground. She had did a series of trusts and kicks to the ribs and head, taking his breath away as the trick dropped to the floor, face first.

"Stop, please, you're killing me!" The infamous trick screamed. "Somebody, please help me. Murder!"

"Jimi, I'm trying to kill you, you two-timing motherfucker," she yelled. "You've never sucked my pussy Jimi, but you're going to suck it tonight," she continued.
Oh my goodness, the horrified trick thought as he pissed on himself. I've picked up a hope-to-die nut tonight. This whore is totally insane. I'm going to die tonight.

A light was turned on from behind the closed door. An elderly woman glared from behind the glass door. Red stayed on the trick's head, rubbing her wide-open pussy all over the trick's face and baldhead.

"Murder!" The bloody trick managed a muffled scream.

Seeing the light and the curious elderly woman, Red dashed from the darkness into the bright lights and neon signs of the Hollywood night for her freedom and her survival.

In the distance, the faint sound of sirens began to wail as the ambulance zigzagged its way through the Friday night Hollywood stagnant and gridlock traffic. The flashing red light revealed the shocked and horrified tourists and neighborhood passer-bys. The siren grew louder as it approached its destination. The ambulance came to a stop at the intersection of Sunset and La Brea. Police cars lined both sides of the street. Open mouthed, curious on lookers pointed their fingers in disbelief, while others gasped in dismay and surprise.

Red sat in the rear seat of the black and white police car directly in front of the darkened doorway with her head dropped. She was crying. The tears ran from her eyes as she laughed hysterically. Her scuffed and bruised hands were cuffed behind her. On a stretcher, the paramedics rolled the bald, bloodied movie star into view. The curious crowd gasped at the sight.

The television cameras from a local news station focused in on the half-dead star and rolled. The black helicopter with bright roving searchlights lit up the darkness like the morning sun, circled overhead as its spinning blades made a beating sound.

The T.V. news commentator placed the microphone to the battered movie star's once handsome face. "Sir, can you tell us what happened?" asked the commentator.

The bald, bloodied, battered, and bruised celebrity pulled the microphone closer as he attempted to smile for his millions of adoring fans. He did not know his diamond front tooth was missing.

Weakly, he began to speak. "I stepped from the restaurant and lounge. I had just had dinner. Three streetwalkers ran out of the darkness and began assaulting me. I was pushed into the darkened doorway at gunpoint. I was gagged, robbed, and beaten. At that point, the desperado whores escaped into the darkness, leaving me for dead. I thank God someone came along and found me or I may have bled to death. There are hoards of thieving whores and other vicious unsavory characters roaming the city. The streets aren't safe for good people like us anymore."

The bald, raggedy-mouthed movie star looked away from the camera and towards the curb and the police car.
"Yeeee," he cried, screaming and cringing in fear and horror. "That's her!" He shrieked, trembling. "That's one of the bitches who tried to kill me!"

"There will be film and details at eleven," the television news commentator said excitedly as the camera zoomed in on Red just before he signed off the air.

I stepped from the restaurant into the warm spring darkness of the Southern California night. The stars twinkled like diamonds in the black Hollywood skies. I drove along Sunset Boulevard. Three police cruisers zoomed past with their lights flashing as their sirens blared. The black helicopters hovered low in the dark skies. Their search lights illuminating the intersection of Sunset and La Brea with the brightness of the midday sun.

Damn, this is serious! I thought to myself. Some poor son-of-a-bitch is in serious trouble. The three cruisers screeched to a halt one block away. Damn, I thought to myself-an ambulance, six police cars, two helicopters, and a news team. Someone must have been assassinated. I inched along in the Friday night traffic towards the hovering helicopters with shining searchlights and the news team. Paramedics brought a familiar looking bloody, balding fellow out of a darkened doorway on a stretcher.

He looked into the police car, pointed his finger and screamed, "That's her! She tried to murder me!" Crying real tears, he grabbed his knees with both arms and began to rock back and forth as if he were in shock.

Slowly, I passed the police car. Looking in, I was unable to believe my eyes. Red sat in the rear seat handcuffed with a maniacal grin on her face.

She looked out of her window and up at the full moon that sat in the vast blackness of the Hollywood skies and began to speak, "Hey! Hey, Moon Doggie. I finally got some of Jimi's head. Yeah, and I got some dick, too. What's that you say, Moon Doggie?" she asked as she squinted her eyes and turned her ear to the moon as if she were listening. "Yeah, you heard right, Moon Doggie. I had to whip his ass. That's right, a bitch has got to do what a bitch got to do to keep her man. I tried to kill that nigger tonight. Yeah, Moon Doggie, Jimi loves me now. I'm going to have his baby," she was saying.

Momentarily, I stopped my car and looked and listened in shock and disbelief as she continued to babble, rant, and talk gibberish to the moon. My beautiful whore was no more. Although her skill level never diminished, her mental stability was never quite the same. In my mind, I had done all that a man is supposed to do. I had wined her. I had dined her. I had spent a gang of time with her. Where had I failed her? Oops, I had forgotten to fuck her.

The clock on the wall read 9:00 a.m. as the judge entered the courtroom. Red wore a black two-piece suit. On her face, she wore an expression of innocence. She had been placed under psychological observation for the last seventy-two hours. Today the court would hear her plea. In a show of support, I put in an appearance. I pulled my hair back into a ponytail and put on a pair of dark glasses. I sat directly behind her. The infamous Hollywood trick sat front-row center. He had chosen not to file charges against Red. However, because of Red's prior record and the trick's notoriety, the district attorney pursued the case, which ultimately brought more publicity to the case and exposed the fact that the famous movie star was a first-class degenerate. The courtroom was packed with the media and curious fans.

The courtroom was sparsely filled. There were two huge deputy sheriffs at the door. The bailiff stood up and said, "All rise for the Honorable Joe Joseph Smith," bringing everyone in the courtroom to their feet. It was 9:00 a.m. when the judge entered the courtroom. By 9:15, it was all over with for any hope of retrieving Red's sanity, and the realization that this was the end of a lucrative five-year run. Red's lawyer approached the bench. Citing her psychological issues, he asked that the nature of her condition be considered in this case.

The judge spoke, looking over his wire rim glasses, "I knew one day you would come before me again on some serious charges, Miss Gonzales," the judge said dryly as he flashed all thirty-two of his denture teeth. "I am not only going to prosecute this case within the spirit of the law, I am also going to prosecute this case to the letter of the law."

With cold, blue, vindictive eyes, he looked down from his bench at Red. In his black robe, the judge proudly sat confident of the events that would follow, sticking out his chest with his gavel in his hand.

He sneered at the psychologically diminished defendant, "Sooner or later," he said, "all criminals end up here in front of me or in front of someone just like me," he arrogantly announced, again flashing all thirty-two of his yellow-stained denture teeth. "Yes," he said, "justice is going to be served today, and then, young lady, you're going to serve justice," he sarcastically stated with an air of biased authority. Damn, poor Red is fucked, I thought to myself. She has lost her mind and now she's losing her freedom.

The judge wasn't finished yet. It has been brought to the attention of the court that Miss Gonzales, the defendant, has possession of certain pertinent information and would like to address the court before sentencing is invoked." With the face of a lost child, she sat staring into space, unaffected by the judge's biased statements. The bailiff assisted Red in standing. The two huge deputy sheriffs manned the double doors of the courtroom.

"Your Honor," Red softly said as she began to rock back and forth, smiling, rolling her eyes to the ceiling as the tears flowed freely from her confused face. As she looked towards the clock on the courtroom wall, her lips began to quiver.

She began to speak, "Moon Doggie, are you out there? What's that you say, Moon Doggie? Have you seen my man?" Red asked her invisible associate in a mumbling tone.

"What's that? What did she say?" The judge asked. Astonished, the wide-eyed judge stood up and spoke, "What kind of gibberish is she ranting?" The judge asked as he came into the realization that Miss Gonzales was not only quite sincere, but also quite mad.

"Yes," the judge said, "who is your man and where is he?" He observed her activities with his steel-blue eyes peering over the top of his wire-rimmed glasses as she continued to rock back and forth, swaying from side to side.

"Hey, Moon Doggie, if I tell them we'll be snitches, but will they let me go?" Red asked her invisible confidant.

"Oh yes," the district attorney said, speaking to her as if she had the mind of a child, "we'll let you go," he said, but I could tell by his face that straight to the nut house was what he was thinking.
"But first, you must tell me who and where your man is."

Oh shit, it's all over with! I thought. Red is going to give me up. I looked at the double doors of the courtroom. The two huge deputy sheriffs appeared to have swollen, doubling in size. Red turned and pointed with her index finger of her bruised hand directly at the famous movie star.

"That's him over there! Get him, he's violent! I'm pregnant with his baby." Everyone in the courtroom gasped. "He's been forcing me into a life of prostitution. He's made me suck strangers' dicks and fuck them for money. He beats me." She pointed her bruised finger at her firm, round ass, "and he's been doing it to me right here." Mr. Hollywood, the famous movie star, turned beet-red and dropped his celebrated face in shame. "He has six other whores just like me," Red continued.

The judge turned beet-red, slammed his gavel, and yelled, "You're in contempt, young lady!" The two huge deputy sheriffs didn't know what to do. Yes, the Game had rendered Red as quite mad.

The proof is in the pudding. The Game is not for everybody. In her twisted mental state, Red believed that the bald-headed movie star was yours truly. Red's current and incurable mental disorder abruptly brought to an end a prosperous five-year run. It had been a harsh and unsuspected ending to an otherwise beautiful and prosperous relationship. In view of her psychological condition, the judge modified the charges, sending her to the Camarillo State Mental Institution for six months.

Reader, there is an old pimp's cliché that reads, "A pimp is not really pimping until he has sent a whore to the graveyard or the nut house." In retrospect, I can only assume it is safe to assume that at that point, I was truly pimping. I have always believed in friendly competition and rivalry. Unfortunately, Red couldn't take it. Ultimately, it assisted in pushing her over the edge. No two whores are exactly alike. It is for that reason that I rejected group pimping and treated each whore as an individual.

Although Bianca was my main woman and I had placed her on a pedestal, I treated each individual whore as my main woman, minus the coveted pedestal. This enabled me to pimp them all with a passion, demanding maximum dividends and receiving them. If I wanted to fly seven whores to New Orleans to the Mardi Gras, so be it. If I decided to fly my sweet baby and me to Waikiki, let it be. If I made the call to fly them all to Montreal and have a ball, I did it all. I had a rare passion for pimping and for life, and I pimped and lived as if there was no tomorrow. Why? A man can never be bigger than his dreams. The absolute best he can ever hope to do is realize and live his dream to the fullest.

What do you do when the dream is over? The process of life is a great deal like a Hollywood premiere with a 7:00 p.m. showing and a giant movie screen. You pay for your ticket of entry and stop in the mezzanine. Then in the darkness, you find a seat and the movie begins. For two hours or the length of the movie, you are the hero, the star of the show. The movie's over, the dream ends here. If you are lucky, you just might get a standing ovation. You place your popcorn box, soda, and other debris on the floor. You stand and begin to exit. As the people from the 7:00 p.m. show are pushing out, the people for the 9:00 p.m. show are pushing in. On the way out in the mezzanine, you make eye contact with someone who looks vaguely familiar; as a matter of fact, he looks identical to you. However, you know it can't be you. No, it couldn't be, you nonchalantly think to yourself.

In reality, there are many people with a mindset similar to your own. You acknowledge and greet the passing stranger with a gracious nod. He continues to push into the theater and finds the seat that you just vacated, just in time for the next showing. You continue to push out of the theater into the fresh air and a new world. Yes, there are as many Jimi Starrs as there are many people just like you.

Madrid, Jimi Starr, and Rosebudd Bitterdose

Jimi Starr

Chapter 17

Revelations

From over the San Gabriel Mountains came the early morning rays of sunshine, along with the undisputed revelation of the truth.

Bianca and I sat eating breakfast and watched the first morning light of the Creator's brilliance. We dreamed dreams and made plans for tomorrow.

The phone rang. "Good morning," I said.

"Hello Jimi, how's everything going this morning? How's the weather there in Los Angeles?" Frisco's voice asked.

"Good, it's going to be a bright and sunny day," I said.

"It's raining here. It's been storming all week," Frisco reported. "I saw Red's ordeal on the Six O'clock News. That was a heart felt misfortune. Dedicated moneymaking whores like her don't grow on trees. She was one of the good ones. That was truly a tough break. It's also a shame about Little Lulu choosing Solo, the drug dealer turned pimp. I was so hoping that you would be able to groom her, turning her into something proper that a father could be proud of," Slim stated. "Oh well Jimi, whores will be whores." Slim couldn't possibly know how relieved I was that Little Lulu had chose.

"I hate to be the bearer of bad news, however, I'm calling you this morning with some new and unfortunate news. Jimi, this morning, around 3:00 a.m., two junkie vandals parked a U-Haul Truck in front of your penthouse and went to the back of the building. They shimmied up the drainpipe and entered your house through your bathroom window. Jimi Starr, they cleaned you out, man."

There was something strange in Slim's voice, something that raised the hair on the back of my neck. "Jimi Starr, early in the Game I told you to beware of Bay City Fats." My mind raced back into the vivid past to that occasion and than went blank. Frisco had warned me, but I didn't listen. I had lost everything that I had pimped so hard for. All of my dreams were instantly gone with one phone call.

"Jimi," Slim continued. "They took all your furniture and clothes. They even took the pictures off the wall and the saltshaker. Starr, your house is bare," his voice echoed through my mind.

I shook off the fog of this distasteful mental dilemma and spoke, "I want a reward put out for any information leading to the whereabouts of my belongings," I said.

"How much will you pay?" Frisco asked.

"Whatever it takes," I replied.

"What about the vandals? How far are you willing to take this?" he asked.

"All the way Slim," I spat angrily. "I'm going to tie up any loose ends I have here in Los Angles and be on the highway by early afternoon. I'll see you at some point tonight." Getting off the phone, I prepared for a date with Slim and did a reality check.

From my penthouse in the Hollywood Hills, I sat in contemplation of my unscheduled journey to San Francisco. Bianca busily packed our bags for the trip. Soft melodic jazz floated through the air as I sat, watching the sprawling and congested traffic on Sunset and Hollywood Blvd. Suddenly, the hair rose on the back of my neck. All my life I had keen perception, a sixth sense, some people call it. It was the sure sign of a cross. The phone began to ring. I answered it.

"Hello," I began.

"Jimi Starr, is that you?" a frantic female voice asked.

"Yeah," I replied.

"It's me, Sable," the frantic voice said. "Jimi, I told you that Fats was the dirtiest nigga on earth; you refused to believe me. When I tried to give you that money the other morning you should have taken it. I just left Fats' house and he and his crack head whores were moving your furniture and all your personal belongings into his penthouse. Jimi, Jimi," she continued excitedly, "are you still there?" My mind was reeling and then snapped from the mental fog.

"Jimi, whatever you do, don't say you heard it from me," Sable went on. "That nigga, Fats, is as crazy as a sack full of shit house rats," she said. "I just wanted to let you know what was going on. Don't tell anybody you talked to me. Just remember, Fats fucked me, he fucked Honey Boy, and if you're not careful, he'll fuck you, too."

With her last statement, she hung up the phone. Sable's words confirmed my inner most thoughts. In the latter years of Fats' career, the aging, one-time master pimp had turned out to be a crack head, a burglar, and a common junkie, second-story boy.

Slowly, we forged our way through the rain slick streets of San Francisco. At the intersection of Divisadero and Fell, I pulled my car to the curb and parked. I turned out my headlights. Under the cover of darkness and the falling rain, we sat and watched a seemingly endless parade of dope fiend derelicts and crack head junkies enter and exit the building on Fell Street.

It was 12:15a.m.when I rang the doorbell of Bay City Fats' apartment building. Bianca and I were buzzed in and started up the long flight of stairs. The hallway and staircase of this once immaculate building were lined with strange, glassy and wide-eyed characters with quivering mouths. A junkie squatted in the corner and defecated at the bottom of the stairs. A tall, slender, blue-eyed blonde woman in a navy blue pinstriped business suit, carrying a black briefcase, feverishly pleaded with a young drug dealer for another $20 rock of crack cocaine.

Relieving her of the briefcase and smiling, the young, baggy-pants drug dealer said, "You've already given me your cash, your watch, and your ring, what else do you have that I might be interested in?" He sneered, handing her his personal pipe. Taking a hit from the drug dealer's pipe, her eyes widened and perspiration appeared on her forehead. Raising her navy blue pinstriped skirt, she exposed her white lace designer underwear. Hurriedly, she stepped from her panties, dropping them to the filthy, urine-stained carpet as if like they were hot or on fire.

Bianca and I continued up the stairs. The stench of urine and human feces in the hallway reeked to high heaven. On the dimly lit staircase, crack heads held flickering flames to small glass pipes. Men and women on their hands and knees, searched for non-existent rocks that they believed they or someone else had dropped.

Bay City Fats stood at the top of the stairs with his mouth quivering. His eyes and face shone as if he had just left the mountaintop and had seen the face of God Almighty.

"Come on up Starr," Fats said invitingly like the spider said to the fly. It was nothing short of ironic that Bay City had once stood in that spot and had reigned supreme over his pimpdom. Tonight, he stood in that very same spot, dictating to an assortment of curb creatures, crack heads, and derelict junkies. This was nothing short of retribution. The Game had an ugly ending for all those who didn't play fair. This once immaculately kept palatial manor had been the White House of West Coast pimping. It had now become a rock house for curb creatures and common crack head derelicts.

I remembered poor, departed Honey Boy and Sable's words, "Jimi, Bay City Fats is one of the dirtiest niggas alive." Now he was on drugs, making him one hundred times more vicious and making him one thousand times more deadly.

Religiously, I carried my pistol everywhere I went. I pushed my hand deep into my London Fog pocket. Yep, it was there. Bianca and I continued to climb the steps that led to Bay City's penthouse.

Bay City Fats' main whore, Chocolate, greeted us at the front door and escorted us into the living room. Chocolate was short, dark skinned, and muscular. Except for her blonde wig, she could have been Mike Tyson's identical twin sister. She was known for knocking tricks out with one punch and taking their money. In her time, she had also knocked out a pimp or two. She would never win a beauty contest, not even if it was for gorillas.

"Jimi," Bianca said excitedly, "that's my couch and there's my table too." Bay City entered the room and sat down in his black easy chair. Through wide glassy eyes, he began to speak in his harsh Southern drawl.

"Jimi," Fats began, "I called this meeting between us because we have a bone to pick."

His normally firm voice was shaky. His wide eyes were searching mine for emotion. He was, to the knowing eye, noticeably shaken. I had only seen him like this, out of his character, once before. I knew I had to be careful or die.

There is an old pimp cliché' that reads, "A desperate man will do desperate things." Checking my mental notes, my mind flipped through the past, looking at Fats through eyes of disgust, disbelief, and shame.

He started, "Starr, it seems I have come into some merchandise that belongs to you." His mouth and his words were out of sync, like a bad scene from a cheap Japanese movie. How could this be? The once infamous Bay City Fats, the legendary pimp, had somehow became a crack head, burglar, and a raggedy- mouth, prick licking, dick-in-the-booty faggot.

"I have your furniture and some other personal items of yours. I'll let you have them cheap," Fats said.

I couldn't believe my ears! I wanted to believe they were lying! Adding insult to injury, this nigger wanted to sell me my own personal belongings. I had taken all I could take. I pushed my hand deep into my pocket, wrapping it around the butt of my steel-blue friend. Tonight, Bay City Fats was going to pay for the things he did to Honey Boy and for every whore he ever abused in life.

In the heat of passion, I realized I had to either kill Bay City and run the risk of going to the penitentiary or kill our relationship. By the grace of God, I chose the latter.

"Nigger, you ain't no pimp, you're a burglar!" I harshly snapped. "You're a raggedy-mouth, prick- licking, dick-in-the-booty faggot. Yeah nigger, I know all about you burying your deformed dick in Honey Boy's ass." Fats dropped his head in shame.

I roared at the Mike Tyson-look-alike, "Open that door you monkey-face bitch and let a real pimp out of this crack house! The crack house is where relic pimps come to die. Let me the fuck out of here so I can get on with my pimping, and so that Fats can go climb into another one of his unsuspecting pimp friend's bathroom window."

Chocolate, watching my every move and realizing that perhaps I had a pistol, hurriedly unbolted the door. With that, Bianca and I left Bay City Fats' penthouse.

Men and women still searched on their hands and knees, scouring the carpet for nonexistent rocks that they believed they or someone else had dropped. A lone crack head stood in the stairwell with his pants dropped around his ankles, masturbating. At the foot of the stairs, for a puff of rock cocaine, crack head derelicts lined up to take turns sticking their soiled dicks into the asshole of the geeked blonde, former businesswoman, while others waited to stick their filthy unwashed dicks into her hot, wanton mouth. No, it doesn't take long, I thought to myself.

Bianca and I stepped from this morally condemned building into the freedom of God's creation, the fresh air, and falling rain. This night marked the end of my close acquaintance with the infamous Bay City Fats.

I never returned to the building on Fell Street, and Bay City Fats and I have rarely spoken since that day. There's an old pimp cliché that reads, "Old pussy and old asshole have two things in common, nobody wants it and you can't give it away."

Jimi Starr

Rosebudd Bitterdose

Chapter 18

The Last Hurrah

Excitement was in the air. One-arm bandit jockeys stood by gawking as the old lady shrieked, jumping up and down, excitedly pointing at her machine. Lights went off and on, bells rang as silver dollars were mechanically spat from the machine in rapid succession, making a clacking sound as they hit the metal bucket.

"Seven, lucky seven," the stickman called as the red dice struck the end of the green felt table.

I made my way from the bar through the casino to the parking lot. With my windows opened, I slowly cruised down Las Vegas Boulevard towards Fremont Street. I diligently observed the unexpectant tourists, laden with cameras and jewelry, in summer dresses and short-sleeve shirts as they innocently made their way across the intersection. The ladies of the night openly worked both sides of the boulevard, waving and making suggestive body gestures in the hopes of separating some unsuspecting tourist from his wallet.

It was an exceedingly warm summer night as the stars studded the beautiful moon lit desert sky. The signal light turned red. I came to a screeching stop at the intersection of Las Vegas and Desert Inn Boulevard. A platinum blonde, blue-eyed white woman with a mole on her cheek, driving a white Thunderbird, pulled along side my customized Eldorado. At first glance, she appeared to be a Marilyn Monroe look-a-like. But my knowledge of police tactics forewarned me to proceed with caution.

She pulled along side of me and began, "Excuse me," she began, "aren't you Jimi Starr?" Sexily she implied as she licked her thin pink lips in suggestive fashion, while flashing her humongous breasts, held in place by a sheer halter-top.

In an instantaneous flash, I mentally summed up all that I could see and all that she projected. The average player would have literally turned a flip just for a chance to pop the pimping at this platinum blonde, blue-eyed doll, but I had to be careful. Across America, the police are famous for sending decoy whores to undermine a pimp and then arresting him for 266H and 266I; soliciting for the purposes of pimping and pandering, or maybe even the Mann Act, interstate transportation of known whores. At first glance, I could make no defining determination.

So I looked deep into her pool-blue eyes and calmly replied, "No, lady, I'm not Jimi Starr, you've got the wrong guy," and screeched through the intersection as the light turned green.

I was determined not to lose one moment out of my career in the cruel penitentiaries of America, as so many other pimps had before me. In lusting after and pursuing choice young white girls, the pimp would expose his game demeanor, only to find out later that the choice young white girl was really Officer O'Reilly, an undercover detective from the Vice squad. No, I wasn't going out like that. Pimps didn't go to jail for pimping, they went for the ignorance of "mispimping." My Eldorado glided to a stop as the signal light, at Las Vegas and Dunes Boulevard, turned red and the movie star blonde once again pulled along side of my customized Eldorado.

"Hey, Jimi," she began, "you're not some kind of faggot or afraid of money are you?" This bitch really has a bad mouth.

In an attempt to shake her, I got loud, yelling from my open window, "Look here Lady," I snapped, "I don't know any fuckin' Jimi Starr! Now, officer, why don't you leave the pimping alone and go give somebody a speeding or jaywalking ticket."

I pulled into the valet section of The Dunes Casino and the persistent movie star pulled in behind me, pursuing me. I approached her car and she opened the door waving a spread of one hundred dollar bills.

"What in the fuck did you say, nigger?" She said in an elevated tone as she attempted to get out of her car. "Nigger, I'm whoring, I'm whoring for real! What in the fuck do you mean I'm the police? I was trying to like you, nigger. You're trying to give a bitch a bad name. Nigger, you can't be Jimi Starr. If I had a knife I'd cut you."

I realized I had obviously misread her intentions and her identity. Leaning into her opened door I smiled, and with the charm of Don Juan, I began to speak, "Hello, pretty blue eyes," I said softly. "It seems as if this just might be a case of mistaken identity. You know, a fella of my profession and persuasion can never be too careful. For the record darling, why yes, I'm Jimi Starr."

I ran my eyes over the seasoned blonde bombshell and then waited for her verbal credentials. With an air of confidence and determination, she fanned her face with 41 one hundred dollar bills.

"Oh, excuse me sir, I mistook you for the man of my dreams." I greedily eyed her cash. Sliding across the seat, she continued sexily, "I thought you were my Dream Nigger."

Eager to get my hands on the cash, I slid in besides her. "Shall we forego the formalities?" Reaching out my hand I spoke, "Is that my money?" If she was the police, she had me now. Searching for police backup, I eagle-eyed my surroundings. "Now, what's your name, bitch?"

"My name is Angel and yes, this is your money, but there are some stipulations that go along with it," she said. "I've been in town for about a week. I don't have anyone. I left my last man because he hurt my baby."

"Oh, a child abuser," I remarked. "You should have sent that nigger to the fucking joint."

"I've been hearing about you all across country and when I heard that you were in town, I decided to look you up," she spoke, eyeing my crotch and licking her lips. "Before you take my money, know this; my baby must be taken care of. You can hurt me, but never hurt my baby."

That's when I noticed the dog. The feisty little poodle growled and pulled at the pants-leg of my tailor- made silk slacks. I wanted to slap his little ass right out of the open window, but I refrained. I'm glad that I did.

"Oh, I see that you like animals," Angel said. Our eyes met and with a wicked glance she spoke, "I've already been some nigger's whore. Now I want to be some man's woman. So there it is, Jimi. If you accept this money, I want to be your woman. I want you to fuck me, and I want you to walk my little dog."

Oh shit, my mind screamed. This bitch is nuts! With that, she handed me the cash. I folded it and placed it in my pocket. The little black poodle continued to pull my slacks and gnawed on the heel of my alligator shoes. Now that I had the money, I was going to choke his black ass.

"Oh Jimi," Angel said proudly, "Catch is my baby." she said proudly.

Leaning over, I scooped him up, "Come here son," I said as the little black dog excitedly licked my face.

Reader, you and I know this white bitch was crazy if she thought that little black poodle, with a little white tam and sports jacket was her baby! But you must understand this; different whores pay for different reasons. Some pay because it's "Pay a Nigger Season", while others pay because they're paying for a reason.

The next day, I proudly paraded Catch through the barbershop, the neighborhood, and all around town. It was the least I could do for 41one hundred dollar bills. If Angel chose to believe that this black poodle was her baby, it was OK with me.

Angel Moore was her name. For some whimsical and unknown reason, I attracted nuts, which produced large amounts of cash. Angel and I left the soul food restaurant on Wilcox Boulevard in Hollywood, California. We were there for a mini-vacation. She had been my woman for a little over a year, and in that time, she had never given me a moment's grief. And as far as getting my money was concerned, she possessed some hidden talents. Not only was she a thief, she was a paperhanger as well. At her craft, perhaps she was one of the best in the country. Angel did have one small quirk besides Catch. Each and every Tuesday morning, religiously, without fail, this crazy white bitch attempted to commit suicide.

. Catch, our delightful and dutiful son, waited in the car until we returned. Slowly we rolled down Sunset to the Hyatt Hotel, watching the tourists watch the stars, the fancy cars, and whores along Sunset Boulevard. The room faced the boulevard and the beautiful red Los Angeles sunset. Angel showered, and I stood alone on the balcony enjoying the view and the cool California breeze. The phone began to ring; it was Bianca calling from my Las Vegas house. I could hear the excitement in her voice.

"Daddy, somebody broke into the house and stole some cash and jewelry. The next door neighbor says he saw that rat-bitch, Diane, leave in a cab." The phone went silent. "Jimi," Bianca said, "I know I'm in big trouble. Yesterday Diane saw me stash some money in the house. I trusted her. I know you told me to trust no one, nigger nor bitch."

"Don't say another word," I said firmly. "I'll be back some time tomorrow evening in time for the champion fight at Caesar's Palace. When I get there, have that bitch and have my money." The phone clicked as I hung up the receiver.

Yes, Diane truly was a rat. She had witnessed Bianca stash cash in the house and returned later, under the cover of darkness, and shimmied up the drainpipe and kicked in the bathroom window. I reflected on the old pimp cliché, "The same whores that will give it to you will take it away." Now I personally realize the validity of this statement. It had only been $1,500, but it could have been a lot worse. The Rat's larceny confirmed in me a life long lesson. The Rat's blatant actions had brought my trip to an instantaneous halt. Angel loaded our bags into the car. We were on the highway within an hour. It was only a four and one-half hour drive to Las Vegas. In my customized Eldorado, I rocketed east on Interstate 10. Taking in the desert scenery, Angel and I made small talk as we raced into the seemingly endless miles of desert nothingness. There was truly only one thing on my mind. That cutthroat bitch, Diane, had stolen from me. She had to be punished! If it got out that she had robbed me and got away with it, every stick-up kid, and larcenous whore in the country would consider me an easy mark.

Reno

Reno was a long-time personal associate; often times we passed ourselves off as brothers. He was a former drug dealer who had turned pimp. He was the kind of guy who loved to clown, especially if it was at someone else's expense or he had the upper hand. Unfortunately, as with most people who gloat at the misfortune of others, time proved he could shuffle, but he couldn't deal.

Having had breakfast in the restaurant of the Stardust, we stepped into the casino area. The slot machines made clacking sounds as they spat coins into waiting tubs and elated tourists leaped and danced in excitement.

The stickman on the crap table in the center of the floor, yelled, "Twelve, pay that lucky man who placed the high-low eleven. Thirty to one." the stick man yelled.

With his cat like demeanor, Reno flashed a grin that was reminiscent of the Cheshire cat from Alice in Wonderland. He excitedly scooped up his chips and dashed for the cashier's window.

Sitting at the bar was most probably one of the most gorgeous women I have ever seen before in my life. She had a bronze tan. She wore a white vest and slacks. With her piercing ice-blue eyes and straw-blond hair, she could have passed as a double for Bo Derrick and been that perfect 10. I was in complete cognito, wearing a Panama hat and dark glasses. I sat without speaking. From behind dark glasses and a cocktail, I observed this vision of loveliness. Was she a movie star or perhaps some prominent politician's wife? With a mental zoom lens, I observed her closer. No, she was definitely someone's whore, I thought to myself.

Reno returned from the cashier's window. He sat at the end of the bar next to the Bo Derrick look-a-like. I saw them make eye contact and I saw Reno's cat-like smile. He whispered something into her ear. She laughed as they stood up and left the bar and exited the casino. My brother Reno always was a terrible cum freak. He would fuck a snake if you held its head so it would not bite him.

This chance encounter changed the course of my brothers' career. As the story unfolded the mystery lady turned out to be a thousand-dollar-a-day white girl. And my brother Reno never looked back. This mysterious whore had come from the stable of Thurman, a premiere California pimp and personal associate with some renown. Her whoring had soured fast and she went bad in Maui, Hawaii. A rich, regular trick of hers brought her to Las Vegas directly into Reno's hands. Three weeks later, after taking $3,500 at the Ali Fight, she left just like she came.

Any woman who will leave one man will leave another. After all, human beings are all creatures of habit. Having had been Thurman's latest turnout, she was an attention freak. As Thurman's crew of whores and his notoriety grew, the less attention she received. She rebelled against Thurman's inattention by running away with that pimp-hating trick, leaving isle of Hawaii and flying to Las Vegas where she met and chose Reno, thereby disrupting Thurman's cash flow. Out of nowhere, she came, and into nowhere she returned. The way a whore comes is the way a whore goes. However, by the time she left, Reno was a multi-thousandaire.

People flowed into Las Vegas, Nevada from all over the world. By jet, by bus, or car, they came to this magnificent and stellar once in a lifetime historical event. It had been billed as the Fight of the Century, the Last Hurrah.

For Mohammed Ali, the people's champion, that's exactly what it was. It was fight night. It was one of those strange moments in time. Religiously, I had watched the champ train in the desert. Ali was getting older, but in my opinion, Ali is and was the greatest of all time. Besides that, he was only fighting his former sparring partner, right? A virtual unknown named Larry Holmes. For Ali, it was going to be just another day in the gym, right? WRONG!!! That night, the one-time sparring partner, Larry Holmes, then the current champion, all but beat Ali to death. It had been one of the most vicious assaults I had ever seen on a human being. Holmes did everything to Ali that night but take him to bed. An unbelieving crowd cheered and roared, as Ali became the outclassed recipient of the beating that, in my opinion, ended his celebrated career.

The Last Hurrah had not been just a bad night for Las Vegas or the champ; it had also been a bad night for me. Believing Ali was a sure thing, I bet my entire wad and the deed to the proverbial farm and found myself experiencing the age-old saying, "There's no such thing as a sure thing." I was flat broke. Like Ali, I had gambled and I had lost. I was there, at Caesar's Palace, sixth row center. I personally witnessed this historic event. I sat ringside in the same row as John Travolta and Gladys Knight. After the third round, it was apparent that the Greatest was a beaten fighter. However, it was the eighth round before the Champ's corner threw in the towel; by that time it was too late. The damage had already been done.

Having had witnessed the impossible, buzzing hoards of excited and unbelieving fight fans left the arena, many throwing the receipts of lost multi-thousand dollar bets to the floor. Many squares and players alike, from around the world, lost fortunes that warm summer night, including myself. Later that evening at the circular bar in the casino area of Cesar's Palace, the Champ's famed trainer, Boundini, sat crying real tears over the career-ending beating that had been administered to the greatest. On the far side of that same bar, I sat alone wanting to cry myself, but not over what happened to the Champ. I wanted to cry over what happened to my briefcase full of cash.

I was sitting at the bar in my living room, starring at an empty glass, wishing someone would had come along and beaten my ass with a baseball bat, stopping me before I had placed those costly bets on the fight. Daily, Reno and I had visually monitored the Champ's workouts. I had bet every dime my women had given me. The streets and the Game were becoming passé to me. If I could place a proper bet and win, I could retire. It was an extreme thought for a rational man, but at this point in my career, I was anything but rational. All I wanted to do was win and retire. Pimps and other players of the Game don't get any retirement. At some point, they had to try something clever or play the long shot. I had attempted the latter and I had lost.

. It was not uncommon for Wayne to stay at my home when he was in town from Phoenix. He and Judy, his latest white girl, had been staying at my place for the last three weeks.

Wayne and Reno floated into my living room. They glided across the room as if they were on a cloud, feet never touching the floor. You could always tell when real pimps were doing swell just by the way we carried ourselves. I sat at the bar in my living room.

It was a strange thing about Insane Wayne and me and the relationship that we shared. Although we could be bitter rivals, in reality, we were the absolute best of friends. I understood him and he me. In a clutch situation, we would give each other the shirts off of our backs.

Reno finished his drink, stood, and spoke. "The atmosphere here is too depressing for me," he began. "The best way to get over a lost whore or a lost bankroll is to get a fresh one," he concluded as he headed for the door.

Wayne momentarily disappeared into his bedroom, only to reappear seconds later, carrying a brown paper bag. In a concerned and cold tone, he began. "Jimi, a fool and his money are soon parted. Never do this to yourself again." I sat and listened curiously.
"I'm probably the only real pimp you know and definitely the best friend you have," he continued. He reached into the bag and extracted his hand, producing bundles of one hundred dollar bills. "Help me count this money and I'll do something for you," he said.
Wayne arrogantly began, "Nigga, I'm going to fly to Los Angeles in the morning and buy a Rolls Royce. I might even pay for that Rolls Royce in cash," he concluded.

Reader, I tell you for a surety and a certainty, there is nothing on earth like having a real friend in a time of need. We counted in excess of one hundred thousand dollars in one hundred dollar bills that night. In conclusion, Wayne slid me a stack of bills containing five thousand dollars.

"Jimi Starr, this is seed money. Take it and keep pimping. I know it will grow for you like it grew for me. I'm booked on an early morning flight to Los Angeles," Wayne said. "Before I leave, I'd like to place a bet on the black jack tables downtown," he concluded.

Again, it was customary for Wayne to stay in my home when he was in town. However, I found it strange that he would be traveling with that kind of money.

Slowly, we rolled along Fremont Boulevard. There was a giant neon cowboy who stood over the Pioneer Casino waving in the tourists. At the intersection of Main and Fremont Streets, we pulled into the parking lot of the Las Vegas Club and got out of the car. It was 5:00 a.m. and the tourists still crowded the brightly lit streets. Well-dressed, high priced whores in evening gowns drifted in and out of the casinos and paraded up and down the boulevard in search of their next high roller.

Wayne was a compulsive gambler; he didn't like to talk while he was gambling. He sat down at a black jack table and immediately began to play two hands at five hundred dollars a hand. I took a seat at the bar, had a drink, making small talk with the local players.

It was two hours later that a cocktail waitress whispered into my ear. "Jimi, your friend is losing big." By the time I got from the bar to Wayne's black jack table, it was all over.

Reader, you can believe it or not, but in the course of two hours, Wayne had gone from a Wonder Mack to a common street pauper, not having possession of a Chinese nickel or a Canadian dime.

Scrutinizing security surrounded the table. A smiling pit boss and grinning black jack dealer stood over Wayne as the dealer dealt the last card to himself, then turned his hand up and said, "Black jack, sir. Sorry, you lose," he swept away Wayne's last five hundred dollar chip.

In complete disbelief, Wayne stood from the black jack table, trying to maintain his composure. As he stood, his legs wobbled and he swayed from side to side, as if he were about to faint. Tears welled in his eyes and he stared at me in disbelief. In the last two hours, the man had lost in excess of one hundred thousand dollars.

"Jimi, I'm going to need that five G's," he said.

"I don't have it," I replied. "While you were playing, I lost here this morning, just like you did. Let's get the fuck out of here," I concluded.

In complete bewilderment, Wayne and I headed for the nearest exit. Wayne didn't know it at the time, but I not only still had his five G's, but I had doubled it on the tables on the other side of the casino. It didn't make any sense to give it to him right now; he was in the middle of a losing streak. There is an old cliché that reads, "The deeper in debt, the bigger the bet." It was as Wayne had earlier implied, a fool and his money are soon parted.

We left the casino into the predawn darkness. There would be no early morning flight to Los Angeles this day. In complete and utter silence, we drove away from the glitz and glamour of the casinos of Las Vegas towards my home near the desert on Jones Street.

Only a man who has been in a similar position might understand the true impact of such a devastating event. We rode into the desert sunrise as I pondered the ramifications of this distasteful situation on Wayne's emotions. I didn't have to wait long. In an air of confusion, Wayne broke the silence. Tears welled in his eyes as he began to speak.
"Jimi, I can't believe it's all gone," he began in a raspy tone.
His distraught voice broke as he said, "Give me a quarter so I can call my mother in Phoenix and have her wire that one hundred and thirty-five dollars she's holding for me. Then I'm going back to that casino and get my money back."

I tried to keep a straight face and show compassion and concern; however, the surrounding circumstances leading to this event, in conjunction with his last statement, caused me to roar with laughter.

"What's so fucking funny, nigga? Are you laughing at me? Are you laughing because I lost my money?"

"No, I'm laughing because just two hours ago, you were telling me that you were a multi-thousandaire and the only real man on the planet. The only pimp I ever knew. Now just two short hours later, you're asking for twenty-five cents for a phone call. Motherfucker, I think that's funny," I concluded.

In that same instant, wide-eyed, he hysterically screamed, "Nigga, you're glad I lost all of my money!" Insane Wayne had been one of my closet friends that I ever encountered throughout the coarse of my life. However, he was always one disturbed motherfucker.

In that same instant as my automobile hurtled down Decatur Boulevard, my long time friend did the unthinkable.

With an expressionless gaze on his face he growled, "The entire world is glad that Wayne is broke."

At that point, the chimes went off in my car, which alerted me that my door had opened. I heard and felt the rush of the warm, roaring wind. Dumbfounded and amazed, I turned my attention to Wayne, but he wasn't there. I looked into the rear view mirror only to see Wayne skidding down the center lane of the boulevard, as if he were surfing. The man led a charmed life. He never fell and wasn't injured. It was then that I truly realized why they called him Insane Wayne. Slamming on the brakes, I fishtailed to an abrupt stop. In reverse, I raced to the assistance of my troubled friend; however, he refused to get in the car.

"I know the Game was rigged. They robbed me Jimi," he cried, the tears from his eyes streaking his face. "I'm going to have money again, in a big way. I know where they keep it."

Losing that money really shook my pal Wayne. But hell, in retrospect, when I think about it, anyone who loses in excess of one hundred thousand dollars in two hours is capable of this same foolishness, including myself.

Later that day Judy, Wayne's prize and last white girl, became the focal point of Wayne's anger. In his unprecedented and violent behavior, the normally suave and debonair Wayne, became an enraged gorilla pimp. He almost beat her to death.

Las Vegas

Bianca and Little Angel had given The Rat the ass whipping of her life. She sat bound in the chair gagged. My long time sadomasochistic pimp pal, Insane Wayne, couldn't have done it any better. The Rat had been savagely beaten and bruised from head to toe. Diane was dazed and confused as I stood over her, ripping the duck tape from her lips. The Rat wept as I removed the panties the revengeful, sadistic whores had stuffed into her terrified and screaming mouth.

Diane's once romantic bedroom eyes were now bugged in sheer horror. She managed to rattle these words from her trembling lips, "Jimi, don't kill me," she pleaded.

Bianca had savagely beaten The Rat until her mind was finally right. This one would never steal again, not from me anyway, I confidently concluded.

"What do you mean kill you sweetheart," I mischievously questioned. Conniving I said, "I'm here to save you."

I reached down and released the knot from the rope that bound her to the chair. Sobbing, she fell from the chair to her knees, clutching me around the waist.

Her bitter tears poured like wine as she wailed hysterically, "I just want to be a good whore. You've never paid me any attention. I'm sorry about your money Daddy. I'll get you some more," she pleaded. "Please don't let those crazy whores kill me. Don't let them hurt me anymore, please," Diane cried as she writhed in pain.

Pressure will bust a pipe. The mental stress and psychological strain of Wayne blowing his bankroll had rendered him temporarily out of sorts. As formidable as his skills were, like a trick, he became a prize sucker when he lost his money and attempted suicide.

I can only write of that which I have knowledge of through personal observation or experience. For all of his cunning, suave, and mind manipulations, Wayne's addiction to gambling had rendered him a "Class A" trick and a victim and to that end. He had become an unpredictable prize sucker.

Wayne sweated profusely as he stood in the center of the living room floor. In his hand he held a wire cloths hanger. Nude, Judy laid cringing and sobbing on the floor, begging for mercy. She was welted from head to toe.

"Bitch!" Wayne barked. "You are the reason that I lost my money and now I'm going to murder you!"

I sat on the couch in my living room, nonchalantly looking out into the desert. Murder! My mind reeled and exploded on Wayne's last words.

Picking up the pistol from the table, Wayne placed a lone bullet into the chamber and spun the cylinder in Russian roulette fashion.
With tears in his eyes, he spoke in a cold mechanical growl, "Now I'm going to kill you, bitch!"

I rose from the couch, face to face with Wayne.

"I am not a 'Will Save A Bitch nigger,' however, you're not going to kill anybody here, not at my house," I began. "As a matter of fact, pal, you were just about to leave," I said firmly.

His eyes widened as he pondered the thought of multiple homicides and attempting to cause additional confusion, "So now, bitch-ass nigger," he barked, "I don't have any more money, so I have to leave, right?"
His chest heaved as he squeezed the butt of the pistol.

"No, Wayne," I calmly and firmly instructed him. "You don't have to leave because you don't have any more money, you have to leave because when you lost your money and you stopped pimping." I concluded.

I took the stack of one hundred dollar bills comprising the 5Gs that I had been holding for him, from the pocket of my silk robe and threw it on the table. I walked to the front door and opened it for Wayne's exit.

"Look me up when you start pimping again, pal," I said sarcastically.

Wayne maniacally grinned, scooped up the stack of one hundred dollar bills, and grumbled some form of gibberish as he angrily rushed passed me and out of the door.

In the weeks that followed, I neither saw nor heard from my old pimp pal. However, there was a rash of bank robberies throughout the Las Vegas Metropolitan area. The media headlines read, "Gentleman Bandit Strikes Again."

The sun was setting on the city of Las Vegas. It was another sweltering desert evening as I left the cold shower. Bianca was preparing my evening meal.

"Jimi," she loudly exclaimed as she rushed into the bedroom and turned on the television set to the Six O'clock News. "Daddy, you're not going to believe this," Bianca exclaimed.

A revealing picture that bore a strong resemblance to an old pal of mine flashed across the screen, and the news commentator said, "This is the Gentleman Bandit. Do you know this man?"

I can only assume that someone, who looked a great deal like my old pimp pal, had found a new occupation and way of life in the form of armed bank robbery. Pimping is not for everybody. Pressure will bust a pipe.

My old pal was and is one of the best Mack men that the country or perhaps the world has ever seen. By contrast, throughout the years, through my personal ups, downs, and turn arounds, I've never sold a grain of cocaine, played any form of con, nor run any hustle of any kind, and I definitely never took a pistol and ran into anyone's bank!

Pimps simply pimp. I was a straight up Mack with no chaser. That was it and that was all. If a whore doesn't give me mine, then I'll never have it! For me, it had to be whore money or no money at all.
It had been a weekend to remember. The Greatest had been the recipient of the ass whipping of his life. I had lost my entire fortune. Insane Wayne had truly gone mad. Yet life and the Game persevered and time moved on.

The Rat

Bianca and Little Angel had given The Rat the ass whipping of her life. She sat in a chair, bound and gagged. My long time sadomasochistic pimp pal, Insane Wayne, couldn't have done it any better. The Rat had been savagely beaten and bruised from head to toe. Diane was dazed and confused as I stood over her, ripping the duct tape from her lips. The Rat wept as I removed the panties the revengeful, sadistic whores had stuffed into her terrified and screaming mouth.

Diane's once romantic bedroom eyes were now bugged in sheer horror. She managed to rattle these words from her trembling lips, "Jimi, don't kill me," she pleaded.

Bianca had savagely beaten The Rat until her mind was finally right. This one would never steal again, not from me anyway, I confidently concluded.

"What do you mean kill you, sweetheart?" I mischievously asked. Conniving, I said, "I'm here to save you."

I reached down and released the knot from the rope that bound her to the chair. Sobbing, she fell from the chair to her knees, clutching me around the waist.

Her bitter tears poured like wine as she wailed hysterically, "I just want to be a good whore. You've never paid me any attention. I'm sorry about your money, Daddy. I'll get you some more," she pleaded. "Please don't let those crazy whores kill me. Don't let them hurt me anymore, please," Diane cried as she writhed in pain.

My dear Reader, the Rat and Squirrel had two things in common, they were both rodents and they were both destroyers. Understand and realize that I had possession of these two whores during the same period of time, but never at the same time. As considerable as I would like to believe, my talent and skills were, during this era of my life, at my best. I would have been no match for the combined larceny and depravity. Truly, these whores were two of the dirtiest whores who ever squatted and pissed between two feet. Some whores come to build. Some whores just come along. While others, though small in numbers, come to destroy!!! Mimi, the Squirrel, and Diane, The Rat, were destroyers.

A destroyer will enter a pimp's stable with one thing in mind, to see the pimp whore-poor. That is their mission and they will attempt to complete that mission by any means necessary. They will attempt to run off his other whores, thereby cutting off the pimp's cash flow, which will ultimately lead to his downward spiral in the Game. Case in point, his ultimate demise and ruination.

There is only one way to productively have a whore of this stature and demeanor. They had to be pimped on hard and fast, made to produce large amounts of cash fast, fast, fast. They had to be led to believe in their false reality that the pimp trusted and depended on them implicitly. Once she believed this false truth, in her mind, the destroyer's mission was accomplished. She would run off, attempting to cause dissension in the rank and files of the pimp's family of whores. After all, she was a destroyer. Three or four months down the road, when she realized that she had been psychologically played once again, she would return with a vengeance and greater determination to undermine the pimp, only to wind up producing another shit load of cash. For this reason, whores with the mentality to destroy had to be kept off balance.

(from left to right)
Tenderloin Slim
Filmore Slim
Daring Don Dupré
Jimi Starr

Nikki Dee

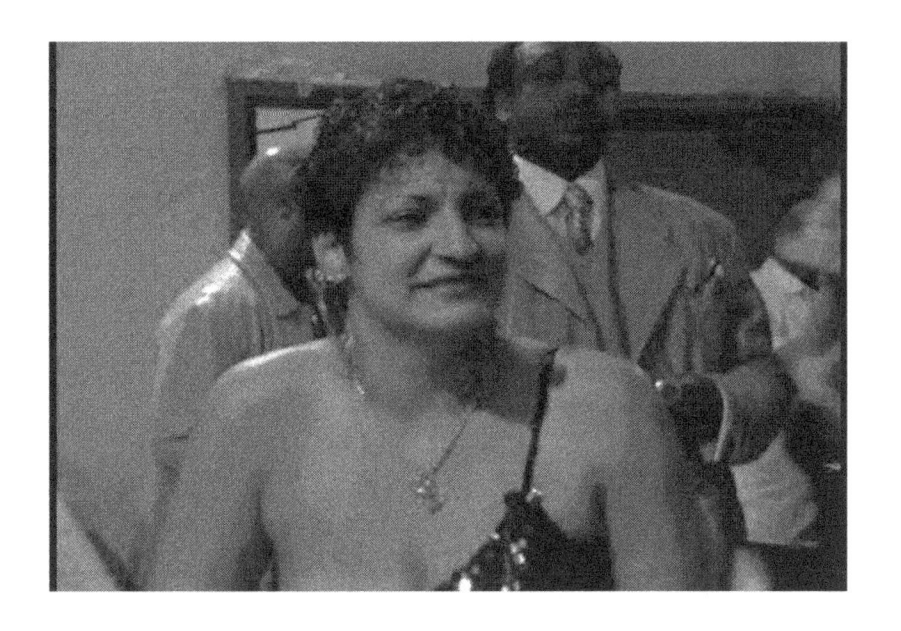

Nicole and Jimi Starr

Chapter 19

The Judas Package

I've always found that jazz soothed me. Angel and I relaxed in the lounge of Cesar's Palace as a talented lounge pianist played a melodic tune. It was Tuesday and without fail, on any given Tuesday for the last six months, Angel had brought me some kind of problem. Tonight she was trying to say she had lost her money. This meant only one thing to me, another man. Angel was about to betray me in my time of need.

I sat poised, holding a snifter of fine cognac, enjoying the fine craftsmanship of the skilled pianist. The well-tanned and voluptuous cocktail waitress with piercing blue eyes, wearing the apparel of a Roman slave girl and balancing a tray with one hand, made her way to our table.

Placing the drinks on the table, she smiled and slipped me her phone number, written on a napkin and said, "The blonde lady at the bar is buying you a drink." The cocktail waitress smiled, winked, turned, and pranced away with the tray over her head in true slave-girl fashion. Oh, so you want to be a slave, I thought to myself as I watched her serving drinks to the high rollers that stood around the crap table.

"That's what I'm talking about," Angel began. "I never get your full attention. It's been two months since you touched me," she bitterly spat.

Whoop's, I had forgotten to fuck her, I thought to myself. The baby doesn't even recognize you anymore. I think he wanted to bite you when you picked me up this evening. Without a word, I stood from the table, straightened my apparel, and started for the door. Angel followed.

Although Angel was a top-flight whore, she was also crazy as a rabid shit house rat. As if she had a printing press, she made money hand over fist. Without doubt, she was one of the most productive whores I had ever had, or for that matter, I had ever known. However, in the bitter end of her prosperous scenario that old pimp cliché rang true, "The way a whore comes is the way a whore goes." The night that I met Angel, she chose me with money that was intended for another man. Tonight it was my turn. When I wasn't looking, another man with a fast pimp hand gave Angel some new pimping and a new direction. For the time that I had her, she paid like a triple crown winner, like Secretariat, Citation, or Seattle Slew. I can honestly say I never missed her, but Reader, I'd be a mother fucking liar if I told you I never missed that whore's money.

Most whores, who pay in a big way, usually have psychological problems. Like I mentioned earlier, it seemed as if every Tuesday night, like clock work, Angel would create some kind of problem. On this particular Tuesday, it went something like this.

Streams of curious tourists drifted into and out of the magnificence that is known as Cesar's Palace. We sat poised at the circular bar near the main entrance of this premiere establishment. From my vantage point, I could see the pimps, movie stars, professional athletes, and other high rollers as they entered and left the building.

On the far side of the casino, an elderly woman leaped for joy and began to scoop the coins into her oversized purse as the lights began to flash off and on and as the bells of a one-armed bandit rang and mechanically spit silver dollars into a metal pot with a thud. The well-manicured stickman and the pit boss stood and looked on nonchalantly; it was just another day to them. The old lady's persistence and perseverance had paid off in a prolific way. The lights flashed on and off throughout the entire casino. Security and tourists ran from everywhere, rushing towards the old lady and her machine. She had hit the big one.

Angel had excused herself and went to the ladies room. I approached the blonde-haired, blue-eyed Jamaican sitting at the bar. Sitting down besides her, I introduced myself and bought her a drink. Her name was Opal. I jotted my number down on a napkin and returned to my table. I knew I would see this novice whore again. Then the hair stood up on the back of my neck, a sure sign that something was wrong.

Angel had returned to the table. I stared studiously into her slightly aging movie star's face. It had been a little over six months, and during that time she had paid me royally. When her sexual needs and my apparent duty deemed it necessary, I would stand up in her stinking Diego pussy like the Pope stands up in the Vatican.

Reader, to me the pimping was and is a mind game. You can never let a woman think that she can have you simply because she sold her pussy and gave you the cash. After all, selling pussy was her job. If a whore wanted to fuck me, she had to pay. Yes, most indeed, she had to pay in a prolific way.

"Jimi," Angel began, "I know I've paid you well, probably better than most." She continued, "I think I deserved more attention and more dick than you gave me."

The hair rose on the back of my neck again. This bitch was speaking in the past tense. Before I could get the words out of my mouth, there was a gentle tap on my shoulder. I turned to see Pretty Phil from Georgia. Angle flashed a conniving smile across her movie star face. Phil served me the pimping in the middle of the casino floor of Caesar's Palace.

"Jimi Starr, this whore is no longer with you," he confidently began as Angel stood up from the table.
"I broke this whore for the last two nights straight and she had the good sense to follow her money." He continued, "The word is out around town that you squandered your fortune," he sarcastically implied as Angel mischievously snickered. "I'm serving you face-to-face and in front of the bitch so that there is no misunderstanding that she is with me now," Phil concluded as he sternly studied me for reaction.

One is never quite prepared for a situation like this. With my current cash flow crisis, this was the last thing that I needed. However, it was the first thing that I suspected. I knew I had to keep it pimping, no matter what.

"Mr. Pretty Phil, the name of the Game is cop and blow," I began. "I never saw a pimp have any whore forever. I sent that whore to get my money until my run was done. No Phil, there will be no misunderstandings about this whore or any other." I concluded, "When an ignorant whore leaves me, I celebrate, because it gives a smart whore a chance to get at me." With those words I smiled, turned, and strolled out of the casino through the door, and into the night.

Reader, I have an old pimp cliché' that goes, "There was never a horse that couldn't be rode and never a cowboy that couldn't be thrown". On any given night, under the proper circumstances, any pimp could be had. The name of the Game is "Cop and Blow".

Until this day, I do not believe that Angel truly understood that I was not her boyfriend, nor was I Catch's daddy. I was her pimp. I truly didn't give a rat's ass about a shot of her stinking, once-a-month-bleeding pussy. The ultimate climax for a man like me was the captivation, manipulation, and the cash flow he received from his whores. In my tenure as a pimp, I had mastered the psychology of reversing the mental perspective.

All whores see their man as God. Any time a whore can summon up and reach out and touch God at will, sooner or later, that God will cease to be God; it was obvious that I had become common to Angel. Divinity exists outside the range of sight and just beyond the physical grasp of man.

Reader, some pimp's pimp for the season. I was pimping for a reason. A whore had to be made to realize and differentiate between her man and a trick. If the pimp were consistently sampling his own supply of flesh, eventually, like a drug addict, he would become addicted to his own product. No man addicted to anything is at his absolute best. If he was going to be a career pimp, he had to be God Almighty. At my absolute best, I would not have traded my mind set for one hundred productive movie star whores like Big Angel. No, most indeed. I would not have altered my state of mind, not for all the paying pussy in the world.

For the first time in years, I was financially destitute. I was so broke that I couldn't pay attention. At the first hint of my financial dilemma, Big Angel, one of my premiere thieves, had broke bad. For the sakes of notoriety, most whores want to maintain a pimp who is at the top of his game. Only a dedicated whore or a damned fool will represent a nigger's business who has no business to represent. If a whore wanted to get even with a pimp for any past transgressions, I will lay ten to one odds, she would do it when he was broke and or down on his luck.

Unlike most pimps, I did not burden myself with common flat-backing whores. The average whore on my line was also a thief. Having that attribute to my advantage, I took this distasteful situation in stride and kept it pimping. I knew I would not have to wait long. My whores took it all, big and small, from the money in a trick's pocket to a ring, watch, or locket. They specialized in expensive brands.

In order for a woman to be with a man, she must choose him. To choose him, she must come to him with a dowry, a pre-specified amount of money; the greater the pimp's prominence and notoriety in the Game, the larger and more lucrative the whore's dowry. If a pimp were to accept a woman without money, it would lessen his own creditability and renown in the underworld as a pimp.

If a pimp accepts a woman and she has no money, this is attached to her credentials and her persona and locks her into a position of servitude to any and all whores; the pimp might already have or acquire the future, putting her at the bottom of the pecking order in servitude. If she has no "choosing money" and or no dowry, and she was fortunate enough to be accepted, it's only as a servant and a second class member of the family social and pecking order, to be utilized until the end of the run with no possible chance of upward mobility in the structure of the hierarchy of the family. However, there are always exceptions to the rule, but they are far, few, and in-between. Depending on her personal sense of wit, the woman may or may not recognize this scenario. One thing for a surety and certainty, without cash, she will not move up in the family structure, nor the Game.

A whore without choosing money is a bitch with low self-esteem who would be considered of low regard and without reference a tramp, trollop, and a "chippy". A top-flight pimp's mindset on prostitution is that the way a whore comes, is the way a whore goes. The way you catch them, is the way you hold them. The initial dowry is a sign of commitment to the Game and an expression of dedication and devotion to the pimp and his chosen profession, establishing the whore's credibility.

There are checks and counter balances to this sub-culture that pimps call "the Game." Contrary to popular belief, there are rules and regulations to street life, and all who fail to abide by these rules and regulations are shunned and looked down on by the masses of street players. They would be considered "outlaws" or "renegades".

My dear Reader, the Game is a sub-culture of society in and of itself. It is governed by its own separate set of complex ethical and moral rules and regulations. In the Game, once you have been accepted, established, and recognized as a legitimate pimp, strange things begin to happen. In order to be accepted and respected, one must embrace the code of the Game and the lifestyle.

Jimi Starr's First Annual Macks Convention/Filmore Slim and Jimi Starr

Chapter 20

Rescued in the Name of the Game

From my living room, I watched the shimmering reflection of the gleaming golden sunrise, which was mirrored in the pool, as I interviewed a young, tanned, and statuesque blue-eyed Jamaican beauty with flowing blonde hair. Her name was Opal. I had met her and broke her on the night of the fight. This morning, she was attempting to follow her money, as like most smart whores will.

"Darling," I began, "I'm truly flattered that you want to choose me, however, you must try to understand that all whores cannot be with me." She dropped her head in submissive fashion. "Tell me about yourself, your qualifications, and your sexual escapades. Tell me what you can do for me that those seven whores of mine can't. Tell me your story," I concluded. Pimping was my livelihood. It was my business and I respected the pimping, running it like a typical business at all times. There is an old pimp cliché that reads, "If you are true to the Game, the Game will be true to you."

I had evolved to a level in the game where I could virtually pick and choose any whore that I wanted. If a whore could be had, I could have her. In those whores in whom I found offense or disdain, I simply threw them back like a small fish to be caught by some lesser or hungrier pimp. A true pimp had to be selective. All whores were not worthy, nor qualified to represent neither me and my business or the Game.

Opal began to run her spiel. Her father had sent for her to come to America from Kingston, Jamaica. It seems that she was with a local pimp who called himself Prince. Opal had no other relatives in the United States. After she had arrived, her father had assisted her in getting a job in a casino restaurant. Her father unexpectedly died soon afterwards. While working in the restaurant, she met a chili pimp, i.e., a nigger who is pimping for something to eat and a place to sleep, named Prince. In the confusion of her immediate and devastating circumstances, Opal ended up homeless. Prince advised her that she could live with him; she agreed. He took her home, brutalized, sodomized, and made a whore out of her.

"Last night was the first time I ever sold any pussy," she concluded. Hers was a sad but typical story.

I reached into my pocket and peeled a hundred dollar bill off my bankroll, folded it in half, and placed it on the table. "If you really want to be with me," I said, "I want you to pick up that one hundred dollar bill." Reaching out, she retrieved the one hundred dollar bill with her hand and extended it to me.

"No, listen to me, you're not hearing me," I patiently said. "I want you to pick it up with the lips of your pussy."

She childishly blushed and then whispered in puzzlement, "No one can do that."

"Any one of those seven whores of mine can," I told her arrogantly. "Now hop up on the table and let me see what you can do."

Opal took off her clothes and climbed up onto the table. Standing wide-legged, her firm young breasts jiggling as she squatted, she attempted to retrieve the bill. Try as she did, she couldn't retrieve it.

"A real whore can pick that bill up with her pussy or her asshole," I knowingly said. Her eyes widened as she nervously giggled. "It is simply a matter of muscle control," I continued. "Now turn around and face me and try to pick up that hundred dollar bill with your ass hole."

Squatting, her body stiffened as she exuberantly attempted to oblige. Her firm shapely ass was magnificent. Perhaps one might say that I was a connoisseur of a woman's ass. Throughout the years, I had known many women; however, I had never seen an ass quite as firm or curvaceous as this. I do believe it was perfect. Secretly, I relished in the moment.

"I can't do it," she gasped as her novice and untrained ass hole missed its designated mark.

"I can see that," I said, "but in time, I will fix that small, troublesome problem for you." I said.

If Opal believed that the nigger, Prince, had viciously sodomized her, just wait until she gave me some real money. I was going to tear her innocent and unknowing ass smooth off her novice back.

Reflections

During the years that I have had and come to know Bianca Starr, she has been studious, dedicated, and tenacious. There is an old pimp cliché that reads, "A woman is the reflection of her man." Bianca had become one of the most talented and premiere thieves in the country. If there was any money to be gotten, for a surety and a certainty, she was going to get it.

When you send a whore out of the door, she was no longer yours, but she belongs to the world until she returns through the door with your money.

The personal phone in my bedroom rang continuously, arousing me from my deep and much-needed slumber. The only people on the planet who had this number were my mother and Bianca. There was no doubt in my mind that this was a call of some importance. Placing the phone to my ear, I overheard part of Bianca's conversation with the Rat.

"That was good blocking Diane," Bianca whispered.
Excitedly she spoke to me, "Hello, Daddy, I think you're going to be exceptionally proud of me this morning. It seems I have come into possession of a money belt and it's packed full of hundred dollar bills."

Commandingly, I hushed her to silence. "Don't say another word over the phone baby, just head on home," I said.

Bianca had become one of the premiere Black thieves in the nation. From the money in your pocket to a ring, a watch, or locket, she specialized in expensive brands. She was a natural-born thief. It wasn't difficult perfecting her given skills as a professional cannon.

I sat watching in a deep-cushioned seat as they came through the door strutting proudly, heads held high. Bianca stopped in front of me.

"Daddy," she said, "I shouldn't have been so open on the phone, but I got so overly excited."

She reached under her flowing lavender designer evening dress, unsnapping a blue cloth money belt, and extending it to me. A bundle of hundred dollar bills, still in bank bands, protruded from an open snap on the belt. Wow!! Ooh shit!! My mind leaped and screamed in excitement. Hoo, hoo!! But I continued to sit in the chair, expressionless, and calmly emptied the blue cloth belt and I began to count the cash, poker-faced. I removed stack after stack. Oh shit, I thought to myself. You have superseded your wildest dreams.

Bianca, paraded around the room and, with her wickedly sassy sense of humor asked, "Daddy, did we give you enough?"

"No, it'll never be enough," I said sarcastically. Again she lifted her lavender evening dress, only to reveal a second belt. Wow, my mind screamed! It just didn't get any better than this!

Bianca has had this type of tenacity all of her career. She was like the Calvary when I was in distress; from out of nowhere she would, without fail, ride over the hill and save the day. I was blessed the day I found her. My luck has been like that all of my life and all of the Game. Behind every strong man stands a strong woman.

My thoroughly informed and educated Reader, know this now and remember it in times to come. This novel is named The Gospel of the Game because it is the uncorrupted and undisputed truth of the lifestyle known as the Game. It is the Gospel.

There is an old pimp cliché that reads, "The Game is to be sold and never told." It is for that explicit reason that this small informative novel is for sale. My writings, though colorful and descriptive, were meant in no means to glorify the Game, but in fact and to the contrary, they were meant to vilify it. My urban writings represent an era of my life that has long since passed. It is my earnest and most heart felt desire that some mother's son or daughter, who might perhaps may be on the wrong path in life, chance onto my modest writings and read, analyze, and visualize the devastating substance of a real pimp story. The horrific contents contained within should turn them around and send them running and screaming for their very lives, sanity, and moral salvation, and away from this putrid and parasitic life that pimps call "The Game."

Epilog

The day breaks over the face of the world. The gleaming golden sun brings an end to night's darkness with its first rays of early morning light. With perfect timing and perfect pitch, the early birds' melodic song is reflective of the Creators' music flowing through the air, filling the world with the lively rhythmic sounds of life. Our existence is mirrored like the life of a strong, beautiful tree that brings forth lush tender green leaves and delicious sweet-tasting fruit, in its own time, in its own season.

Like the Creator's time for perfection of that sweet fruit, my time and season for having the solution for The Game had come and gone. It didn't seem strange, nor by any means peculiar that the same gentle, whispering, and warm wind that blew the Game into my life, had returned too blow the Game away.

My dear Reader, nor did it seem exceedingly strange or indifferent that, after a lifetime of street success and at the apex of my career, that I would turn my back on the Game, walking into the sunrise of tomorrow.

As before mentioned, like a cycle, there exists a natural order to all things. There is a certain time and season in life for the birth, nurturing, and maturing, and the eventual demise of all things. It is the mind or ego of man that leads a championship fighter to take just one more fight, with the end result, leaving him permanently punch-drunk. It is in fact the spirit of man that leads him to know when it is time for changes and what those changes are to be. All men must know when to walk away. The individual, who possesses this tidbit of knowledge, has all ready won the fight.

But for the goodness and mercy of the Creator's divine providence and spiritual intervention and his raining of the priceless jewels of mercy, compassion, truth, and wisdom into my otherwise miserable and parasitic life, I would have been unable to send forth this small volume before you, which is proof positive that the Creator is magnificent, omnipresent, omniscient, and most merciful, for who but God could forgive a man like me?

The first rays of golden sunlight bring the reality of truth that my tomorrow will never again be like yesterday.

I stood in my bedroom window watching the inhabitants of the world. Scurrying about going everywhere and nowhere. Children left home early in the morning going to school, only to return to their points of origin in the evening, as did doctors, lawyers, and common laborers; sooner or later, we all return to our point of origin.

The trees in Central Park grew from the earth straight up into the heavens, yet the trees dropped its seeds and hopes of new beginnings and better tomorrows back towards the soil enriched Earth and its roots from which it all began.

On the golden sunrise, flying geese made their annual return to the south for the winter. What did it all mean? Mama's words continued to haunt me, "Jimi, it's a long road that doesn't have an ending". Life is a learning excursion. It is a time of physical, psychological, spiritual growth, and expression. It is a season, just that, no more and no less. This ongoing process has been mirrored, reflecting itself since the dawning of time. Yet, most wise men fail to see it. In the end, most people return to the spiritual simplicity of their basic beginnings. Some people, though few in number, don't. It is given like a tree, we must all live, reproduce, and return the essence of our collective growth to our basic beginnings, enriching lives through dropping our seeds of wisdom earned into the soil of life, so that the tree might continue to live, flourishing into another season.

If you are ever in San Francisco, look me up. I'm currently employed as a transit operator. If you can't catch me on the line driving a bus, perhaps you can catch me in the office. I am also the executive director of a community outreach program, designed to feed the hungry and shelter the homeless. Or perhaps you just might find me in church, praying and crying on bended knees for the salvation of mankind, or on a street corner downtown, preaching the gospel of Jesus. I am also an evangelist minister of the Creator's Gospel. By the tender and forgiving mercy of the Creator's infinite love, I have been born again, washed clean of sin in the blood of Christ Jesus. Like the prodigal son, I have returned home. Like the seeds that fall from a strong tree to the earth to replenish itself for another season, I also have returned home to the spiritual atmosphere of my humble beginnings. I too, like that strong tree, will drop my impregnated seeds of wisdom earned back to the earth, enriching the precious and sacred soil of life.

The offer to visit is extended and open to one and all. No whores please, Jimi Starr has retired.

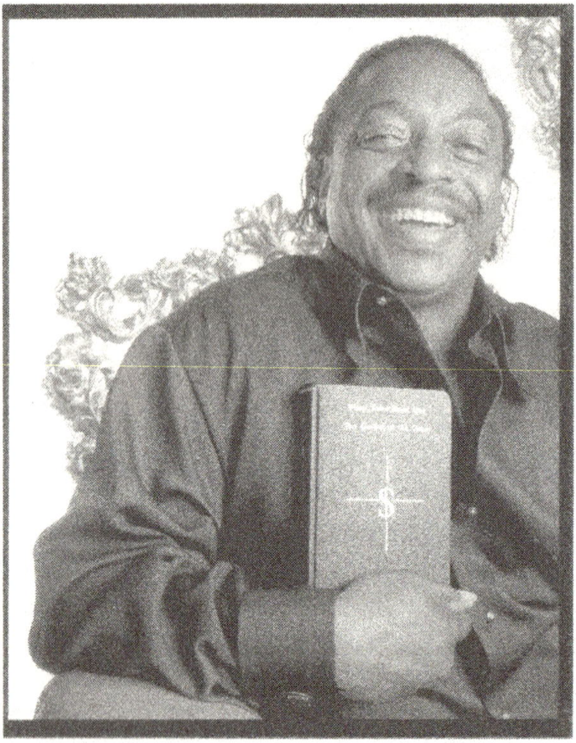

Available Now....
Gospel of the Game Documentary

*Genuine Jimi Starr Pimp Cup
with encrusted diamonds*

coming soon. . . .

> # Who Killed Boukie Bates
>
> by Jimi Starr

CPSIA information can be obtained
at www.ICGtesting.com
Printed in the USA
LVHW091020031119
636175LV00001B/178/P

9 781463 452933